Managing Economic Reforms in Post-Mao China

Managing Economic Reforms in Post-Mao China

KUOTSAI TOM LIOU

PRAEGER

Westport, Connecticut
London

Library of Congress Cataloging-in-Publication Data

Liou, Kuotsai Tom.
Managing economic reforms in post-Mao China / by Kuotsai Tom Liou.
p. cm.
Includes bibliographical references and index.
ISBN 0-275-95792-6 (alk. paper)
1. China—Economic policy—1976– 2. China—Economic conditions—1976– I. Title.
HC427.92.L5624 1998
338.951—DC21 97-34754

British Library Cataloguing in Publication Data is available.

Library of Congress Catalog Card Number: 97-34754
ISBN: 0-275-95792-6

First published in 1998

Praeger Publishers, 88 Post Road West, Westport, CT 06881
An imprint of Greenwood Publishing Group, Inc.

Printed in the United States of America

The paper used in this book complies with the Permanent Paper Standard issued by the National Information Standards Organization (Z39.48-1984).

10 9 8 7 6 5 4 3 2 1

To my father, Jiunn-Jin Liou
and
in memory of my mother, Der-Jy Wann

Contents

Tables

Preface

The post-Mao Chinese economic reforms developed since 1978 have attracted attention from researchers and policy makers from various disciplines in different countries. Researchers are interested in analyzing China's reform and development strategies and verifying their validity in the context of theoretical contributions. Policy makers are concerned about the positive outcomes and changes associated with the reforms and the possibility of incorporating some aspects of the Chinese experience into their own development policy.

As a researcher of public management and policy, I have observed China's reforms and development closely since the beginning of China's open-door policy in the late 1970s. I have focused on issues related to the formulation and adoption of the reform policies and strategies as well as their implementation and interaction. Especially, I am interested in the perception of the reforms from both the official perspective, especially that of the local officials, and the general public's perspective. In addition, I would like to know the impact of the reforms on Chinese society in terms of their direct or indirect, intentional or unintentional, effects. The more I studied, the more fascinated I became about the progress, achievements, and problems of the reforms. I realized the importance of the reforms to the Chinese people, domestic and overseas, with regard to not only the current situation but also the historical status.

It was after 1993 that I decided to write a book about China's economic reforms. In 1993, I served as a co-chair (with Dwight Ink) of the American Society of Public Administration (ASPA) and the Chinese Public Administration Society (CPAS) Bilateral Committee. I arranged the invitation and visit of a high-level Chinese delegate team, including Mr. Zhang Wenshou, then vice president (later the president) of the CPAS, to the 1993 ASPA National Conference in San Francisco. During the visit, we discussed the importance of the reforms to China's development and the contribution of public management to the economic reforms.

The next year, I was invited to attend the CPAS National Conference in beautiful Huangshan in October and gave a speech on the role of government in managing economic development. During the conference, I had the opportunity to meet officials from many provinces, researchers from major universities (e.g., Peking University, People's University of China, Zhongshan University), and administrators and staff of the CPAS and various provincial and local public administration societies and institutes. I was impressed with their enthusiasm and optimism about the economic reforms and development. Especially, I enjoyed the conversations with professors Liu Yichang and Xia Shuzhang (both are vice presidents of the CPAS) and like their modest attitude about suggestions and criticism of the reforms.

I organized and edited a symposium on China's economic development in the *International Journal of Public Administration* after the Huangshan trip. Many researchers of Chinese reforms from China, Hong Kong, Singapore, and the United States responded to and participated in the process of the symposium. The final papers accepted for publication addressed such important issues as China's financial reforms, ethics issues in China's civil service, decentralization and state-society relations, public transportation development, and privatization of the public housing system. I benefited from the intellectual interactions with these researchers and broadened my perspective on Chinese reforms after the editorial experience.

Many important things happened in my personal and professional life during the preparation of this book. First, my mother passed away suddenly in July 1994. Then, I became a father, with the births of my son, Alan, in October 1994 and my daughter, Anna, in April 1996. During the period of 1994-1995, I served as Director of the Graduate Programs for the School of Public Administration at Florida Atlantic University (FAU) and supervised and assisted the graduate work of about 50 Ph.D. students and 150 master's students in public administration. In summer 1996, I accepted a tenured faculty position of public administration from the University of Central Florida (UCF) and moved from Coral Springs to Orlando.

While personal issues and changes delayed the publication of this book, my views and judgments on China's economic reforms and development have matured and are now well established. I found out that many of my earlier observations about China's reforms were correct when recent publications emphasized many important issues and conclusions that are similar to mine. For example, instead of criticizing the Chinese government's partial and gradual approach, many researchers today embrace the Chinese experience and indicate the importance of the government in managing the reforms and development.

Finally, many people provided important support and assistance during the process of writing this book. My colleagues at FAU and UCF provided the intellectual and institutional assistance in my writings, presentations, and publications of my studies. Ms. Rita Kraemer has always been there to help me improve my English writing. Her friendship and assistance for many years have contributed significantly to my career development. My friends in China, Canada, Hong Kong, Singapore, Taiwan, and the United States offered important information and data that are useful in presenting the arguments. Among them, Mr. Zuo Ran of the CPAS has continuously sent me their publications for many years. Strong support from my family has been critical to finishing this book. My father and brothers have always supported me in my career development. My wife, Susan, has spent a lot of time taking care of the children and other family business, which allowed me to concentrate on my research. Her comfort and encouragement were especially appreciated when lower-back injuries kept me from work during the spring of 1997. I am grateful for the assistance and support of all these people.

CHAPTER 1

Introduction: Managing Economic Reforms

Economic development has become one of the popular public policies in many developed and developing countries for many decades. The concern for economic development in the past was mainly related to efforts emphasized in many developing countries. But, with the rapid changes in international politics and technological improvements, the interest in development-related issues has moved to the top of policy priorities for many developed countries. For example, the end of the Cold War and advancements in transportation and communication have changed past isolated economic activities and increased the interaction of many countries, rich and poor, in today's global market economy.

While sharing the same concern for economic development, many countries may have different objectives in their development policies. For most of the developed countries, for example, the objective of their development policy is to increase their economic growth, which refers to such measured output or income as gross domestic product (GDP) or gross national product (GNP). The objectives of economic development policy for many developing countries, on the other hand, include not only increases in the growth rate of GDP or GNP but also changes in their economic, social, and political structures (Goode, 1984). For these countries, an economic development policy is also related to their overall national goal of modernization.

The topic of economic development is especially important for many post-socialist states like China, countries of Eastern Europe, and other countries that were part of the former Soviet Union. To achieve the goal of economic growth, these countries need to be involved in the process of economic transition from a centrally planned to a market-oriented system. For these countries, an economic development policy becomes a part of their economic reforms, which consist of changes in such areas as macroeconomic stabilization, price and trade liberalization, enterprise reform (especially privatization), and the development of the institutional and legal framework for a market economy, e.g., a market-based financial system (Fisher & Gelb, 1991; Fisher, Sahay & Vegh, 1996).

This book examines the economic reform process and issues in post-Mao China. The purpose of this chapter is to provide readers a conceptual framework for the later analysis of China's economic reforms. The chapter begins with a general discussion of issues related to economic development and reform. The discussion especially focuses on the role of government in managing macroeconomic growth during the process of economic development. Then, the chapter provides a brief review of the condition of Chinese development and reforms, which also focuses on the issue of managing economic reforms. Based on the results of the discussion and review, the chapter finally explains the outline of the book, including its approach and the purpose of each chapter. Following this introductory chapter, the book consists of seven chapters covering such topics as the background of economic reforms (Chapter 2), stages and measures of economic reforms (Chapter 3), evaluation of economic reforms (Chapter 4), changes in China's regional development (Chapter 5), changes in China's administrative system (Chapter 6), changes in China's state-society relations (Chapter 7), and lessons to be learned from China's economic reforms (Chapter 8).

ISSUES OF MANAGING ECONOMIC REFORMS

This book attempts to examine China's post-Mao economic reforms by focusing on the involvement of the Chinese government in the process of managing the reforms. The issue of government or state involvement in the process of economic development or reform has recently become very popular in the literature on economic development. The interest in the role of the government in the development process has to do with the past development experience of many developing countries, especially the successful ones associated with those of newly industrialized countries (NICs) in East Asia and the recent emphasis on economic policy reforms (economic stabilization and structural adjustment) by international development organizations (e.g., the International Monetary Fund [IMF], the World Bank) (Haggard & Kaufman, 1992; Hughes, 1988).

Despite their different background issues, studies of economic development have tended to agree that there should be a substantial role for the government in economic affairs such as growth and development (e.g., Caporaso, 1982; Doner, 1992; Stern, 1991; Summers & Thomas, 1993). Similarly, research on economic policy reforms or structural adjustments also emphasized the importance of the administrative and political functions of the state in the successful implementation of an adjustment program or a reform policy (e.g., Haggard & Webb, 1993; Rondinelli & Montgomery, 1990). The present section will provide a brief review of these findings about the role of government in economic activities, especially growth and development, and major policies and conditions that are important for economic reforms.

First, the role of government in the modern economic system is necessary and accepted according to standard microeconomic theory. Government functions and activities are important because of the provision of public goods and the problem of market failure. Public goods, such as the service of national defense, are nonrival and nonexcludable in consumption and benefit of such goods. The market system cannot function well in the presence of such issues as the existence of goods with externalities (positive or negative), the emergence of monopolies and oligopolies (also monopsony and oligopsony), incomplete or nonexistent markets, and information failures.

With regard to specific government functions and activities in the market economy, researchers emphasized three duties of the government (state): protecting the society from violence and invasion by other societies, establishing an exact administration of justice, and erecting and maintaining certain public works and institutions (Adam Smith; see Cannan, 1976). Similarly, Musgrave and Musgrave (1980) promoted three functions of public finance (government): (1) the allocation of social and other goods that the market will not of itself provide, (2) the equitable distribution of income and wealth, and (3) the stabilization of unemployment and control of inflation.

Moreover, public policy researchers (Lehne, 1993; Meier, 1985; Tanzi, 1990) have recently noticed the increasing role of government regulatory activities. Regulation refers to any attempt by the government to control the behavior of citizens, corporations, or subgovernments (Meier, 1985: 1). This may consist of such actions as regulation of competitive behavior, industry regulation, social regulation, and regulation of labor-management relations (Buchholz, 1992). Tanzi (1990) noticed that governments often pursue their policy objectives through regulation and use regulations to replace traditional public finance instruments. The pervasive use of regulation and the growth of regulatory activities resulted in some concerns about regulatory cost and in suggestions for regulatory reforms (Litan & Nordhaus, 1983).[1]

These roles or functions of government have been generally accepted among industrial and developed countries as major economic activities of government. For these countries, economic growth is expected to follow automatically from the pursuit of these functions. The situation, however, is different for developing countries. With low income levels in the developing countries, it has been argued that growth should be an explicit and separate objective of government policy and that government should take the responsibility for speeding up growth and promoting economic development (Goode, 1984; Tanzi, 1990).

Next, with regard to the issue of promoting growth and development, it has been noticed that governments have been very involved in these activities in many developed and developing countries. Government activities in this area include, but are not limited to providing the infrastructure for development, encouraging industrial activities by subsidizing the export sector and providing fiscal incentives for the industrial sector, and reorganizing the productive enterprise. Caporaso (1982) explained that the involvement of government in these activities is based on the consideration of the need for minimum capital and technology inputs to overcome the vicious cycle of poverty, as well as the competitive international environment in which modern countries and firms must operate.

To promote growth and development, researchers of economic development and reform (e.g., Haggard & Webb, 1993; Rondinelli & Montgomery, 1990; Summers & Thomas, 1993) have identified major public policies and critical conditions that are related to the success of many countries. On the side of public policies, governments need to address four sets of policy issues in their efforts to manage development (Rondinelli & Montgomery, 1990: 76-77). The first set of policy issues has to do with economic growth for the purpose of allocating economic resources among investments and expanding productive activities and national output. The second set of policies focuses on social equity for the purpose of reducing the social adversities imposed by class, regional, religious, or ethnic inequalities and affecting the distribution of income and wealth resulting from economic growth. The third set of policies is related to international transactions for the purpose of exporting and importing agricultural and manufactured goods and raw materials to obtain capital, information, and technology from abroad. The last set of policy issues concerns public management for the purpose of creating and maintaining an effective governmental structure and procedures to deliver public services, regulating activities that affect public health and safety, protecting national security, and extending protection of laws to citizens.

On the side of critical conditions, these researchers identified several important environmental factors that are associated with the success of economic development, including, for example, sociopolitical stability; a flexible, pragmatic, and longitudinal approach; the integration of government and market; and institutional development. A stable political and social environment is necessary because it allows policy makers to create structure through which development goals could be established and pursued. The flexible, pragmatic, and longitudinal approach is important for governments to mobilize resources to change priorities based on economic conditions and to allow development policies to be pursued over long periods of time. The appropriate integration of government and market covers such issues as investment in human and physical infrastructures (e.g., education, roads, and bridges), creation of a competitive climate for enterprise (e.g., reducing tariffs and quotas), and emphasis on macroeconomic management to provide sound policies with sustainable fiscal deficits and realistic exchange rates. Finally, sound institutional development is critical because it assures commitments from some effective private corporations and a well-trained (competent and disciplined) government bureaucracy to work together to implement development policies.

In sum, the review of research on the role of government in economic development and reform revealed that government plays an important and leading role in the modern economic system and that government functions and activities are necessary and essential to economic growth and development. The major functions and activities identified include (1) economic management functions such as promoting growth, allocating resources, distributing incomes, and stabilizing the economy; (2) regulatory functions designed for both industry and social considerations; and (3) protection functions in terms of defending the country from outside invasions and maintaining law and order for a stable environment.[2] To assure the success of economic development and reform, governments need to simultaneously formulate and implement all four policies regarding economic growth, social equity, international transaction, and public management. Especially, governments need to consider creating a stable political and social environment, adopt a flexible and practical approach emphasizing long-term development, consider the appropriate relationship between government and market, and develop sound institutions in both private and public sectors to support the development policies.

THE CONDITION OF CHINESE REFORMS

This section provides a review of the condition of Chinese reforms. The review especially focuses on the role of the Chinese government in developing reform policies. In their search for economic growth and modernization, the post-Mao Chinese leaders formulated development policies based on the consideration of the mistakes of their past development, the social and political condition of China, and the development experience of other countries, especially those of China's neighbors (e.g., Japan, South Korea, Singapore).

China's past development history revealed some problems with their central planning system (e.g., imbalances between supply and demand, inefficiency and breakdown of the incentive system) and mistakes of their changing and unstable development policies related to political power struggles (e.g., Mao's revolutionary policy versus non-Mao's revisionary policy) (Dong, 1980; Nolan & Ash, 1995; Prybyla, 1982). The Chinese condition before the reform was basically a society closed and isolated internally within China's rural and urban areas and externally from Western countries. The Chinese Communist Party dominated and controlled all the institutions (including the government) and ideas (especially Mao's revolutionary ideas) of the society. Finally, observing the successful development of their neighboring countries and regions, the post-Mao leaders realized not only the need to improve economic performance but also the way to change economic conditions.

The post-Mao leaders first emphasized decentralization and opening up in their earlier development policies. During the process of the implementation of these policies, Chinese leaders gradually recognized and accepted the need and importance of reforming their past central planning system. In other words, economic development and modernization call for China's system reforms; development policies in China mean reform policies. Since 1978, the leaders have formulated reform policies that gradually introduced private market mechanisms in China's agricultural and industrial sectors, decentralized decision-making power to local administrators and enterprise managers, invited foreign investment in China and opened the country to the world market, and established infrastructures needed for the market economy.

Despite the comprehensive nature of the reforms, Chinese leaders have consistently emphasized the leading role of the government, especially the Party, during the process of the reforms. Attempting to build a system of "socialism with Chinese characteristics," the leaders believe that the Chinese government should play an essential role in the process of transforming economic systems and emphasize that the challenge is to redefine the role of the government when introducing market mechanisms.

In fact, Chinese leaders and researchers have never advocated the idea of a total elimination of state or government involvement in the economy. Their view of the government role in economic development is very similar to that experienced by China's neighbors (e.g., Japan and the NICs). Studies of the development experience of the NICs showed an active role of government, beyond correcting market failures (e.g., Kuznets, 1988; Lim, 1983; Pack & Westphal, 1986; Park, 1990). The economic development experience of the NICs has emphasized government-oriented and export-oriented approach strategies. Specifically, these countries incorporated their national planning with economic development policy and used the development of export-oriented industries to promote and lead the economic growth and development. Chinese leaders promoted the revised role of government by separating the concept of ownership from the practice of management. Based on Marxism's premise that a society's economic base dominates its institutional superstructure, they argued that the role of government in the economy must be reduced because the government represents only part of the superstructure (Ling, 1988). But they insisted that government must still maintain a major role in the economy since the government owns the economy on behalf of "all the people."

PURPOSE AND OUTLINE OF THE BOOK

The previous discussion and review of the literature of government and economic development and the condition of the Chinese reforms provide a conceptual framework for analysis of China's post-Mao economic reforms. Focusing on the management experience and issues, this book examines the economic reforms from a comprehensive and interdisciplinary approach. The book covers various important policy and management issues without considering the limitation of the discipline. This approach also means that the book's analysis uses information and resources not only from publications of Chinese researchers but also from studies of the reforms published in major journals of economics, politics, public administration, sociology, and other disciplines. It is the author's belief that the comprehensive and interdisciplinary approach is important to understand the overall phenomenon of China's economic reforms because of the comprehensive nature and impact of the reforms.[3] It is the author's hope that this book will contribute to both researchers and policy makers the knowledge and experience of China's reforms.

This book basically consists of two parts: the experience of China's post-Mao reforms and major issues associated with the reforms. The first three chapters that follow cover the background, stages, and measures as well as the achievements and problems of the economic reforms. The next three chapters address major issues and changes in China's regional development, administrative system, and state-society relations.

The analyses of the experience and issues in these chapters are related to important development policies and conditions that were reported in the literature and are emphasized in this chapter. For example, the evaluation of China's economic reforms focuses on not only economic growth policies introduced in China's rural-agricultural, urban-industrial, and macroeconomic-structural reforms but also on international transaction policies associated with China's open-door policy and foreign trade and investment. The three changes and issues selected in this book are also related to the identified development policies and conditions. The study of changes in regional development is based on the consideration of the social equity policies because of rising income and regional inequalities in China after the reforms. The analysis of the administrative system and reform is related to the public management policies that are important in the implementation of reform policies. Finally, the examination of changes in state-society relations concerns the political and social conditions that are critical to economic development.

The specific purposes of the following chapters are summarized as follows:

Chapter 2, "Background of China's Economic Reforms," provides an overview of China's past development process and issues before the reform years. The chapter examines seven development stages during the period of 1949 to 1980; economic performance in national income, gross output value of agriculture and industry, and foreign trade during this period; factors related to the disappointing economic performance; and the political environment on the eve of the 1978 reform.

Chapter 3, "Stages and Measures of Economic Reforms," describes major reform policies and measures introduced after 1978. The chapter includes policy measures in the rural-agricultural area (e.g., decentralization, price policies, and institutional changes, 1978-1984); the urban-industrial area (e.g., changes in enterprise management and the dual-price system, 1985-1988); the slowdown of economic reforms (e.g., the problem of inflation, the Tiananmen Square incident, 1989-1991); the macroeconomic-structural reforms (e.g., the tax reform and the banking reform, after 1992); and the open-door policy (e.g., changes in foreign trade and development in China's coastal region, since the 1970s).

Chapter 4, "Evaluation of Economic Reforms," analyzes achievements and problems of economic reforms. The chapter evaluates macroeconomic performance in gross national product, national income, unemployment and inflation rates; agricultural and industrial performance and changes (e.g., increases of gross output value and structural changes); foreign trade and investment; the problem of inflation; regional and income inequality; environmental and resource protection; and crime and social unrest.

Chapter 5, "Changes in Regional Development," addresses policies and issues associated with China's regional development. The chapter consists of discussions about changes in regional development policies; the evaluation of regional and provincial economic performance between 1985 and 1993; and challenging issues related to regional development, including, for example, income inequality between the coastal and interior regions, inequalities between the rural and urban areas, and concerns about political disintegration.

Chapter 6, "Changes in the Administrative System," offers a comprehensive analysis of China's administrative or bureaucratic reforms. The chapter examines the background of administrative reform (e.g., the problem of the traditional cadre system and the motive of the administrative reform); reform measures in decentralization of decision-making power; separation of economic enterprises from administrative agencies; establishment of a civil service system; simplification of administrative structures; and professionalization of public administration activities; and challenging issues of bureaucratic corruption, the role of the Party, and economic and social influences.

Chapter 7, "Changes in State-Society Relations," examines the impact of economic reforms on Chinese society in general. The chapter covers discussions about state-society relations before the reform years, changes in rural areas; changes in urban areas, changes in social mobility, changes in individual and social ideology, changes in social control and stability, and changes in the legal system.

Finally, Chapter 8, "Lessons of Economic Reforms," summarizes the experience and issues of China's economic reforms. The chapter especially identifies ten major lessons or characteristics of China's economic reforms. The lessons identified include the role of a government-guided reform and development, the nature of partial and gradual reforms, the flexible and practical development approach, the two-way development policy, the strategy of decentralization and uneven development, the kindred development model and Chinese social culture, the contribution of a stable political and social environment, the importance of administrative reforms, the balance of economic growth and social control, and the need for monitoring and a control mechanism. The chapter ends with an analysis of the future development of economic reforms and addresses the issues of China's political environment and economic reforms.

NOTES

1. Similar to the functions identified here, Stern (1991: 250-251) also identifies five groups of arguments for state intervention in the economy, including, (1) a concern for market failure (arising from sources such as externalities, public goods, and imperfect information), (2) a concern to prevent or reduce poverty and improve income distribution, (3) the assertion of a right to certain facilities or goods (e.g., education, health, and housing), (4) paternalism (e.g., relating to education, pensions, and drugs), and (5) the rights of future generations (e.g., concerns about the environment).

2. Based on the consideration of these functions, Liou (1998) identifies five major roles of government in his evaluation of China's post-Mao economic development. The five roles are government as a promoter of growth, as a manager of the economy, as a distributor of income, as a regulator of industry, and as a protector of citizens and business.

3. Emphasizing an interdisciplinary approach, the author recognizes a potential problem in the difficulty of integrating theories and arguments from different aspects. But, after reviewing the literature on economic development, the author believes that we need to have an interdisciplinary analysis of China's economic reforms in order to fully understand the whole picture of the reforms.

CHAPTER 2

Background of China's Economic Reforms

INTRODUCTION

Since the founding of the People's Republic of China (PRC) in 1949, Chinese leaders have emphasized the importance of China's economic development. Under the leadership of Mao Zedong, the Chinese Communist Party attempted to eliminate many weaknesses of the old Chinese society and to establish a new system to promote China's modernization and security in the international political arena. Based on the Soviet Stalinist development model, Chinese leaders have developed a central planning administrative system to lead the country to the goal of industrialization and modernization.

The policy of China's economic development during Mao's era (1949-1976) was not a stable one. The economic development policy adopted by Chinese leaders was guided by several five-year national plans. Under the plan, the central planning authority controlled all social resources through the nationalization process and arranged resources distribution through different levels of the administration. The development policy and plan, however, was interrupted frequently by many objective and subjective factors. The objective factors included, for example, the withdrawal of the Soviet assistance in the late 1950s, while the subjective factors were related to Mao's revolutionary politics and class struggles emphasized during the 1960s and 1970s.

The unstable economic development policy and the nature of the central planning system have resulted in many problems in China's economy. For example, the national growth rates were inconsistent and below the target of the plan. Productivity rates in both the agricultural and the industrial sectors were low. The planning system was inefficient in improving economic performance and promoting incentives among peasants and workers. By the time of Mao's death (1996), Chinese leaders recognized that they had failed to achieve their goal of industrialization and modernization. Recognizing these problems, the post-Mao leaders have gradually developed many reform policies that have led to major changes in China's economic system and improvement in economic performance.

To examine the post-Mao Chinese economic reforms, we need first to understand the background of the reforms. The background study covers not only the problems of China's economic development during Mao's era but also the environment of the post-Mao reforms. The analysis of the former issue attempts to provide answers to the question about what went wrong in Mao's regime. The analysis of the latter issue is related to our interest in finding out what motivated the post-Mao leaders to initiate reform policies. Both background issues are important in our study of China's economic reforms and have been emphasized by many researchers of the post-Mao economic reforms (e.g., Cheng, 1982, 1990, 1991; Dong, 1980; Ishikawa, 1983; Naughton, 1995a; Nolan & Ash, 1995; Perkins, 1988; Prybyla, 1981, 1982; Tsao, 1987; White, 1991).

This chapter is designed to provide a brief, but comprehensive, analysis of the background of China's post-Mao economic reforms. The chapter begins with an overview of the process and stages of China's economic development before the reform years. It then follows with an evaluation of China's economic performance during the pre-reform period. The evaluation especially focuses on analyzing economic indicators such as national income and the gross output value of agriculture and industry among different stages of the development. Moreover, the chapter examines factors that are related to the poor economic performance before the reform years. The chapter also reviews China's political environment in the late 1970s to offer answers about the motives and needs of the reforms. Finally, the chapter concludes with summaries and discussions about the implications of the background of economic reforms.

ECONOMIC DEVELOPMENT BEFORE THE POST-MAO REFORM

The history of China's economic development can be described as several stages based on its development policies and plans (Cheng, 1982; Riskin, 1987; Tsao, 1987; Yabuki, 1995). Prior to post-Mao economic reforms, Chinese economic development consisted of seven stages and covered five periods of China's five-year plans, including (1) the period of economic rehabilitation (1949-1952); (2) the period of the First Five-Year Plan (1953-1957); (3) the period of the Second Five-Year Plan (1958-1962); (4) the period of economic readjustment (1963-1965); (5) the period of the Third Five-Year Plan (1966-1970); (6) the period of the Fourth Five-Year Plan (1971-1975); and (7) the period of the Fifth Five-Year plan (1976-1980). The present section will provide a brief review of major economic activities in each of these development periods,[1] as summarized in Table 2.1.

Economic Rehabilitation, 1949-1952

In the first stage of economic development (1949-1952), Chinese leaders emphasized the importance of recovery and rehabilitation. The goals of the recovery were to restore production facilities and activities in both the industrial and agricultural sectors that were severely damaged during both the Sino-Japanese War (1937-1945) and the Civil War (1946-1949). In the agricultural sector, the Chinese leaders successfully started land reform, which was designed to destroy the landlord class and to establish a collective farming system (i.e., Mutual Aid Teams).[2] In the industrial sector, the Chinese leaders postponed their original socialization policies because of their concern about the potential low level of industrial production. Instead, the leaders adopted a liberal policy that used the experience of the existing system and provided incentives to workers and owners.

The First Five-Year Plan, 1953-1957

After three years of recovery, the Party Central Committee considered the development experience of the Soviet Union and gradually adopted a Soviet planning model for long-term economic development. The first plan, entitled the First Five-Year Plan of the People's Republic of China for Developing the National Economy, covered the period of 1953 through 1957 and was designed to build 694 specific large-scale industrial construction projects, especially 156 Soviet-aid projects. During the period of the First Five-Year Plan, the Chinese government successfully attained its political objective of public ownership of the means of production by completing the policy of socialist transformation in both industry and agriculture. The socialist transformation policy included the change from private enterprise to joint state-private enterprise in the industry sector and the introduction of lower-stage producer cooperatives in the agriculture sector.[3]

The Second Five-Year Plan, 1958-1962

Covering the period of 1958 through 1962, the Second Five-Year Plan was interrupted and terminated because of the Three Red Banners. The Three Red Banners, under the direction of Chairman Mao, represented the "General Line for Socialist Construction," the "Great Leap Forward of Production," and the "People's Commune Movement." The Great Leap Forward attempted to achieve high economic growth rates by using China's abundant labor and traditional methods of production. The People's Commune Movement attempted to transform China from a socialist system to a communist one. The communes were considered as both productive units and local governments and were responsible for managing industry, agriculture, trade, education, and military affairs. The policies of the Great Leap Forward and the People's Commune Movement resulted in chaos in China's economy and an open split and confrontation within the Party's top leadership. The economic chaos was further hurt by the unexpected withdrawal of Soviet assistance in August 1960. The political outcome of the economic failure was that Mao gave the presidency of the People's Republic to Liu Shaoqi.

Economic Readjustment, 1963-1965

Following the failure of the Great Leap Forward and the 1960 nationwide famine, the Chinese leaders emphasized four guidelines in the three years (1963-1965) of the readjustment period. The four guidelines in this period referred to adjustment, consolidation, enrichment (filling out), and elevation (raising standards). The adjustment guideline emphasized the importance of agricultural development. To eliminate the chaos caused by the People's Commune Movement and the Great Leap

Forward, the consolidation guideline emphasized changing authorities and functions in both commune and industry management. The guideline of enrichment focused on the strengthening of weak links among different economic units. The guideline of elevation led to the shift of attention from increasing gross output to improving quality and expanding variety to meet user demand.

The Third Five-Year Plan, 1966-1970

During the period of the Third Five-Year Plan, China experienced the Cultural Revolution movement, a major political power struggle among top leaders within the Party.[4] The Cultural Revolution was launched by Mao to strengthen his control over the Party and the government. Under the goal of struggles against the revisionist line, Mao and his supporters (e.g., Red Guards) attacked the so-called anti-party clique, (i.e., Liu Shaoqi, Deng Xiaoping, Peng Zhen, and Luo Ruiqing) because they revised or rejected Mao's development policies and ideologies. For example, unlike Mao, Liu and his supporters emphasized not spiritual but material incentives and allowed some forms of private ownership and market activities.[5] Despite its political nature, the Cultural Revolution also had some negative effects on China's economy and society when the struggle moved from the urban industrial area to the rural agricultural area.

The Fourth Five-Year Plan, 1971-1975

The Cultural Revolution and the power struggle continued and extended in China during the period of the Fourth Five-Year Plan. After the death of Lin Biao in 1971, Premier Zhou Enlai was in charge of economic management and managed to rehabilitate many former officials from the Cultural Revolution purgatory. Especially, after his rehabilitation in 1973, Deng Xiaoping joined Zhou's team to assist in managing the country's economy. To promote China's economic development, Zhou adopted two major policies: the open-door and the Four Modernizations. The open-door policy attempted to improve China's economic relations with Western countries. In 1972, for example, China restored diplomatic relations with Japan and the United States. Closely related to the open-door policy, the Four Modernizations policy attempted to import foreign technology to modernize China's agriculture, industry, science and technology, and national defense. Zhou's policies were immediately under attack by the "Gang of Four" (Jiang Qing, Wang Hongwen, Zhang Chunqiao, and Yao Wenyuan) as the revisionist line. The Gang of Four attempted to seize power by reigniting the spirit of the Cultural Revolution (i.e., the second phase of the Cultural Revolution).

The Fifth Five-Year Plan, 1976-1980

The period of the Fifth Five-Year Plan (1976-1980) was a turning point in the history of China's economic development. The deaths of Zhou Enlai and Mao Zedong and the purge of Deng Xiaoping in 1976 provided an opportunity for Hua Guofeng

Table 2.1
China's Economic Development Stages and Activities, 1949-1980

Stage	Activity
Economic Rehabilitation (1949-1952)	Postponing socialization of industry Land reform in the agricultural sector
The First Five-Year Plan (1953-1957)	Adopting the planned economy model of the Soviet Union Collectivization of agriculture Socialist transformation of industry
The Second Five-Year Plan (1958-1962)	The Great Leap Forward of Production The People's Commune Movement The withdrawal of Soviet assistance The rise of Liu Shaoqi to power
Economic Readjustment (1963-1965)	The agriculture first policy Changes in the commune system Changes in industry management
The Third Five-Year Plan (1966-1970)	Power struggle between Mao Zedong and Liu Shaoqi Phase I of the Cultural Revolution
The Fourth Five-Year Plan (1971-1975)	Formulation of the Four Modernizations The open door policy (improving relationships with the United States and Japan) Phase II of the Cultural Revolution The Gang of Four
The Fifth Five-Year Plan (1976-1980)	The Rise of Hua Guofeng to Power The Ten-Year Economic Development Plan The Three-Year Adjustment Plan The Third Plenum of the Eleventh CCP Central Committee The rise of Deng Xiaoping to power

to take over the position of chairman of the Party Central Committee and of premier. Hua proposed a ten-year economic development plan to continue Zhou's concept of the four modernizations and Mao's policy of high-speed development. The ten-year plan was later revised and replaced by a new three-year adjustment plan (1979-81) proposed by the Third Plenum of the Eleventh CCP Central Committee in December 1978 because of the failure of many projects. Especially, after Deng Xiaoping's rehabilitation in July 1977, the Third Plenum of the Eleventh CCP Central Committee supported Deng's proposals for economic reforms. In addition, the Plenum announced that the era of involving mass movements in political or economic affairs was over and that economic modernization would replace class struggle as the focus of the Party's work (Harding, 1987).[6]

In sum, the brief review of China's economic development during the period of 1949 through 1980 showed major characteristics of instability. The official development policies and plans were interrupted frequently because of political power struggles within the Party leadership. The arguments and changes between the Mao's left, revolutionary policy and the non-Mao's right, revisionist policy had some negative impact on China's economic growth. The following section provides an overall evaluation of China's economic performance before the post-Mao reform.

ECONOMIC PERFORMANCE BEFORE THE REFORM

The unstable political environment and changing development policies significantly affected China's economic growth and development. Based on official Chinese statistical data, the present analyses evaluate China's economic performance by focusing on four major economic indicators and covering the period of 1949 through 1977.[7] The four economic indicators are national income, gross output value of agriculture (GOVA), gross output value of industry (GOVI), and foreign trade.

First, Table 2.2 provides longitudinal data about the value of national income, per-capita national income, and indices of national income. Based on current prices, China's national income increased from about 3.6 billion yuan in 1949 to more than 26 billion yuan in 1977, an increase of 7.4 times. The data of per-capita national income show that it increased from 66 yuan to 280 yuan during this period, an increase of 4.2 times. In addition, the data of national income indices are emphasized here because they measure percentage increases of national income between the current year and the preceding year. Between 1949 and 1977, the national income indices showed that the largest annual percentage increase was 23.3 percent in 1970 and the lowest increase was -29.7 percent (70.3) in 1961. The average annual percentage increase of national income during this period was 7.79 percent.

Next, the longitudinal data about value and indices of GOVA and GOVI are presented in Table 2.3. With regard to GOVA, the data show that the value increased from about 3.3 billion yuan in 1949 to 14 billion yuan in 1977, an increase of 4.3 times. The indices data of GOVA show that the largest increase was 17.8 percent in 1950 and the smallest increase was -13.6 percent (86.4) in 1959. The average annual percentage increase of GOVA was 4.39 percent. The GOVI data show that the value increased from 1.4 billion yuan in 1949 to more than 37 billion yuan in 1977, an increase of 26.6 times. The largest increase of GOVI indices was 54.8 percent in 1958, and the smallest increase was -38.2 percent (61.8) in 1961. The average annual percentage increase was 15.26 percent during this period.

The data on China's foreign trade, including total amounts, exports, imports, and balance, are presented in Table 2.4. The total trade amounts increased from U.S. $1.13 billions of dollars in 1950 to $14.80 billions of dollars, an increase of 13.1 times. During the same period, the exports increased from $0.55 billions to $7.59 billions, and the imports increased from $0.58 billions to $7.21 billions. These increases in exports and imports are 13.8 times and 12.4 times, respectively. The data on trade balance showed that China experienced trade deficits during the period of 1950 to 1955, ranging from $0.03 billions to $0.32 billions. After 1956, China generally maintained trade surpluses except in the years of 1960, 1970, 1974, and 1975. The trade deficit in 1974 was $0.67 billions, the largest amount during the period of 1950 to 1977.

The data about China's major economic indicators are further divided based on the six development stages between 1950 and 1975. Table 2.5 provides a summary of economic indicators from the stages of economic rehabilitation (1949-1952), the First Five-Year Plan (1953-1957), the Second Five-Year Plan (1958-1962), economic readjustment (1963-1965), the Third Five-Year Plan (1966-1970), to the Fourth Five-Year Plan (1971-1975). The stage of the Fifth Five-Year plan was not included in the present analysis because it was the transition period between Mao's system and post-Mao economic reforms.

The distribution of economic indicators among the six stages (Table 2.5) reveals the impact of changing economic development policies. With regard to the data on national income, the largest average annual percentage increase in national income was 19.3 percent, achieved in the first stage of economic recovery (1949-1952). Again, the second largest average increase in national income was 14.7 percent, in the second stage of economic readjustment (1963-1965). As explained previously, Chinese leaders emphasized more liberal and revisionary policies in both stages. During the period of 1958 through 1962 (the Second Five-Year Plan), China experienced an average annual increase of a negative 3.1 percent (i.e., an average decrease of 3.1 percent), which showed the negative impact of the left and revolutionary policies (i.e., the Great Leap Forward and the People's Commune Movement). Similarly, the average percentage of national income declined during the period of the Cultural Revolution (1966-1970), when Mao's revolutionary policies were emphasized.

The distribution of the average annual increase of GOVA and GOVI among six stages shows a similar pattern of development. The largest average annual increase in GOVA was 14.1 percent, and the largest average annual increase in GOVI was 34.8 percent, both occurring in the first economic recovery stage (1949-1952). The lowest average annual increase in GOVA was negative 4.3 percent (i.e., a decrease of 4.3 percent annually), and the lowest average annual increase in GOVI was 3.8 percent, both occurring in the period of 1958 through 1962 (the Second Five-Year Plan). The GOVA and GOVI data also indicate the impact of China's industrial-oriented development policy, because of the greater percentage increases in the industrial sector than in the agricultural sector. Moreover, the data reveal that the revolutionary development policy tended to have greater negative impact on the agricultural sector than on the industrial sector.

Finally, the distribution of the average trade data also indicate the effect of China's economic development policy. During the 1950s, China experienced major trade deficits, and the Soviet Union was China's top trade partner because China emphasized Mao's lean-to-one-side trade policy. The situation gradually changed after the break in the relationship between China and the Soviet Union in 1960 and the influence on Mao's self-reliance policy. The direct outcome of the self-reliance policy was the trade balance, that is, the trade surplus during the 1960s. The total trade amount increased in the 1970s, when Chinese leaders emphasized the open-door and modernization policies. Hong Kong, Macau, and Japan became China's major trade partners during this period of time (Tsao, 1987).

The findings of the present evaluation of China's economic performance are similar to those reported by other Chinese researchers (e.g., Ishikawa, 1983; Prybyla, 1982; Rawski, 1979). These researchers agreed that China had achieved a relatively high level of economic growth during the period of economic recovery (1949-1952) and the First Five-Year Plan (1953-1957).

With regard to the negative impact of Mao's revolutionary policies, the researchers found that both labor productivity (measured in output value per man-day) and factory productivity in agriculture (measured by gross value of output) declined between 1957 and 1975. While the former declined from 15 to 36 percent (depending on the assumption used about labor intensity), the latter declined ranging from 25 to 33 percent over the whole period (Prybyla, 1982: 1206-1214; Rawski, 1979: 119-122). Especially, Cheng (1982: 355-356) estimated that labor productivity in industry rose only 15 percent during the 21-year period of 1957 to 1978, or 0.7 percent per year. This again showed a declining picture when comparing it with an average annual increase rate of 8.7 percent between 1953 and 1957.

The evaluation of China's economic performance also needs to compare its growth and development records with those of other developing countries. Two different findings have been reported. On the one hand, it was noticed that China's official per-capita GNP in 1978 was 379 yuan (about $250), which put China in the upper half of the low-income countries category (including countries such as Uganda, Sudan, and Kenya) with per-capita GNP ranging from $260-$360 (Prybyla, 1981). Among these developing countries, China's economic growth was considered one of the highest (Nolan & Ash, 1995: 981; World Bank, 1983) during the period of 1960-1980.

On the other hand, it was also suggested that China's economic development was considered poor when comparing it with that of East Asian countries. For example, during the period of 1960 to 1976, China experienced an annual increase of 5.7 percent in gross national product (GNP) and 3.6 percent in per-capita GNP. During the same period, China's neighbors achieved much higher percentages of increase, including an annual average of a 9.1 percent of GNP increase and 8.0 percent of per-capita GNP increase in Japan; a 9.6 percent of GNP increase and 7.3 percent of per-capita GNP increase in South Korea; a 9.5 percent of GNP increase and

Table 2.2
National Income, 1949-1977

Year	National Income (100 million yuan)[1]	Per-Capita (yuan)[1]	Indices (Preceding year = 100)
1949	358	66	-
1950	426	77	119.0 %
1951	497	88	116.7
1952	589	104	122.3
1953	709	122	114.0
1954	748	126	105.8
1955	788	129	106.4
1956	882	142	114.1
1957	908	142	104.5
1958	1118	171	122.0
1959	1222	183	108.2
1960	1220	183	98.6
1961	996	151	70.3
1962	924	139	93.5
1963	1000	147	110.7
1964	1166	167	116.5
1965	1387	194	117.0
1966	1586	216	117.0
1967	1487	198	92.8
1968	1415	183	93.5
1969	1617	203	119.3
1970	1926	235	123.3
1971	2077	247	107.0
1972	2136	248	102.9
1973	2318	263	108.3
1974	2348	261	101.1
1975	2503	273	108.3
1976	2427	261	97.3
1977	2644	280	107.8
1949-77	(7.4)[2]	(4.2)[2]	(7.52)[3]

Source: State Statistical Bureau, *Statistical Yearbook of China* (1986: 40-42).
Note: 1. At current prices.
2. The calculated times of increase from 1949 through 1977.
3. The calculated average annual percentage increase from 1949 through 1977.

Table 2.3
Gross Output Value of Agriculture (GOVA) and Industry (GOVI), 1949-1977[1]

	Agriculture		Industry	
Year	Value[2]	Indices	Value[2]	Indices
1949	326	-	140	-
1950	384	117.8%	191	136.4%
1951	420	109.4	264	138.2
1952	461	115.2	349	129.9
1953	510	103.1	450	130.3
1954	535	103.4	515	116.3
1955	575	107.6	534	105.6
1956	610	105.0	642	128.1
1957	537	103.6	704	111.5
1958	566	102.4	1083	154.8
1959	497	86.4	1483	136.1
1960	457	87.4	1637	111.2
1961	559	97.6	1062	61.8
1962	584	106.2	920	83.4
1963	642	111.6	993	108.5
1964	720	113.5	1164	119.6
1965	833	108.3	1402	126.4
1966	910	108.6	1624	120.9
1967	924	101.6	1382	86.2
1968	928	97.5	1285	95.0
1969	948	101.1	1665	134.3
1970	1058	111.5	2117	130.7
1971	1107	103.1	2414	114.9
1972	1123	99.8	2565	106.6
1973	1226	108.4	2794	109.5
1974	1277	104.2	2792	100.3
1975	1343	104.6	3207	115.1
1976	1378	102.5	3278	101.3
1977	1400	101.7	3725	114.3
1949-77	(4.3)[3]	(4.39)[4]	(26.6)[3]	(15.26)[4]

Source: State Statistical Bureau, *Statistical Yearbook of China* (1986: 24-26); (1993: 335-336).

Note:
1. After 1970, there are some differences in GOVA and GOVI numbers between the two sources of statistical data. The GOVA data are based on the 1986 statistical yearbook and the GOVI data are based on the 1993 yearbook.
2. Based on 100 million yuan, at current Prices.
3. The calculated times of increase from 1949 through 1977.
4. The calculated average annual percentage increases from 1949 through 1977.

Table 2.4
Foreign Trade, 1950-1977[1]

Year	Total	Exports	Imports	Balance
1950	1.13	0.55	0.58	-0.03
1951	1.96	0.76	1.20	-0.44
1952	1.94	0.82	1.12	-0.30
1953	2.37	1.02	1.35	-0.33
1954	2.44	1.15	1.29	-0.14
1955	3.14	1.41	1.73	-0.32
1956	3.21	1.65	1.56	0.09
1957	3.10	1.60	1.50	1.00
1958	3.87	1.98	1.89	0.09
1959	4.38	2.26	2.12	0.14
1960	3.81	1.86	1.95	-0.09
1961	2.94	1.49	1.45	0.04
1962	2.66	1.49	1.17	0.32
1963	2.92	1.65	1.27	0.38
1964	3.47	1.92	1.55	0.37
1965	4.25	2.23	2.02	0.21
1966	4.62	2.37	2.25	0.12
1967	4.16	2.14	2.02	0.12
1968	4.05	2.10	1.95	0.15
1969	4.03	2.20	1.83	0.37
1970	4.59	2.26	2.33	-0.07
1971	4.84	2.64	2.20	0.44
1972	6.30	3.44	2.86	0.58
1973	10.98	5.82	5.16	0.66
1974	14.57	6.95	7.62	-0.67
1975	14.75	7.26	7.49	-0.23
1976	13.43	6.85	6.58	0.27
1977	14.80	7.59	7.21	0.38
1950-77	(13.1)[2]	(13.8)[2]	(12.4)[2]	

Source: State Statistical Bureau, *Statistical Yearbook of China* (1993: 633).
Note: 1. Based on current price in billions of U.S. dollars.
2. The calculated times of amount increases from 1950 through 1977.

7.5 percent of per-capita GNP increase in Singapore; and a 9.0 percent of GNP increase and 6.2 percent of per-capita GNP increase in Taiwan (Bell et al., 1993: 9).

Besides the disappointing economic growth, China's economy also showed some signs of structural problems in the late 1970s. Dong (1980) identified these structural problems as serious imbalances in the national economy, including the imbalance between heavy and light industry and agriculture, the imbalance in the accumulation-consumption ratio, and the imbalance in the distribution of investments. Nolan and Ash (1995) provided data to support the argument about the structural problems in China. For example, Nolan and Ash (1995: 983) found that percentage distributions of agriculture, industry, and services in China's gross domestic products (GDP) in the late 1970s were 31 percent, 47 percent, and 22 percent, respectively. The percentage distributions of the three sectors in China's employment were 71 percent, 17 percent, and 12 percent, respectively. The distributions were very imbalanced when comparing them with the distributions in other economies. The imbalance was especially noticed in the services sector because for industrial market economies, the percentage distributions were 62 percent of the GDP and 56 percent of the employment. The imbalances certainly resulted from China's past economic development policies.

In sum, the evaluation of China's economic performance revealed that during the period of 1949 to 1977, China experienced both positive and negative development records. The Chinese development experience was directly related to its changing economic policies and political environment. While the overall records were good compared to low-income developing countries, Chinese leaders felt that the country's economic growth was disappointing because it was lower than those of China's neighbors and did not meet China's own expectations in the development plans. Considering all the problems of low income, low productivity, and structural imbalances, Prybyla (1989; 1990a) concluded that China's economy in the late 1970s suffered serious quality problems, including (1) chronic shortages of wanted goods, including both consumer and producer goods (i.e., shortage of everything useful); (2) massive waste, including misallocations of resources and inefficient use of resources in production and distribution; (3) technological backwardness, including stagnation of research, development, innovation, and diffusion of modern technology, and (4) the breakdown of the incentive system, including deficient incentives to labor, management, and entrepreneurship (Prybyla, 1990a; 1989). These problems stem not only from China's developmental policies and strategies but also from its economic systems and structures. The concern of poor quality and low productivity led to the open-door and Modernization policies that were proposed and emphasized during the 1970s.

CAUSES OF THE ECONOMIC PROBLEMS

The economic problems of disappointing growth and development, low agricultural and industrial productivity, and various structural and quality issues resulted from a combination of interrelated objective and subjective factors (Prybyla, 1989: 1018-1019; 1982: 1214-1225). The objective factors include, for example,

China's huge absolute size and population increase (about 26 additional people per minute), the shrinkage of farmland from an already exigency base (about one million acres a year), the problem of energy shortages, and the weight of traditional feudalism (the authoritarian nature of the political and economic systems and the problems of the bureaucracy).[8]

The problem of population increase is of particular importance to Chinese leaders. After the end of two long wars (the Sino-Japanese War between 1937 and 1945 as well as the Civil War between 1946 and 1949), the Chinese population grew rapidly during the periods of economic recovery and the First Five-Year Plan because of stable political conditions. The natural population growth rate (birth rate minus death rate) was at a high 2 percent per annum. The population growth slowed down during and following the Great Leap Forward (1958 to 1961) because of natural and man-made disasters. Between 1962 and 1971, the population increased again at a rate of natural increase as high as 3 percent per annum. The total Chinese population increased from 540 million in 1949 to about 900 million in 1974, an increase of 1.67 times (Yabuki, 1995: 9-11).

The problem of population increase is also related to China's policy toward population limitation and control. Ma Yinchu, an economist, warned about the crisis of unlimited population increase and advocated a birth limitation policy in the late 1950s (*People's Daily*, 1957, July 5). But the idea of birth limitation policy was directly in conflict with Mao's "mass line" theory, which emphasizes China's big population as an asset to the country's development. In the late 1970s China gradually formulated its population control policy. Chinese leaders started to advocate and promote family planning in 1978 and the one-child policy was adopted in 1979, when the state promoted the ideal family as a couple and one child (Croll, 1991).

While the objective factors limit economic development, China's disappointing economic performance and increasing productivity and quality problems before the reform years were mainly related to such subjective factors as policy errors and system problems. Policy errors are mistakes of "workstyle," which refers to politically induced economic policy cycles-the struggle between the two lines (i.e., rightists vs. leftists, revisionists vs. dogmatists).

For example, the move from the First Five-Year Plan to the Great Leap Forward showed a policy change from the right line to the left line. The three-year adjustment period after the Great Leap Forward was a policy change from the left to the right. During the ten-year period of the Cultural Revolution, the economic policy was first moved to the left line when the Red Guard attacked the so-called anti-Party clique and their policies. The policy was then switched to the right line when Zhou Enlai was in charge of the economy and the open-door policy was adopted. The economic policy made another turn to the left after the 1976 Tiananmen incident and the death of Mao Zedong. The policy finally went back to the right when Deng Xiaoping rehabilitated and gradually controlled the party power at the Third Plenum of the Eleventh Party Central Committee. The continued changes of economic policy certainly put large obstacles in the way of economic development and modernization.

Table 2.5
Major Economic Indicators by Development Stages

Stage	Average Annual Percentage Increases			Average Trade (in U.S. $ billions)			
	National Income	GOVA	GOVI	Total	Export	Import	Balance
1950-52	19.3%	14.1%	34.8%	1.68	0.71	0.97	-0.26
1953-57	8.9	4.5	18.0	2.85	1.37	1.49	-0.12
1958-62	-3.1	-4.3	3.8	3.53	1.82	1.72	0.10
1963-65	14.7	11.1	17.9	3.55	1.93	1.61	0.32
1966-70	8.3	3.9	11.7	4.29	2.21	2.08	0.14
1971-75	5.5	4.0	9.1	10.29	5.22	5.07	0.16

Source: Calculated from previous tables.

There were major differences in economic development strategies between the right-line and left-line policies (Tsao, 1987). The right-line policy was related to the group development strategies (strategies of Liu Shaoqi, Deng Xiaoping, Chen Yun) and emphasized production for market demand. The left-line policy was related to Mao's development strategies and stressed production for political purposes. In the agricultural area, the right-line policy allowed the reserve of a small percentage of arable land as private plots and the left-line policy stressed the reduction of the utilization scope of private plots. In the industrial area, the right-line policy focused on the consumption industry and the left-line policy emphasized the defense industry. With regard to production incentives, the right-line policy used wages as incentives and allowed overtime pay and awards for over-quota production; the left-line policy used Mao's thoughts as spiritual incentives and emphasized an equal pay scale.

System problems refer to the nature of China's central administrative command planning system, which has been characterized as having vertical information flows, centralized coordination and property, and limited and concentrated participation in economic decisions (Prybyla, 1982). In the command planning system, resources allocation decisions are made in response to commands from planners in the administrative hierarchy, rather than in response to prices from the market. The system was based on the Soviet Development Model, which emphasizes a high rate of investment, collectivization of agriculture, priority to heavy industry and military, reliance on large-scale and capital-intensive technology in industry, and the relative neglect of investment in agriculture and consumer goods industries (Cheng, 1991; Tsao, 1987; Yeh, 1967).[9]

The problem of the command planning system was that planning did not eliminate the shortcomings of the capitalist system (e.g., anarchy) but generated problems of its own (e.g., the built-in, permanent imbalance between supply and demand) because of the complexity involved in constructing a material plan. It did not abolish waste but generated it on a grand scale. It abolished production for profit, but failed to replace it with production for use. Especially, it produced economic activity in socially undesirable directions and was unable to alter the underlying pattern of economic behavior (Nolan & Ash, 1995: 981). The system led to allocative inefficiency because of such problems as (1) the misallocation of both investment goods and of inputs and outputs; (2) the restriction on the use of material incentives; and (3) the destruction of the energy and enthusiasm of workers, managers, and farmers (e.g., Perkins, 1988: 602; Prybyla, 1982: 1234).

While sharing a similar command planning model of development, China's economic and social backgrounds are different from those of the Soviet Union and the Eastern European countries. In addition to the common problems of the planning model explained earlier, China differed from these countries in many important factors, which caused additional problems for development and modernization. These factors include China's shortage of arable land; its larger rural sector; its level of underemployment; its educational deficiencies and lack of scientific and technical expertise; and its lower levels of per capita income, industrialization and urbanization. In other words, China was much poorer and not so developed as its socialist counterparts (Naughton, 1995a: 38-46; Nolan & Ash, 1995: 996-997).[10]

Moreover, to make the command planning system work, it is necessary and important to maintain a climate conducive to the routine administrative process and avoid disruptions in it. Unfortunately, this was not the case of the Chinese development experience because of the radical policies advanced by Mao. Mao's policies emphasized the primacy of class struggle and the need for continuous revolution, the promotion of mass participation in decision making and disdain for intellectuals and experts, the use of movements or campaigns instead of normal economic measures, and the importance of egalitarianism and normative incentives instead of material rewards and profits (Cheng, 1982; 1991). Based on the influence of Mao's radical policies, the history of the five-year plans in China was a history of violation and disruption, especially related to mass mobilization political movements (the Great Leap Forward and the Cultural Revolution) (Ishikawa, 1983). During the political movements, the economic development programs and goals were not followed, the institutions and factories were closed frequently, and many of the planning bureaucrats were purged because of the power struggles within the Party.

Recognizing serious economic problems and poor economic performance, the post-Mao Chinese leaders addressed such issues as the structural problems of the command planning system, the negative consequences of the policy mistakes, power struggles in the Party, and class struggles in the society. They decided to reform the economic system; overcome the quality problems; and promote economic growth, modernization, and development. Considering the issue of political stability, the leaders supported reform policies that consisted of such characteristics as (1) developing a greater and supplementary role of the market mechanism in the existing planning system, (2) readjusting the traditional macro-economic imbalances (i.e., from heavy toward light industry, from industry toward agriculture, from investments toward consumption, from state toward collective and private business), (3) reducing the traditional emphasis on egalitarianism and balanced regional growth, (4) decentralizing the economic decision-making power to raise efficiency, and (5) promoting closer integration of China into the world economy (Nolan & Ash, 1995; White, 1991).

THE POLITICAL ENVIRONMENT IN THE LATE 1970s

In addition to the economic issues, the analysis of the background of China's post-Mao economic reforms also needs to examine the political environment in the late 1970s to understand the political motivations underlying the reforms (White, 1991). After Mao's death and the coup against the Gang of Four in 1976, the Chinese political system was in crisis. The credibility of the Communist regime was seriously shaken by the ideological confusion and power struggles among the top Party leaders. The Chinese people were angry about the social disorder caused by the Cultural Revolution. Especially, they felt frustrated about their social and economic life because of the increase of restrictions in daily activities and the lack of improvement in living standards.

Chinese leaders first supported Hua Guofeng, then head of the Ministry of Public Security, to assume the top Party, military, and government posts based on a short note, "as long as you do the job, I am not worried," that Mao had given to him. To maintain his political power and position, Hua continued to endorse Mao's decisions by emphasizing a "two whatevers" policy, namely, "firmly upholding whatever policy decisions Chairman Mao made and unswervingly adhering to whatever instructions Chairman Mao gave." To deal with economic problems and to enlarge his power base, Hua also tried to redefine national policies by emphasizing a "new leap forward" and introducing a ten-year development program.

Hua's ambivalent position, liberal in economic activities and conservative in political activities, was not successful. People criticized his economic programs as too aggressive, causing high investment costs and trade deficits. His attitude toward Mao and especially his defense of the Cultural Revolution were challenged by many cadres who were victims of the movement and wanted a decisive repudiation of the event. One critical issue here was whether or not to rehabilitate Deng Xiaoping, who was unfairly dismissed from office in 1976 and had wide support among the Party leaders. Facing pressure from the provincial and central Party committees, Hua finally agreed to Deng's return to his previous political positions.[11]

After reassuming his positions in the party and military posts in 1977, Deng moved quickly to challenge Hua's policies and leadership. Recognizing the widespread dissatisfaction with Cultural Revolution type politics, Deng united pre Cultural Revolution officials into a reform coalition and used this coalition to challenge Hua's policies and to lay the foundation for his own reforms. In addition to get support from the highest level of the Party, Deng also mobilized support from vocal sectors of the broader population through the "Democracy Wall" movement. In the late 1970s, most of the wall posters called for a redress of grievances resulting from the Cultural Revolution.

Facing pressures from within and outside the Party, the Third Plenum of the Eleventh Party Central Committee in December 1978 made several policy decisions that supported and encouraged several key elements of Deng's ideologies and programs. These elements include, for example, the end of class struggle and mass movements, the emphasis on economic development, the philosophy of "seeking truth from facts," and the reassessment of Mao and the Cultural Revolution. The last two issues were formerly endorsed in the Fourth Plenum of the Central Committee in 1979. These issues further weakened Hua's political basis because the philosophy of "seeking truth from facts" was directly in conflict with Hua's "two whatevers" policy and because Hua is a political beneficiary of the Cultural Revolution.

Besides challenging Hua's ideological and programmatic issues, Deng also worked to strengthen his own power base within the leading organs of the Party. On the one hand, Deng gradually secured the appointment of his supporters to influential positions in the Party (especially the position of members of the Central Committee), army, and government. On the other hand, Deng tried to create new Party and state agencies to assume power and to replace the original positions that were occupied by Hua's supporters. After he built a strong power base in the Party, military, and government, Deng removed Hua's closest supporters, the "little Gang of Four" (Wang Dongxiang, Chen Xilian, Ji Dengkui, and Wu De), from their administrative and party positions in 1980 and forced Hua to step down from his leading positions, including giving up his premiership to Zhao Ziyang and his Party chairmanship to Hu Yaobang (both Zhao and Hu were Deng's supporters). In 1982, Hua was dismissed from the Politburo at the Twelfth Party Congress, and Deng became chairman of the Military Affairs Committee.

Finally, it is important to recognize the change of political philosophy emphasized by Deng and his reformers. Since 1978, the primacy of ideology under Mao has been replaced by the pragmatic philosophy of Deng (Pye, 1986). The pragmatic attitude of Deng is evident in his remarks about the cat and the mice (i.e., it does not matter about the color of the cat so long as it catches the mice). The impact of this pragmatic attitude on the post-Mao economic reforms is especially evident when the reformers emphasize the principle of "practice is the sole criterion of truth." This principle means that pragmatism and empirical experimentation rather than ideologies are to provide the basis for economic reforms (Prybyla, 1981; Solinger, 1981). The change from doctrinal politics to pragmatic politics received support from the majority of cadres and the general public, who had suffered decades of class struggles. The pervasion of pragmatism in the Chinese society is essential to the cultivation of the positive psychological environment, which was lost after the Cultural Revolution but was necessary for the time of economic reforms.

In sum, the Chinese political environment in the late 1970s was the power struggle between Hua Guofeng and Deng Xiaoping. Both Hua and Deng recognized the importance of maintaining political stability and improving economic performance to restore the authority of the Party and the credibility of the regime. Hua and his restorationists adopted the traditional approach to economic management and some positive attitudes toward Mao's policies and the Cultural Revolution. Deng and his reformers, on the other hand, emphasized the importance of readjusting economic structures and criticized Mao's policies and the mistakes of the Cultural Revolution. The rise of the reformers means the end of the past class struggles and mass movements and the beginning of pragmatic politics and economic development.

CONCLUSION

This chapter examined major background issues related to China's post-Mao economic reforms. The review of China's economic development policies and activities during Mao's years showed that China's past economic development policy was based on the central planning development model learned from the Soviet Union. The economic development before the reform years covered four five-year plans reflected in six development stages. The development was characterized by unstable policies and abrupt changes due to power struggles among top leaders within the Party.

The evaluation of China's economic performance between 1949 and 1977 revealed that economic growth records were relatively good when comparing them with those of other similar developing countries. The growth records, however, were considered very disappointing when based on the expectation of Chinese leaders indicated in their national plans. The development records were also very poor when compared with those of China's neighboring countries and regions (Japan, South

Korea, Singapore, Hong Kong, and Taiwan). The differences of economic development between China and Taiwan were especially important because of the political and ideological confrontations between the Communist Party government and the Kuomintang government.

The analysis of causes of disappointing economic performance identified some problems associated with the central planning economic system. The analysis further pointed out major differences between Mao's left, revolutionary development policies and the non-Mao's right, revisionary development policies. Based on the development experience, the post-Mao Chinese leaders recognized that both the system problems and Mao's revolutionary policies negatively affected China's economic growth and development. To improve economic performance and promote development, the leaders first emphasized the open-door and modernization policies and gradually proposed and implemented policy measures to reform China's economic system.

The discussions about China's political environment in the late 1970s focused on the power struggles between Deng Xiaoping and Hua Guofeng. Both Deng and Hua understood that China faced many economic and social problems and that the Party was in political crisis because of the impact of the Cultural Revolution. But they had different ideas about the needed changes and reforms. While Hua took a limited and compromising approach, Deng emphasized a comprehensive and practical approach to economic development. The success of Deng in the power struggle was related not only to Deng's experience and strategies but also to the attitudes of the cadres and the Chinese people.

Finally, the outcome of the background examination is important for readers to understand the post-Mao economic reforms. The outcome provides the necessary information to study the motives, scope, approach, and expectation of the reforms. For example, the combination of both economic and political motives indicates that the post-Mao reforms will cover both economic issues and other related political and social activities that are important to economic development. The rise of Deng in the Party indicates that the reforms will be not only comprehensive in nature but also practical in their implementation. After many years of experience with political and power struggles, the Chinese leaders will pay special attention to the issue of political environment and try to maintain a stable social and political environment as the first consideration of implementing any reform policies. The frustration associated with the failure to meet past unreasonable goals during Mao's years also teaches Chinese leaders to be realistic about any expectations of the new policies. All of these issues become important components of China's post-Mao economic reforms.

NOTES

1. For more information about China's economic development experience before the reform years see, for example, Cheng (1982), Riskin (1987), and Tsao (1987: 11-38).

2. The earliest Mutual Aid Team (MAT) consisted of three to five households that banded together to help each other during the heavy farming seasons; the more advanced MAT was larger (up to twenty households) and worked together year-around in such activities as labor power and farm tools (Riskin, 1987: 68).

3. The feature of the lower-stage agricultural producer cooperatives (LAPCs) was that

their members' land and large tools, while still owned privately, were pooled and used collectively. Members were paid for their work and a rent for their property investment. The size of the LAPCs consisted of between 10 to 20 households, and some reached 200 households (Riskin, 1987: 68).

4. For more information about the Cultural Revolution Movement, see, for example, Lee (1978) and Selden (1979: 107-133).

5. For a good comparison of development strategies between Mao's and the non-Mao's, see Tsao (1987: 34-35).

6. For more information about the period of the Fifth Five-Year Plan, see the section on political background before the reform in this chapter.

7. In the past, Chinese economic statistics were regarded as secrets. To provide correct documentation and data for China's development, the Chinese government has emphasized the importance of statistics and improved the quality of the official statistics since the beginning of the reforms. For more information about the scope, the quality, and the development of Chinese official statistics see, for example, Chow (1994: 101-111, Chapter 10).

8. For additional discussions about objective and traditional problems, see Prybyla (1982: 1214-1216) and Riskin (1987: 11-37).

9. For more information about the Soviet Development Model, see Cohn (1970), Desai (1983), and Treadgold (1967).

10. Researchers (Naughton, 1995a; Nolan & Ash, 1995) emphasized the different background and experience between China's development and that of the Soviet and Eastern European countries. They maintained that the differences led to the later adoption of different economic reform strategies.

11. For more information about the power struggle between Deng Xiaoping and Hua Guofeng during 1978 and 1982, see Harding (1987: 57-66) and Lieberthal (1995: 122-137).

CHAPTER 3

Stages and Measures of Economic Reforms

INTRODUCTION

The Chinese economy in the mid-1970s showed poor and disappointing performance in many aspects of economic measures. As discussed in the previous chapter, China's economy revealed such problems as low income and poor living standards, deficient incentives to labor and management, low quality of industrial products, inefficiency in resources distribution, declining productivity in both agriculture and industry, disproportionate rates between investment and consumption, and imbalances between heavy industry development and agriculture and light industry development (Dong, 1980; Nolan & Ash, 1995; Prybyla, 1981, 1982). These economic problems became one of the major policy issues that challenged the survival of the Communist regime.

China's poor and disappointing economic performance resulted from both system problems and policy errors. The system problems were related to the nature of China's central administrative command planning system, characterized as centralized control and coordination of economic activities and decisions by planners in the administrative hierarchy. The policy errors had to do with not only mistakes related to both the Soviet development policy and Mao's revolutionary policy but also instabilities and changes associated with the power struggles within the Chinese Communist Party. The economy suffered during the period of the Great Leap Forward (1958-1960), the Socialist Education Campaign (1963-1965), the Cultural Revolution (1966-1970), and the radical campaigns of the 1970s.

The death of Mao Zedong in 1976 provided an opportunity for the Chinese leaders to develop new policies to address economic issues and problems. After a short period of internal power struggles, Deng Xiaoping's ideas and policies have emerged as the major force to guide China's economic reforms, since the Third Plenum of the Eleventh Party Central Committee in December 1978. Since then, the post-Mao leaders have given up the past class struggles and mass movements and focused on economic growth and development. They have emphasized not political ideologies but pragmatism and empirical experimentations as the basis for economic reforms. They have gradually reformed various aspects of China's economic system and opened the door to allow foreigners to invest in China on the one hand and China to access the world economic market on the other.

The purpose of this chapter is to examine major stages and policy measures of economic reforms during the post-Mao development period. The period covered China's four five-year plans: the latter part of the Fifth Five-Year Plan (1976-1980), the Sixth Five-Year Plan (1981-1985), the Seventh Five-Year Plan (1986-1990), and the Eighth Five-Year Plan (1991-1995). Closely related to the five-year plans, the present examination of China's post-Mao economic reforms is based on five stages that represent major emphases of the reforms. The five stages consist of the rural-agricultural reform (1978-1984), the urban-industrial reform (1985-1988), the slowdown of economic reforms (1989-1991), the macroeconomic-structural reform (after 1992), and the open-door policy (since the 1970s). The five stages of economic reform are similar to those emphasized by other researchers of China's economic reforms (e.g., Perkins, 1988; Yeh, 1993).[1]

The examination of reform stages and policy measures is critical in our understanding of China's post-Mao economic reforms for two reasons. First, the examination of China's major reform policies is directly related to the importance of economic growth and international transaction policies to economic development. As identified and explained in the review of economic development literature, the effective formulation and implementation of both policies contributed to the success of reform and development in many developing countries. Among the successful countries, the Chinese government is especially interested in the development experience of both the growth and trade policies of China's neighboring countries and regions, such as Japan, South Korea, Singapore, Taiwan, and Hong Kong.

Next, the reform stages developed represented the Chinese leaders' intention to reform China's economic system through changes in one aspect of the system that gradually extended to another. The changes and extension of the reform stages were also related to the social and political environment of each stage. The policy measures introduced during the reform years were methods that the Chinese leaders used to improve economic conditions and operations. While some of the earlier policy measures were based on suggestions in the 1950s and 1960s (Solinger, 1981), many of the late measures are new ideas and programs to Chinese people and their leaders. The scope and implementation of the measures are certainly important to the fate of the economic reforms.

This chapter begins with the study of reform issues in the rural, agricultural sector, including the problem of the old commune system, changes in both policy and institutional areas. Next, the chapter focuses on the issues related to the urban, industrial reform, including the expansion of enterprise autonomy, the creation of markets for some goods, and the change of prices for certain industrial products. The speed of economic reforms slowed down in 1989 because of disagreements about the pace and depth of the reforms and especially the impact of the Tiananmen Square incident. The chapter further introduces major proposals suggested in the 1990s to reform China's macroeconomic structure, including reforms in the fiscal system, the bank system, and the legal and market infrastructure. After examining the reforms in the internal economic activities, the chapter also addresses the open-door policy and reviews changes in China's foreign trade and new development policies in the coastal region. Finally, the chapter concludes with discussions about the nature and characteristics of China's economic reforms.

THE RURAL-AGRICULTURAL REFORM, 1978-1984

The post-Mao Chinese leaders started their economic reforms by first focusing on the rural-agricultural sector. The decision to reform the farming system was based on the consideration of the agricultural stagnation problem. The stagnation problem here referred to the serious situation that agricultural production could not provide enough food to feed the growing population. The agricultural stagnation problem was evidenced in Yeh's (1993: 19) analysis that during the period of 1952 to 1978, China's net agricultural output grew at an average of 1.8 percent per year, whereas the population grew at an average of 2 percent.

The problem of agriculture production was directly related to China's development policy. First, based on the Soviet development model, China's development policy in the past focused on industrial development. The heavy disproportion of the investment in the industry area was at the expense of agriculture and light industry. During the period of 1950 to 1977, the average annual increase of the gross output value of agriculture (GOVA) was only 4.39 percent, while the gross output value of industry (GOVI) was 15.26 percent, about 3.5 times the average GOVA.[2]

But the primary cause of the low growth in agriculture was the peasants' lack of incentive under the people's commune system. The people's commune system was introduced in 1958 during the Great Leap Forward period. The commune was composed of brigades and production teams and designed to provide additional political, administrative, social, economic, and military functions in China's rural society (Crook, 1986; Tuan & Webb, 1993). The production teams consisted of about 20 to 30 households and were the basic unit of production. Production decisions were made by a higher authority and often did not consider local conditions. The commune system operated under a big-bowl (*da guo fan)* distribution mechanism. The big-bowl distribution means that a group of people share a similar amount of food in a big bowl no matter how much each person has contributed to the production of the food in the bowl.

The commune production system and the big-bowl distribution mechanism significantly reduced and destroyed any incentives for peasants to increase their farming production (Wang, 1994: 67-69). On the one hand, the commune system, under the central planning quotas mechanism, did not allow peasants to make rational or the best decisions on any issues related to agricultural production. The agricultural production decisions were handled vertically (top-down), from a superior planning committee down to a county, then to a commune, and finally down to a brigade and a team. The decisions made, however, were not efficient because they did not always consider the local condition and fit for the local interest. On the other hand, the big-bowl mechanism eliminated incentives for improving production because there is no relationship between work production and work rewards. As indicated earlier, the result of the commune system and the big-bowl mechanism was that agricultural growth in the pre-reform period was barely sufficient to keep up with population growth.[3]

The rural-agricultural reform consisted of both policy and institutional changes.

Major changes in the two areas included opening up of labor and commodity markets in rural areas, raising procurement prices of agricultural products, decentralizing production rights to local collectives, and gradually implementing the household responsibility system (HRS) (Gao, 1996; Perkins, 1988; Prybyla, 1989; Riskin, 1987; Tuan & Webb, 1993).

Changes in Decentralization and Price Policies

The first step of this program was to free up the rural trade fairs or free markets in 1979. By allowing some degree of free markets in the rural area, this policy provided needed incentives for peasants and resulted in the increase of their income through individual efforts outside the farming collectives.

Next, to increase peasants' living standards, the government also raised procurement prices of agricultural commodities many times. In December 1978, the Third Plenum of the Eleventh Central Committee decided to increase grain quota purchase prices by 20 percent. Purchase prices of cotton, oil-bearing crops, sugar, and other farm and sideline products were also raised significantly. Smaller price increases followed in subsequent years and the share of the output purchased at above-quota or negotiated prices also increased.

To decentralize production decisions, the Third Plenum also proposed to limit any intervention by higher authorities in the rights of local commune production teams. In the past, higher-level cadres often intervened in the production teams on regulating labor, funds, materials, and targets. The changes indicate that the production teams have the right to decide to grow what they think fit, to make decisions concerning production methods and income distribution, and to ignore arbitrary orders from leading organs or leaders (Riskin, 1987: 286-287).

Changes in the Institution

Moreover, the government gradually decollectivized the agricultural commune system by introducing various forms of responsibility systems. These included the system of "contracting output to the group" (*baogan daozu*), which arranged work-points, inputs, and output between the group and the production team. This system attempted to improve peasants' incentive and raise their productivity by relating the work reward to the work performance. To achieve this, the system provided work-points for completing specific tasks to meet the obligations to the collective and the state. The system of contracting output to the group was quickly changed to "contracting output to the individual household" (*baogan daohu*), which allowed the household the use of a particular piece of land and the decision to give its output to the team in exchange for an agreed number of work-points. Finally, the household responsibility system (HRS) (i.e., the individual household farming component) gradually replaced most of the collective forms of the contract responsibility system by 1983. It was estimated that by November 1983, about 98 percent of basic accounting units in China were under the HRS (*Beijing Review*, 1983; Lin, 1992; Riskin, 1987). Under the new HRS, nuclear farm families were allocated a portion of the formerly collective land for a period of 15 years in exchange for meeting certain tax and crop delivery obligations to the state.[4]

The decollectivization of agriculture eventually led to the dismantling of the people's communes and the creation of some 91,000 village (town) governments and 92,500 village committees by the end of 1984 (Gao, 1996: 62). The reform activities in the rural, agricultural area have continued after 1984. Since then, major reform measures introduced have included the increase of the role of markets and prices in the agriculture structure, the relaxation of the growth of nonstate business, the change in the agricultural trade system (i.e., the import or export of nonvital or nonsensitive commodities by local trade corporations), the reform of the rural financial and credit system, and the fast growth of township and village enterprises (Gao, 1996; Tuan & Webb, 1993).

In sum, the policy and structural changes introduced in China's rural, agricultural area have successfully transformed the old system with its tight bureaucratic controls to one based more on market principles and forces. The success of these reform measures has been evident in the rise of agricultural output and productivity (Ash, 1992; McMillian, Whalley & Zhu, 1989; Perkins, 1988; Wiens, 1983). For example, Ash (1992: 547) indicated the average annual percentage increase of gross output value of agriculture (GOVA) during the period of 1981 to 1990 was 6.4 percent, which is better than the 4.7 percent experienced during the period of 1971-1980 and the 3.05 percent during the period of 1952-1970.[5] In fact, it was the success in the agricultural sector that provided the basis and the momentum for reform efforts in the urban and industry areas.

THE URBAN-INDUSTRIAL REFORM, 1985-1988

The urban-industrial reforms started piecemeal during 1978-1984 and expanded significantly in 1984 after the success of the rural-agricultural reforms. The reform measures introduced before 1984 focused on the reform of the industrial management system and the expansion of the enterprise power. These reforms, however, were partial ones and covered some experiments in state enterprises (Halpern, 1985). These urban industrial reform programs were emphasized and outlined in the "Decision of the Central Committee on Reform of the Economic Structure," adopted on October 20, 1984. The Party was determined to carry out an urban economic reform program that was similar to the one developed in the countryside. The industrial reforms proposed covered changes and issues in both production management and the distribution system, including planning, prices, wages, cadres, and other components.

The urban-industrial reform programs emphasized an expansion of enterprise autonomy and incentives and the reduction, but not elimination, of the government within-plan allocations (Perkins, 1988; Riskin, 1987; Tidrick & Chen, 1987). The reform programs consisted of several important policy measures. First, they emphasized the expansion of enterprise autonomy, which not only freed enterprises from the past control of the state administration (i.e., the separation between government administration and enterprise management) but also gave enterprises the right to share profits and control issues in operational management. Next, the reforms gradually created and introduced markets for inputs and outputs of certain goods (e.g., steel, machinery, and raw materials). The reforms also developed several mechanisms to make enterprise managers act in accordance with market rules. These mechanisms included, for example, the use of repayable bank loans (bearing interest) to control the capital provided to enterprises free of charge and the introduction of a bankruptcy law designed to move away from the guaranteed bailout. Moreover, the reforms gradually introduced the idea of competition by abolishing the monopoly power of governmental agencies in some areas of urban services. Finally, the reforms further brought price changes for various industrial products (e.g., coal and iron ore in 1979-1982, consumer durables, chemical products, and railroad freight in 1983).[6]

Reform of Enterprise Management

For enterprise managers, the industrial reforms provided policy measures that were designed to improve incentives and productivity. These measures included, for example, the emphasis of multiyear management responsibility contracts (i.e., the contract responsibility system) that set various management targets for profits, profit remittance, and taxes. The reforms also gave enterprise managers the right to retain profits and the authority to invest and distribute bonuses out of these retained profits. With regard to the internal operation and management, the reforms allowed enterprise managers to use their authority to choose the level of production, to sell output and acquire material inputs on the market, and to set or negotiate prices. With regard to the external business activities, the reforms gave enterprise managers the right to develop lateral economic associations across different trades and regions as well as to permit the exchange of capital and technology and to cooperate in production matters. Finally, enterprise managers have the right to control activities related to employment, including, for example, the right to recruit laborers openly and to determine the level of skill or qualifications required (Gao, 1996: 70-73; Koo, 1990).

One of the major policy measures in China's industrial reforms was the introduction and emphasis of the contract responsibility system (CRS). The CRS was first introduced and experimented in 1978 in the Nanjian Machinery Factory and five other state enterprises in the Sichuan province and was expanded later to other state enterprises in various forms. The CRS was based on the theory that ownership and management should be separated. The degree of responsibility and authority held by the state and by the enterprises are defined by contract. Usually, the contract would specify such issues as (1) the minimum amount of profits that the enterprise must remit to the state; (2) the mechanism to share additional profits above the base level among the government, the enterprise, and the workers; and (3) a commitment by the enterprises to make up any shortfall in income (Gao, 1996: 73-76; Koo, Li & Peng, 1993: 42-44). Over the years, a number of variants of the CRS have been developed, including, for example, contracts based on quotas, trade-specific contracts, and the managerial responsibility system. In general, smaller industrial and commercial enterprises use some simpler contracts, while large and medium-sized state-owned industrial enterprises adopted more complicated contract arrangements. It was estimated that in 1988, 93 percent of the industrial enterprises in China were operated under various forms of the CRS, covering a period of three to five years. This number included 95 percent of the large- and medium-scale enterprises (Gao, 1996: 73).[7]

The Two-Track System and Policy

Moreover, it was during this stage of industrial reforms that the Chinese economy moved toward a two-track (two-tier) system. Two-track policies existed in the stage of the agricultural reforms and gradually prevailed in the industrial reforms. Two-track policies refer to the coexistence of both central planning and market mechanisms (i.e., one track for each mechanism). They included the coexistence of such characteristics as planned and market prices for goods and services, planned distribution and market allocation of resources, and state enterprises and private or joint-venture firms. The gradual establishment of the two-track system represented a compromise that the post-Mao Chinese leaders made to preserve planned allocations on the one hand and to draw incremental output into a market system on the other. In other words, the two-track system provided a dynamic process that permitted the central planning system to work while transforming it into a new market-oriented system. The two-track policies and system certainly revealed the characteristic of risk aversion that the leaders emphasized in their overall strategies during the process of economic reforms (Wang, 1994: 172-175; Wu & Zhao, 1987).

One of the major components of the two-track policies was the dual-price system (i.e., the two-track pricing system). The dual-price system was first introduced in the rural areas, where peasants would sell their products (e.g., grains) up to the quota amount to the state at the state-fixed price and then could sell the above-quota amount on the open market or to the state at negotiated prices. Over time, the dual-price system was extended to cover a wide range of agricultural commodities (e.g., meat, vegetables). In early 1985, the government established the dual-price system in industry and permitted producer goods (e.g., coal) to be exchanged at two different prices: a state-set price for centrally rationed supplies and a higher free-market price for nonrationed goods. During the period of 1985 to 1988, free market exchanges expanded significantly. For example, Wiemer and Lu (1993: 120) estimated that the amount of retail sales based on market prices increased from 34 percent in 1985 to 49 percent in 1988. During the same period of time, the amount of sales based on state-set prices dropped from 47 percent to 29 percent and the amount of sales based on state-guidance prices remained at about 22 percent. In other words, the increase of sales based on market prices was at the expense of the decrease of sales based on state-set prices.

The implementation of the dual-prices system had both advantages and disadvantages. On the advantage side, the system stimulated the production of enterprises, alleviated the pressure of excess demand, and encouraged energy conservation and high quality management. On the disadvantage side, the system resulted in such negative outcomes as promoting hypocritical enterprise behavior (i.e., hiding production capacity but requesting allocation of materials), inducing smuggling in distribution, and promoting irrational and inefficient utilization of resources. The dual-price system allowed China to implement both price reform and enterprise reform on the one hand and to reduce the risk of reform by "changing a big earthquake into several small tremors" on the other (Wu & Zhao, 1987).[8]

In sum, based on the success of China's agricultural reforms, Chinese leaders expanded reform initiatives and measures from the rural, agricultural area to the urban, industrial area. Emphasizing similar measures used in agriculture, the industrial reforms also separated governmental agencies from enterprise management, gave enterprises more autonomy, allowed enterprise managers to make decisions about the management of enterprises, and established the contract-management system to improve incentive and productivity. In addition, the Chinese economy gradually became a two-track system, with one part of the system under the traditional command planning operation and the other part under the newly established market operation. One example of the two-track system was in China's price reforms. By introducing a dual-price policy, Chinese leaders planned to reduce the risk of instability and uncertainty associated with reform measures. Despite some negative side effects, the industrial reforms have successfully produced rapid growth and structural changes in the industrial sector. For example, Field (1992: 588-591) noticed that China's gross output value of industry grew at an annual average rate of 12.6 percent between 1980 and 1990 and that the primary beneficiaries of the new policies were enterprises at the township level and below (i.e., township, village, cooperative, and individual industry). The increase of the enterprises at the township level and below indicated a change in the structure of industry because they rose from 10.5 percent of the total in 1980 to 31.8 percent in 1990.[9]

THE SLOWDOWN OF ECONOMIC REFORMS, 1989-1991

The movement of China's economic reforms slowed down during the period of 1989 to 1991. The slowdown of the reforms resulted from several interrelated factors, including different views on economic reforms between the conservatives and the reformers in the Party leadership, problems associated with economic growth and modernization, and, especially, the incident that happened in Tiananmen Square. The direct outcome of these factors was the change of leadership in economic management and the beginning of hard-line dominance of economic policy (e.g., Naughton, 1995a; White, 1993; Yeh, 1993).

First, there were disagreements on the pace and depth of economic reforms within the Party leadership. While agreeing with the importance of economic development and modernization, the conservatives, including such revolutionary veterans as Chen Yun, Bo Yibo, Peng Zhen, and Wang Zhen, believed that the planning (both directive or guidance) is a fundamental characteristic of socialism and that the operation of markets should be kept within the limit of central planning (i.e., Chen Yuen's explanation of a bird in a cage). On the other hand, the reformers, including such members as Hu Yaobang and Zhao Ziyang, argued that the traditional planning system should be dismantled and that state planning should be redefined in terms of a regulatory framework of macroeconomic policy (i.e., Zhao Ziyang's explanation of the state regulating the market and the market guiding enterprises)

(White, 1993: 61-65).[10]

Then, the differences between the conservatives and the reformers widened as China's economic reforms experienced such problems as inflation, overinvestment, budgetary deficits, and widespread corruption. The conservatives saw these problems as evidence that the reforms were being pushed too quickly and urged the importance of stabilizing the economic situation before any further reforms (White, 1993). Especially, they criticized the situation of institutional and ideological erosion in the Party, the emergence of bourgeois liberalization (ideas related to political reforms), and the increase of social ills and unhealthy tendencies (Sullivan, 1988). The conservatives' criticisms resulted in the resignation of Party Secretary-General Hu Yaobang, the highest-ranking advocate of political reform, in January 1987.

The economic crisis of 1988 further strengthened the position of the conservatives and led to the change of economic policy and management. Since 1985, the Chinese had experienced high rates of inflation, with the retail price index ranging from 8.8 percent in 1985 to 6 percent in 1986 and to 7.3 percent in 1987. But inflation skyrocketed in 1988 and reached an unprecedented high of 18.5 percent. The other side of the inflation was the stagnation or decline of real income. Accelerating inflation resulted in urban dwellers' reduced confidence in economic policy and led to the replacement of Zhao Ziyang with Li Peng to assume direct management of the economy. Li postponed the policy of price decontrol and announced the slowdown of reform activities.

Finally, the incident that happened at Tiananmen Square in June 1989 further complicated the situation and resulted in a power struggle. The incident began in April 1989, when students demonstrated over Hu Yaobang, who died of a heart attack in the middle of April. Students demonstrated to recognize Hu's status as a reformer because of his support for greater political and intellectual freedom. The student demonstration quickly spread to other cities and expanded to include not only intellectuals but also workers, entrepreneurs, and even some communist officials. The demonstration also changed from criticism of the conservative leaders and the bureaucratic corruption to a call for a democratic movement. The demonstration ended on June 4, when the Party used military troops to crack down on the protests. After the incident, the new leadership, including Premier Li Peng and Party Secretary-General Jiang Zemin, attempted to slow down the scope of both economic and political reforms. During the next two years, except for several ongoing experiments in some cities, there were no major economic policies and programs developed.

THE MACROECONOMIC-STRUCTURAL REFORM, SINCE 1992

The reform movement was regenerated and accelerated in 1992 after Deng Xiaoping's trip to South China. During that trip, Deng attacked conservative options and called on the country to accelerate its growth and pursue more vigorously its policy of reform and opening up. In October 1992, the Fourteenth National Congress of the Party endorsed Deng's views and called for the establishment of a "socialist market economy." The goal of establishing a socialist market economy was adopted in China's constitution during the first session of the Eighth National People's

Congress in March 1993.

The reform plans and measures introduced in the 1990s attempted to broaden and deepen the reform process. These plans and measures covered not only the reform activities emphasized in the earlier stages of reform (e.g., the stages of agricultural and industrial reforms) but also major issues related to China's macroeconomic structures. The macroeconomic-structural issues are important to the post-Mao economic reforms because Chinese researchers recognized that many problems of the macroeconomic management system were related to the lack of an effective framework and the wrong sequencing of reform elements. The problems specifically refer to the importance of changing the fiscal and monetary system before the enterprise reform (Fei & Reynolds, 1987; McKinnon, 1991; Tsang & Cheng, 1994). Macroeconomic-structural reforms represented the intention of the Chinese government to further marketization of the economy.

Reforms initiated and emphasized in the 1990s included, for example, (1) reforming the exchange rate system (allowing the yuan to be devalued without formal government action); (2) adjusting the fiscal system (introducing a new tax assignment system that separates central and local taxation authorities); (3) reforming the bank system (intended to establish an effective central banking system and to commercialize the state banks); (4) opening the stock markets (in Shanghai and Shenzen); (5) emphasizing state-owned enterprises reform to improve the efficiency of state enterprises; (6) adopting systems of accounting, laws on property rights, and patent protection; (7) reforming the social security system; (8) reforming the circulation system; and (9) accelerating housing reforms (Bell et al., 1993; Bhalla, 1995; Gao, 1996; Kaye, 1994a; Zhang, 1995). Recognizing the comprehensive nature of the recent reforms, the present section will review and examine three important reforms in China's macroeconomic structures: the tax reform, the banking reform, and the legal and market infrastructure reform.[11]

The Tax System

The tax reform of 1994 represented the Chinese government's intention to restructure its overall tax system. Before the economic reform, China's tax system was highly centralized and provided few incentives to local governments and state enterprises. During the reform years, the Chinese government tried a tax-for-profit experiment in 1984-1985 and intended to establish an effective direct tax system for state enterprises. The experiment, however, failed due to the difficulty of developing impartial rules that cover state enterprises with wide levels of profitability among them. The situation changed in the 1990s because, on the one hand, state enterprises no longer dominated the whole economy and, on the other hand, most state enterprises did not have a lot of profit after taxes and bank loans were paid (Naughton, 1995a: 293).

The tax reform covered three major aspects: central-local fiscal arrangements, income taxation on enterprises, and reforms of indirect taxes (Tsang & Cheng, 1994: 776-786). First, in the central-local fiscal arrangement, the Chinese government abandoned the old fiscal contract system. The old fiscal contract system allowed the central and local governments to share revenues according to a pre-agreed ratio. Instead, the government developed a tax assignment system. The new tax system divided taxes into three categories: central taxes (e.g., tariffs, income tax on central enterprises, tax on revenues from railways, banks and insurance companies, and consumption tax), local taxes (e.g., business tax, income tax from local enterprises, personal income tax, capital gain tax on land and property sales, estate duty, and stamp duty), and shared taxes (e.g., value-added tax for central and local governments and stock transaction gains tax for central and local governments).

Next, the income taxation on state enterprises became possible because of the expansion of the nonstate sectors of the economy (i.e., the proliferation of various nonstate and foreign-invested enterprises). The reform introduced the income (profit) tax at the uniform rate of 33 percent for all enterprises (state and nonstate). The reform also abandoned the lump-sum income taxes and the income adjustment taxes (the preferential rate of 15 percent for foreign-invested enterprises in the special economic zones remained the same).

Finally, in the area of indirect taxes reform, the government emphasized the Value Added Tax (VAT), the Business Tax, and the Consumption Tax. The VAT became the principal tax on sales or imports of goods at the rate of 17 percent. The Business Tax is the major indirect tax on provision of services, with rates ranging from 3 percent to 5 percent in general and 5 percent to 20 percent for entertainment. The Consumption Tax is levied on luxury items (e.g., alcohol and jewelry), with rates ranging from 3 percent to 45 percent, and is imposed before the VAT is levied.

The Banking System

The Chinese banking system in the pre-1978 reform followed the Soviet Union's Model. Under the central planning system, funds were provided by the state budget and the banking system. The People's Bank of China headed this system as a source of funds to support state enterprises when they tried to achieve the output goals of the central plan. With this type of accommodating credit policy, the People's Bank of China acted as a monobank (functioning as both central bank and commercial bank) and had little impact on the allocation of resources in China (Bell et al., 1993; Wolken, 1990).

During the 1980s, the Peoples' Bank of China was allowed to grant medium- and short-term equipment loans because the post-Mao reform required productive units to pay for their resources used in the production process in addition to the resources allocated by the government. In addition, the branches of the People's Bank of China were given greater autonomy and independence in their credit activities such as increasing the amount of loans if the branches increased their deposits. The bank was also allowed to make loans to street cooperatives, factory cooperatives, and individuals to start small-scale enterprises (Hsiao, 1984; Wolken, 1990). Finally, in January 1984, the People's Bank was established as a central bank, and its commercial banking functions were transferred to a newly created bank, the Industrial and Commercial Bank of China. As China's central bank, the People's Bank instituted a deposit reserve system in 1985 and started to develop the nation's monetary policy, supervise its implementation, control the issuance and circulation of currency, determine interest rates, assist in setting foreign exchange rates, and formulate and ratify the individual plans for credit rationing for the specialized banks under its control (Chinese Academy of Social Sciences, 1989; Wolken, 1990; World Bank, 1988). The specialized banks (e.g., the Agricultural Bank of China, the Communications Bank of China) were gradually allowed to engage in general banking activities.

Despite the changes introduced, the state banks are still regarded essentially as administrative organs of the state responsible for mobilizing and providing funds to finance important activities of the state-owned enterprises. As a result, the specialized banks were obliged to provide policy-based loans that were not based on commercial criteria. In addition, because of the decentralized structure of the banking system, the banks were susceptible to local political pressure to provide loans for investment projects and to give credit to loss-making enterprises to keep them afloat. In late 1992, the Chinese government announced plans to reform the banking system to transform the specialized banks into competitive, autonomous, and self-accountable commercial entities. The major components of the plan are separating commercial from policy-based lending; separating quasi-fiscal from commercial operations; funding long-term loans for investment projects from long-term funds; and encouraging banks to improve their loan assessment and portfolio management. Finally, the Third Session of the Eighth National People's Congress adopted the Law on the People's Bank of China on March 18, 1995. The law, containing 51 articles in 8 chapters, stipulates the nature, status, organization, business scope, finance and accounting, and legal responsibility of the People's Bank of China. It also indicates the issuance and protection of the Renminbi and the bank's role in supervising and controlling the nations' banking sector (Li, 1995: 14).

The Legal and Market Infrastructure

Finally, the Chinese government also focused on the development of a legal and regulatory framework and the establishment of markets and related infrastructure in the 1990s. The legal and regulatory framework is critical to a market-oriented system because, unlike administrative decrees in the central planning system, it sets the rules for enterprises and individuals to compete fairly and freely. In the area of legal and regulatory framework, several important economic laws and regulations have been enacted. The former include, for example, a patent law, a copyright law, the Import and Export Commodities Inspection Law, and a trademark law; while the latter include the Regulations on Changing the Operating Mechanism of Enterprises, Regulations on the Formation of Share-holding Companies, a code for the implementation of a new accounting system for enterprise, and the Interim Provisions on the Management of the Issuing and Trading of Stocks (Bell et al., 1993: 23).[12]

With regard to the market infrastructure, the Chinese government has established several regional and national wholesale markets and trading centers (the circulation system). The wholesale markets include, for example, the garment market in Shengyang, the clothing market in Suzhou, the meat market in Chengdu, and the sugar market in Guangzhou. The trading centers for commodities and services include the national grain trading center in Zhengzhou, the nonferrous metals exchange in Shenzhen, the metals exchange in Shanghai, the securities exchanges in Shanghai and Shenzhen, the petroleum market in Nanjing and Shanghai, and the national foreign exchange trading center in Beijing (Bell et al., 1993: 26). The establishment of the market infrastructure also included the investment in transportation and telecommunications and the development of professional services such as accountants, lawyers, management consultants, and marketing agents.

In sum, the reform measures implemented after 1992 not only continued the spirit of earlier reforms but also extended to major structures in China's economic system. For example, the suggested reform of state-owned enterprises was based on and related to the industrial reforms implemented in the 1980s. To deal with the increase of budget deficits, the tax reform was intended to improve China's financial condition and establish a market-oriented fiscal system. Similarly, the banking reform was designed to address the past irrational banking activities and to establish a market-oriented monetary system. The changes in legal and market infrastructure provided needed bases for sound economic order and circulation to meet demands from a growing and complicated economy. All of these reforms are important to China's further modernization and development. Despite their comprehensive nature, the structural reform programs have not been examined seriously because most of them are still in the early stage of implementation. However, some researchers (e.g., Tsang & Cheng, 1994) have already noticed that similar to the previous reform measures, the new reform measures introduced do not fundamentally address all the problems and are still characterized by cautiousness, concessions, and compromises.

THE OPEN-DOOR POLICY, SINCE THE 1970s

In addition to the agricultural and industrial reforms, Chinese leaders have also expanded the open-door policy adopted by Zhou Enlai in the early 1970s. The expansion of an open-door policy became an important part of the post-Mao economic reform policies in 1978 when Chinese leaders recognized that the achievement of the Four Modernizations would require the encouragement of foreign investment and the importation of foreign technology. The leaders emphasized not only the "reforms" but also the "opening up." While the reforms referred to policy changes that introduced decentralization and marketization, the opening up related to policy changes that increased the integration of the Chinese economy into the international economy.

The adoption of the open-door policy indicated a change of China's economic development philosophy and principles. During the Mao era, China implemented a self-reliance development policy. The self-reliance (*zili gengsheng*) policy emphasized that China's development depends on resources not from its external relations but from its internal activities (Riskin, 1987: 204-205). In other words, the self-reliance policy stressed the importance of utilization of domestic resources (labor, skills, and capital) in development, rejected the policy of indiscriminate imitation of foreign methods of development, and supported the idea of accumulating indigenous experience that suits the Chinese condition.

To promote modernization and development, China's post-Mao open-door policy emphasized such key policy measures as increasing foreign trade, returning to the World Bank and the IMF and borrowing from these institutions, and encouraging foreign investment from joint ventures to wholly owned foreign-investment firms (e.g., a joint venture law formulated in 1979) (Cheng, 1993; Gao, 1996; Riskin, 1987).[13] The present section focuses on two major aspects of the open-door policy: the changes in foreign trade and the development in the coastal region.

The Changes in Foreign Trade

First, before 1978, China's foreign trade was centralized at the national level and was conducted by state-owned foreign trade corporations (FTCs) associated with the producing ministries (i.e., a total of twelve FTCs in 1978). The items and quantities that FTCs exported and imported were directed by the central trade plan and the profits and losses were absorbed by the state budget. Trade growth and development were not directly related to domestic demand and supply, despite the fact that domestic trade was also controlled by the state planning authorities.

With regard to China's trade, the economic reform measures developed since 1978 included, for example, changing organizational structure (i.e., increasing the number of FTCs), moving from trade planning to trade restrictions (e.g., reducing the scope of mandatory planning), establishing an exchange retention system in 1979, introducing a contract responsibility system (i.e., foreign-trade contract management responsibility) for FTCs in 1987, and extending the foreign-trade contract system to provincial governments in 1991 (Cheng, 1993: 208-223).

The changes in organizational structure in China's foreign trade were very important because they represented China's decentralization of trade controls. The FTCs were gradually given greater autonomy and made more accountable for their operations. The management of the trade system was also decentralized from the central government to the provincial governments. Central ministries and departments and provincial and municipal governments were allowed to establish their own FTCs. By the end of the 1980s more than 5,000 FTCs were in operation. Moreover, large state-owned enterprises and foreign-funded enterprises were also given the right to export on their own account (Fukasaku, Wall & Wu, 1994: 27-29; Lardy, 1992a: 39).

The decentralization of trading organizational structures and processes did not mean that Chinese trade became market-determined. Trade in products covered by mandatory plans and by guidance plans were still subject to governmental controls. Like the production and distribution of steel, petroleum, coal, and grain, foreign trade is regarded so crucial to the national economy that the government would like to keep it under close regulation and control (Fukasaku, Wall & Wu, 1994: 28; Shen, 1993: 198).

The Development of China's Coastal Region

Next, in addition to the changes in the foreign trade system, Chinese leaders also adopted several policy measures to develop open economic zones in China's coastal region to attract foreign investment and to promote outward-oriented activities. These reform measures included (1) four special economic zones (SEZs), Shenzhen, Zhuhai, Shantou (Guangdong Province), and Xiamen (Fujian province), in 1979; (2) the 14 opened coastal cities, from Dalian in Liaoning province in the north to Beihai in Guangxi province in the south, in 1984 (Weihai in Shandong province was later added to make a total of 15); (3) the opened coastal provinces, from Liaoning to Guangxi and Hainan provinces, comprising a total of 288 *xian* (counties); (4) the three deltaic areas of the Zhujiang, South Fujian, and the Changjiang (Yangtze); (5) the conversion of Hainan Island into an independent province and making it a special economic zone in 1988; (6) the development of Pudong New Area (in Shanghai) in 1990; and (7) the opening of inland areas that run along the Yangtze River valley and on the borders with neighboring countries (Bell et al., 1993; Fukasaku, Wall & Wu, 1994; Kueh, 1992; Sit, 1988; Tzeng, 1991).

The emphasis on investment and development in China's coastal region represented a shift in its regional development policy. Before 1978, the regional development policy during Mao's era stressed the importance of a balanced-development approach. To mitigate the difference between the coastal and interior regions, the Chinese government in the past emphasized a centrally directed investment in the interior region and distributed about 60 percent of China's investment in fixed assets in the interior region (Yang, 1990). The result of the past balanced development was not only inefficient distribution and utilization of resources but also severe limitations on China's overall development. By switching to the imbalanced, coastal-oriented development, the post-Mao Chinese leaders expected that the faster development in the coastal region would lead to the development in China's other regions.

The development of the SEZs is critical to China's economic reforms in general and the open-door policy in particular because the SEZs provide a function of "windows and bridges." In other words, the SEZs not only provide opportunities for introducing foreign capital, advanced technology, and equipment but also promote competition between regions and trades. In addition, Chinese leaders used the SEZs to serve as experimental units for testing policy measures in the economic structural reform and as schools for learning the value and rules of the market system (Stoltenberg, 1984).

Unlike other areas in China, local governments in the SEZs have the authority to make various investment decisions that are outside the state plan. The local governments in the SEZs are allowed to provide preferential policies to attract foreign investors and to undertake their own infrastructure development and other investment, as long as they can raise the funds. The preferential policies that the local governments offered to foreign-funded enterprises included, for example, lower tax rates than those firms located outside the SEZs, tax holidays for several years, and exemptions of import licenses and customs duties on imports of machinery and equipments as well as on their export (Bell et al., 1993: 39-40).

Moreover, China's SEZs differed significantly from the export processing zones (EPZs) of East and Southeast Asia, even though the original idea for SEZs derived from the EPZs. The major differences between SEZs and EPZs are in size, structure, and role. The SEZs are much larger than the EPZs, as the former range from the 23.4 square km of Zhuhai to the 34,000 square km of Hainan, while the latter are within several hectares. The SEZs are government units in their own right, while the EPZs are governed by management boards controlled by central government units. Especially, the SEZs have many objectives (i.e., the window-and-bridge function, the economic laboratory function) and play many roles (e.g., balancing the economic and production role with those of providing education, sanitation, security, and infrastructure services), while the EPZs have only one single objective and role (e.g., the economic role of promoting exports) (Fukasaku, Wall & Wu, 1994: 47-48).

In sum, the open-door policy emphasized the increase of foreign trade and investment, the importance of China's role and activities in the world economy, and the development of China's coastal region. The policy measures emphasized are similar to those used in the agricultural and industrial reforms. These included the emphasis on decentralized activities and the introduction of market ideas. The open-door policy fundamentally changed China's past self-reliance economic policy and balanced regional development approach. Despite some negative side effects, the open-door policy has resulted in the increase of foreign trade and investment, the growth of the coastal region, and the improvement of China's overall development (e.g., Cheng, 1993; Fukasaku, Wall & Wu, 1994; Zweig, 1995).[14]

DISCUSSION AND CONCLUSION

This chapter examined stages and policy measures developed in China's post-Mao economic reforms. Based on the time of the development and their special characteristics, five major reform stages were identified and reviewed: the rural-agricultural reform (1978-1984), the urban-industrial reform (1985-1988), the open-door policy (since the 1970s), the slowdown of economic reform (1989-1991), and the macroeconomic structural reform (after 1992).

Despite the author's intention to separate reform stages for the purpose of discussion, it should be noted that these stages overlapped and are interrelated during all the reform years. First, the characteristic of overlap means that some reform issues and activities were recognized beyond the period of the individual development stages. For example, after the first stage of the rural-agricultural reform, policies that attempted to improve agricultural conditions were identified in the later reform years. Similarly, some reform issues in the industrial sector were also noticed before the period of the urban-industrial reforms. Next, the characteristic of interrelation indicates that the experience of each reform stage contributes to the development of other stages. For example, the experience of the open-door policy (foreign trade and investment) is closely related to China's agricultural and industrial reforms. The increase of trade and investment also calls for some changes in China's macroeconomic structure identified in the reform of the legal and market infrastructure.

The first stage of rural-agricultural reform was related to decisions made at the Third Plenum Session of the Eleventh Central Committee of the Party in December 1978. Major policy measures developed in this stage included policy and institutional changes. The former refers to decentralization of agricultural decision-making power and the increase of procurement prices for agricultural commodities. The latter has to do with the dismantling of the people's commune system and the establishment of the household responsibility system. The interrelated policy and institutional changes contributed to the improvement of agricultural productivity in peasants' living standards and led to the foundation for the other reforms.

The stage of urban-industrial reform was related to the resolution adopted at the Third Plenary Session of the Twelfth Central Committee of the Party in October 1984. Major policy measures emphasized in this stage consisted of the separation of enterprise management from government administration, the expansion of authority and responsibilities of enterprise managers in their operations, the introduction of the contract responsibility system to state enterprises, the development of a competitive system, and the gradual introduction of price reforms. It was during this stage of reform that China's economy moved toward a two-track economic system. The two-track system means the coexistence of activities in both central planning and market mechanisms, including, planned and market prices for goods and services, planned and market allocation of resources, and state-controlled and joint-ventured private enterprises.

The economic reform movement slowed down during the period of 1989 to 1991. Despite its success in improving agricultural and industrial output, the reform movement also produced negative effects such as inflation, corruption, and social disorder. The major factors that caused the disruption of the reform movement were the different views on scope and pace of the reform between conservers and reformers within the Party, the inflation crisis in 1988, and the Tiananmen Square incident. The outcome of these factors was the change of leadership in economic management and the slowdown, not the elimination, of many reform measures.

The economic reform movement was regenerated and accelerated in 1992 after Deng Xiaoping's call for further reforming and opening up in his trip to South China. Major policy measures emphasized in this stage of reform were related to China's macroeconomic structure and included, for example, changes in the tax system, the banking system, the state-owned enterprises, and the legal and market infrastructure. These measures represented the intention of Chinese leaders to address many structural problems associated with economic reforms on the one hand and to establish a socialist market economy.

Finally, the stage of the open-door policy should be considered as a separate process because it covered all the reform stages identified here. The open-door policy was first emphasized by Zhou Enlai in the early 1970s and was significantly expanded after 1978. Major reform measures emphasized in the open- door policy included the increase of foreign trade and investment, the role of China in the world economic system, and the development of China's coastal region. These reform measures are, of course, closely related to the issues and activities discussed in the reforms of agriculture, industrial, and macroeconomic structure.

The forgoing review of stages and policy measures shows some general characteristics of China's post-Mao economic reforms.[15] First, it is clear that Deng Xiaoping plays a major role in the development of the reform. While not personally involved in economic management, Deng's attitude and position affect the development of economic reforms. For example, Deng's practical philosophy provides the guidance of economic reform by emphasizing not ideology but empirical examination of reform ideas. Deng's interest in reforming economic not political structure certainly limits the reforms in noneconomic areas. Especially, Deng's support for reforms in some critical movements not only renewed the momentum of the reforms but also offers the opportunity to expand the scope of the reforms.

Next, the process of the economic reforms are closely related to China's political and social environment. The development of the reforms was based on the agreement of Chinese leaders on the need for modernization and development. The leaders, however, have different views on the scope and pace of the reforms and are concerned about many negative effects of reforms on Chinese society in general and the Party in particular. The stop-and-go nature of the reforms represents the impact of political and social environment on the process and speed of economic reforms. The stop-and-go approach certainly affects the overall effectiveness of economic reforms.

Finally, it is also clear that the post-Mao Chinese leaders did not have a grand strategy or master plan when they initiated and developed the economic reforms. Instead, they took a trial-and-error approach and proceeded with the reforms in a gradual manner. Many reform measures were first tested partially in several selected sectors or regions. Based on the experience of these tests, a formal policy may be developed and implemented nationally later. Clearly, this approach was related to the leaders' concern about the impact of reforms on China's political and social environment. This kind of approach certainly eliminated uncertainties and risks associated with reform measures. But, this approach is inefficient from the economic consideration. Learning from the past experience of revolutionary policy and mass movements, Chinese leaders certainly would like to approach any reforms gradually and cautiously and ignore criticisms of irrational arrangements, insequential orders, ineffective controls, and inefficient use of resources.

NOTES

1. The divisions of the five stages in China's economic reforms were based on the consideration of presenting major reform measures emphasized in each stage. The five stages identified, of course, are not isolated but closely related. For example, after the first stage of the rural-agricultural reform, Chinese leaders continued their efforts to reform the agricultural sector. Similarly, some reform measures in the industrial sector were introduced simultaneously with the agricultural reforms. Especially, since its adoption in 1976, the open-door policy has been emphasized during all stages of economic reforms.

2. For more information about the value and growth of GOVA, see the data in Table 2.3 and discussions in Chapter 2.

3. For more information about China's past agricultural system, policies, and performance see, for example, Riskin (1987: 169-179) and Tuan and Webb (1993: 82-84).

4. For more information about major reform policies in China's rural, agricultural area see, for example, Ash (1992), Gao (1996: 57-68, Chapter 4), Perkins (1988: 607-613), Prybyla (1989), Riskin (1987: 284-315, Chapter 12), Shue (1984), Tuan and Webb (1993: 84-89,

especially a comparison of the commune system and the HRS), and Wiens (1983; 1987).

5. For more information about the impact of China's economic reforms on its agricultural sector, see analyses and discussions in Chapter 4.

6. For more information about policy changes introduced in China's urban and industrial area see, for example, Field (1992), Gao (1996, Chapter 5), Halpern (1985), Perkins (1988: 613-621), Rawski (1994), Tidrick and Chen (1987), White (1987), and Wu and Zhao (1987).

7. For more information about the contract responsibility system see, for example, Koo (1990), White (1987), and Gao (1996: 73-76).

8. For more information about the two-track and dual-price system see, for example, Byrd (1987), Wiemer and Lu (1993), Wu and Zhao (1987), and Naughton (1995a: 220-227).

9. For more information about the impact of economic reforms on China's industry, see analyses and discussions in Chapter 4.

10. The differences between the conservatives and the reformers are related to their attitudes to economic change, to political change, and to the relations between the two. For more information about the differences see, for example, Bachman (1986), Sullivan (1988), and White (1993: 61-68).

11. For more information about China's macroeconomic structural reforms, see Bell et al., (1993), Bhalla (1995), Gao, (1996), Kaye (1994a), Naughton (1995b), and Zhang (1995).

12. For more information about issues related to China's legal reform, see discussions about the legal system in Chapter 7.

13. For more information about China's open-door policy see, for example, Cheng (1993: 197-230), Fukasaku, Wall, and Wu (1994), Gao (1996: 36-56, Chapter 3), Huang (1987), Kamath (1990), Potter (1995), and Riskin (1987: 316-340, Chapter 13).

14. For more information about the impact of China's open-door policy on China's economy, see analyses and discussions in Chapter 4. For more information about the impact of the open-door policy, especially the coastal development strategy, on China's regional development, see analyses and discussions in Chapter 5.

15. For a complete discussion of characteristics and lessons of Chinese economic reforms, see Chapter 8.

CHAPTER 4

Evaluation of Economic Reforms

INTRODUCTION

Economic reform has been considered by the post-Mao Chinese leaders as one of the country's major national policies since 1978. The purpose of the reform is to promote China's modernization and economic development. To achieve this purpose, the reform leaders first recognized both policy errors and system problems related to the development experience during Mao's years. They then developed and implemented several reform policies that addressed major economic problems and issues. As reflected in different stages of the economic reform, these policies covered many sectors of China's economy, including agriculture, industry, macroeconomic structure, and foreign trade. Lasting almost two decades, the reform policies have extended from one sector of the economy to another. The reforms have gradually adjusted China's economic structures and improved its economic performance.

The present analysis of China's post-Mao economic reforms adopted a comprehensive and systematic approach. The comprehensive and systematic analysis provides an organized framework for examining some complex and dynamic policy issues. This type of analysis usually consists of such policy components as inputs (causes), processes, and outputs (effects). The three components are highly interrelated and interact with changing environment factors. Emphasized by many policy analysts and evaluators (e.g., Easton, 1965; Rivlin, 1971; Rossi, Freeman & Wright, 1979), the systematic approach is considered as necessary and important in the comparative study of policy reform and administrative development (Katz, 1971).

After the review of the input and background issues in Chapter 2 and of the process stages and measures in Chapter 3, this chapter is designed to examine the output and effects of China's post-Mao economic reforms. The examination of economic reforms focuses on both positive and negative effects. The positive effects refer to major achievements of economic reforms, which may include improved economic growth, income, and productivity. The negative effects have to do with some problems and challenging issues associated with the reform. These problems may be related to both economic and noneconomic activities and consist of such issues as increased inflation, corruption, and crime.

The evaluation of economic reforms is very important for both policy makers and researchers. For policy makers, the results of the evaluation, both positive and negative, provide needed information to justify and support some reform policies on the one hand and to revise and improve some policies on the other hand. In other words, the evaluation of economic reforms helps policy makers to maintain the momentum of the reforms and to improve the content of the reform. For researchers, the evaluation outcome provides an opportunity not only to examine the effectiveness of the reform policies but also to test the validity of major theories related to economic reforms. That is, the evaluation of economic reforms assists policy researchers to test and improve reform theories.

To evaluate China's post-Mao economic reforms, this chapter begins with the analysis of major achievements of these reforms. The achievement analysis focuses on the performance of China's economy in such aspects as macroeconomic conditions, agricultural and industrial conditions, foreign trade, and investment. These aspects are not only important components of any economic system but are also related to the reform stages discussed in the previous chapter. Next, the chapter examines major challenging issues that occurred during the reform years. These challenging issues include both economic and noneconomic problems. The former refers to the threat of rising inflation, while the latter refers to the increase of environmental problems, corruption cases, and social crimes. Finally, the chapter concludes with discussions about policy implications related to the achievements and problems of economic reforms.

ACHIEVEMENTS OF ECONOMIC REFORMS

The evaluation of the major achievements of the economic reforms is based on several analyses of major economic indicators in China during the reform years. Specifically, the economic indicators cover such aspects and areas as macroeconomic performance, agricultural and industrial performance, foreign trade, and investment. The evaluation of China's macroeconomic performance provides an overall assessment of the country's economic condition during the reform years. The evaluation of economic indicators in the agricultural, industrial, and foreign trade sectors attempts to relate China's sectorial economic performance to various reform stages that were identified in our analysis of China's economic reform. The results of these evaluations will certainly provide information and evidence to verify the effectiveness of economic reform policies.

Macroeconomic Performance

This evaluation of China's macroeconomic performance during the reform years focused on four important economic indicators. These indicators represent China's economic conditions of growth, income, employment, and inflation. First, Table 4.1 provides information about values and indices of China's gross national product (GNP) and per-capita GNP. During the period of 1978 to 1995, China's GNP annual percentage increases ranged from the smallest of 4.2 percent in 1989 and 1990 to the largest of 14.7 percent in 1984 and achieved an overall average annual increase of 9.8 percent, which is relatively high when compared with the average growth rate of 6 percent achieved in the previous two decades (Yeh, 1992: 502) Similarly, the per-capita GNP annual percentage increases during this period ranged from the smallest of 2.6 percent in 1989 to the largest of 13.2 percent in 1984 and achieved an overall average annual increase of 8.3 percent. The record of economic growth is very impressive.[1]

The data in Table 4.1 not only show the growth of China's economy but also indicate the impact of the country's economic reform policies. For example, both the largest annual GNP and per-capita GNP increases occurred in 1984, which provided the strong basis and momentum for Chinese leaders to move economic reforms to the second stage of the industrial reform. The smallest increases of GNP and per-capita GNP occurred in 1989 and 1990, which certainly related to the slowdown of economic reforms started in 1989. In addition, the calculated average annual increases during the four stages of economic reform also provided evidence to support the impact of reform policies and stages. The annual GNP increases averaged 9.3 percent in the first stage of reforming the rural, agricultural sector (1978-1984), jumped to 11.1 percent in the second stage of reforming the urban, industrial sector (1985-1988), dropped to 5.8 percent in the third stage of slowdown of reforms (1989-1992), and rebounded to 12.2 percent after 1992.

Next, the excellent performance of China's economy during the reform years was also reflected in the data on the country's national income. As revealed in Table 4.2, China's national income achieved an average annual increase of 9.5 percent during the period of 1978 to 1993, which is better than the average annual increase of 7.5 percent during the period of 1950 to 1977.[2] Again, the distribution of the income increases showed the impact of economic reform policies. The average annual increases of national income reached 8.9 percent in the first stage, moved to 10.7 percent in the second stage, dropped to 5.5 percent in the third stage, and rebounded to 15.3 percent after 1992.

Besides the growth and income data, the evaluation of China's macroeconomic performance during the reform years also analyzed the data of the country's unemployment and inflation rates. The rates of unemployment and inflation are important economic indicators because the combination of the two rates generally is referred to as the misery index. Table 4.3 shows China's urban unemployment rate and retail prices index during the period of 1978 to 1995.[3] First, during the 18 years of reform, the urban unemployment rate ranged from 5.4 percent in 1979 to 1.8 percent in 1985 and maintained an average rate of 2.9 percent. Especially, the unemployment rates were constantly below 3 percent after 1982. While the official unemployment rates were relatively low, many Chinese researchers noticed a growing number of "floating populations" in the urban area. These include new graduates waiting and hunting for jobs and people migrating from the country to urban areas because of the changes in the traditional household registration system.[4]

On the inflation side, China has continuously experienced sharp price rises during the reform years. The official retail price indices ranged from the smallest of 1.5 percent in 1983 to the largest of 21.7 percent in 1994 and showed an average annual increase of 7.5 percent between 1978 and 1995.

Table 4.1
Gross National Products (GNP), 1978-1995

	GNP		Per-Capita GNP	
Year	Value[1]	Indices[2]	Value[1]	Indices[2]
1978	3624.1	111.7	379	110.2
1979	3998.1	107.6	413	106.1
1980	4517.8	107.8	460	106.5
1981	4773.0	104.4	480	103.1
1982	5193.0	108.8	515	107.2
1983	5809.0	110.4	568	108.8
1984	6962.0	114.7	671	113.2
1985	8989.1	113.2	855	111.7
1986	10201.4	108.5	956	106.9
1987	11954.5	111.5	1103	109.7
1988	14922.3	111.3	1355	109.5
1989	16917.8	104.2	1512	102.6
1990	18598.4	104.2	1638	102.7
1991	21662.5	109.1	1882	107.6
1992	26651.9	114.1	2288	112.7
1993	34560.5	113.1	2933	111.8
1994	46532.9	112.6	3904	111.4
1995	57277.3	109.0	4754	107.8
Average annual increases (%)[3]				
1978-1995		(9.8)		(8.3)
1978-1984		(9.3)		(7.9)
1985-1988		(11.1)		(9.5)
1989-1991		(5.8)		(4.3)
1992-1995		(12.2)		(10.9)

Source: State Statistical Bureau, *China Statistical Yearbook* (1996: 42); *Statistical Yearbook of China* (1993: 31).

Note: 1. Values of GNP are based on current prices in 100 million yuan, and values of per-capita GNP are based on current prices in yuan.
2. Both GNP indices and per-capita GNP indices are based on preceding year = 100, comparable prices.
3. Numbers in parentheses are calculated average annual increases in the specific period.

The calculated average price increases also revealed that the retail price indices increased about 2.5 percent in the first stage of reform, jumped to 10.2 percent in the second stage of reform, dropped to 7.6 percent in the third stage, and moved to 13.8

Table 4.2
National Income, 1978-1993

Year	Value[1]	Indices[2]	Per-Capita Value[1]
1978	3010	112.3	315
1979	3350	107.0	346
1980	3688	106.4	376
1981	3941	104.9	397
1982	4258	108.2	422
1983	4736	110.0	463
1984	5652	113.6	545
1985	7020	113.5	668
1986	7859	107.7	737
1987	9313	110.2	859
1988	11738	111.3	1066
1989	13176	103.7	1178
1990	14384	105.1	1267
1991	16557	107.7	1439
1992	20223	115.4	1736
1993	24882	115.1	2111
Average annual increase (%)[3]			
1978-1993		(9.5)	
1978-1984		(8.9)	
1985-1988		(10.7)	
1989-1991		(5.5)	
1992-1993		(15.3)	

Source: State Statistical Bureau, *Statistical Yearbook of China* (1994: 33-34); (1993: 33-35).
Note: 1. Values of national income are based on current prices in 100 million yuan, and values of per capita national income are based on current prices in yuan.
2. Indices of national income are based on preceding year = 100, comparable prices.
3. Numbers in parentheses are calculated average annual increases in the specific period.

percent after 1992. Again, the distribution of the data is related to the reform policies.

In sum, based on official Chinese statistics, it is very clear that China has achieved a high growth rate of production and income, maintained a low unemployment rate, and experienced an increasing inflation rate since the beginning of the economic reforms. The present findings about the rapid growth of China's macroeconomic condition are similar to those reported in other studies (e.g., Chen, Jefferson & Singh, 1992; Perkins, 1994; Yusuf, 1994).

Table 4.3
Urban Unemployment Rate and Retail Price Indices, 1978-1995

Year	Urban Unemployment Rate[1]	Retail Price Index[2]
1978	5.3	100.7
1979	5.4	102.0
1980	4.9	106.0
1981	3.8	102.4
1982	3.2	101.9
1983	2.3	101.5
1984	1.9	102.8
1985	1.8	108.8
1986	2.0	106.0
1987	2.0	107.3
1988	2.0	118.5
1989	2.6	117.8
1990	2.5	102.1
1991	2.3	102.9
1992	2.3	105.4
1993	2.6	113.2
1994	2.8	121.7
1995	2.9	114.8
Average annual increases (%)[3]		
1978-1995	(2.9)	(7.5)
1978-1984	(3.8)	(2.5)
1985-1988	(2.0)	(10.2)
1989-1991	(2.5)	(7.6)
1992-1995	(2.7)	(13.8)

Source: State Statistical Bureau, *China Statistical Yearbook* (1996: 114, 255); *China Statistical Abstract* (1990: 20).

Note: 1. Urban unemployment rate = (number of urban unemployed)/(total urban social labor force + number of urban unemployed) x 100%.
2. Retail price indices are based on preceding year = 100.
3. Numbers in parentheses are calculated average annual increases in the specific period.

Agricultural and Industrial Performance

In addition to the general macroeconomic indicators, the evaluation of China's economic achievements during the reform years also needs to examine the country's agricultural and industrial performance because they are the major targets of the first and second stages of the reform, respectively. Table 4.4 shows some summary information about gross output value of agriculture (GOVA) and industry (GOVI) during the period of 1978 to 1995. The values of GOVA and GOVI showed the improvement of both the agriculture and industry sectors, with a GOVA increase of about 14.6 times (the ratio of 20,341 in 1995 to 1,397 in 1978) and a GOVI increase of about 21.7 times (the ratio of 91,824 in 1995 to 4,237 in 1978). The indices of GOVA ranged from the smallest annual increase of 1.4 percent in 1980 and the largest annual increase of 12.3 percent in 1984, while the indices of GOVI ranged from the smallest increase of 4.3 percent in 1981 to the largest increase of 27.3 percent in 1993. During the 18 years, the average annual increases for GOVA and GOVI were 6.6 percent and 15.0 percent, respectively. Clearly, the industrial sector has outperformed the agricultural sector during the reform years.

Moreover, the data in Table 4.4 further reveal the impact and gradual progress of agricultural and industrial reforms explained earlier. For example, during the period of agricultural reform (the first stage of economic reforms, 1978-1984), the increase of GOVA averaged an annual rate of 7.7 percent, which was larger than the average 4.1 percent and 4.8 percent reported in the second (1985-1988) and the third (1989-1991) stages of economic reforms, respectively. The GOVA data showed the largest increase rate of 12.3 percent in 1984, which provided the momentum for the proposed industrial reform. Similarly, the distribution of GOVI increases also showed the impact of economic reform policies as the average GOVI increased 10.2 percent in the first stage, jumped to 17.9 percent in the second stage, dropped to 10.4 percent in the third stage, and rebounded to 24.1 percent after 1992. The excellent performance in the agricultural and industrial sectors was especially noticeable after 1992, with the average annual increase of 8.4 percent in GOVA and 24.1 percent in GOVI.

The interaction between the agricultural and industrial reforms is also evidenced in the analysis of the ratio between the GOVI and GOVA (i.e., the column of I/A in Table 4.4). It is clear that there is a U-shaped relationship between the development of China's agriculture and industry during the economic reform years. It started with a ratio of 3.03, indicating about 3 times the industrial output value to the agricultural output value. The ratios gradually declined to 2.37 in 1984, which indicated the increase of agricultural output value because of the agricultural reform. The ratios moved upward again after 1985 and reached 4.51 in 1995, which indicated the increase of industrial gross output value after the industrial reform.

In addition to the growth record examined previously, the post-Mao economic reforms also brought structural changes in China's agricultural and industrial sectors. In the agricultural sector, there was a structural change of agricultural activities from crop cultivation toward other farm tasks such as animal husbandry and fisheries (Ash, 1992: 551). As revealed in Table 4.5, the share of crop farming has declined since the reforms, from about 80 percent of GOVA in 1978 to about 58 percent in 1995. During the same period, the shares of animal rearing and aquatic products increased after the reforms, from about 15 percent of GOVA in 1978 to about 30 percent of GOVA in 1995 for animal rearing and from about 2 percent of GOVA in 1978 to about 8 percent of GOVA in 1995 for aquatic products.

Table 4.4
Gross Output Value of Agriculture (GOVA) and Industry (GOVI), 1978-1995

Year	GOVA[1]	GOVI[1]	I/A[2]	Indices[3] Agriculture	Industry
1978	1397	4237	3.03	108.1	113.5
1979	1698	4681	2.76	107.5	108.8
1980	1923	5154	2.68	101.4	109.3
1981	2181	5400	2.48	105.8	104.3
1982	2483	5811	2.34	111.3	107.8
1983	2750	6461	2.35	107.8	111.2
1984	3214	7617	2.37	112.3	116.3
1985	3619	9716	2.68	103.4	121.4
1986	4013	11194	2.79	103.4	111.7
1987	4676	13813	2.95	105.8	117.7
1988	5865	18224	3.11	103.9	120.8
1989	6535	22017	3.37	103.1	108.5
1990	7662	23924	3.12	107.6	107.8
1991	8157	26625	3.26	103.7	114.8
1992	9085	34599	3.81	106.4	124.7
1993	10996	48402	4.40	107.8	127.3
1994	15750	70176	4.46	108.6	124.2
1995	20341	91824	4.51	110.9	120.3
Average annual increases (%)[4]					
1978-1995				(6.6)	(15.0)
1978-1984				(7.7)	(10.2)
1985-1988				(4.1)	(17.9)
1989-1991				(4.8)	(10.4)
1992-1995				(8.4)	(24.1)

Source: State Statistical Bureau, *China Statistical Yearbook* (1996: 356, 403); *Statistical Yearbook of China* (1993: 57, 59).

Note: 1. GOVA and GOVI are based on current prices in 100 million yuan.
2. Numbers of I/A indicate the calculated ratios between GOVA and GOVI.
3. Indices are based on preceding year = 100, comparable prices.
4. Numbers in parentheses are calculated average annual increases in the specific period.

Clearly, the increase of shares of animal rearing (about 15 percent) and aquatic products (about 6 percent) were at the expense of decreasing shares of crop farming (about 22 percent).

Table 4.5
Structural Changes in China's Agriculture, 1978-1995

Year	Farming[1]	Forestry[2]	Animal husbandry[3]	Fishery[4]
1978	80% (109.4)	3% (105.5)	15% (104.9)	2% (100.0)[5]
1979	77 (107.2)	4 (101.4)	17 (114.6)	2 (96.6)
1980	76 (99.7)	4 (112.2)	18 (107.0)	2 (107.7)
1981	75 (105.9)	5 (104.1)	18 (105.9)	2 (104.4)
1982	76 (110.3)	4 (108.5)	18 (113.2)	2 (112.3)
1983	75 (108.5)	5 (110.2)	18 (103.9)	2 (108.6)
1984	74 (111.5)	5 (119.0)	18 (113.4)	3 (117.6)
1985	69 (99.8)	5 (104.5)	22 (117.2)	4 (118.9)
1986	69 (102.7)	5 (96.4)	22 (105.6)	4 (120.5)
1987	67 (106.4)	5 (99.7)	23 (103.2)	5 (118.1)
1988	62 (101.4)	5 (102.3)	27 (112.6)	6 (111.6)
1989	63 (102.4)	4 (100.4)	28 (105.5)	5 (107.2)
1990	65 (108.0)	4 (103.1)	26 (107.0)	5 (110.0)
1991	63 (100.9)	5 (108.0)	26 (108.8)	6 (107.6)
1992	61 (104.2)	5 (107.7)	27 (108.8)	7 (115.3)
1993	60 (105.2)	5 (108.0)	27 (110.8)	8 (118.4)
1994	58 (103.2)	4 (108.9)	30 (116.7)	8 (120.0)
1995	58 (107.9)	4 (105.0)	30 (114.8)	8 (119.4)
(Average)[6]	(5.3)	(5.8)	(9.7)	(11.9)

Source: State Statistical Bureau, *China Statistical Yearbook* (1996: 356); *Statistical Yearbook of China* (1994: 330); (1993: 336).

Note:
1. Farming activities include planting, sideline products, and other farming.
2. Forestry activities include afforestation and its added value, forest products, lumbering in and below village.
3. Animal husbandry activities include animals, poultry raising, hunting, and other.
4. Fishery activities include seawater aquatic products and freshwater aquatic products.
5. Percentage numbers are based on the total gross output values of agriculture (100%). Numbers in parentheses are indices of gross output value in each agricultural sector, based on preceding year = 100.
6. Average numbers are calculated average annual increases of indices in each sector during the period of 1978 through 1995.

The structural changes in China's agricultural sector is also evidenced in the calculated average annual increase of GOVA indices in the four areas of agriculture (also in Table 4.5). During the period of 1978 to 1995, the average annual increase of GOVA indices for farming, forestry, animal husbandry, and fishery were 5.3 percent, 5.8 percent, 9.7 percent, and 11.9 percent, respectively. The average annual

Table 4.6
Structural Changes in China's Industry, 1978-1995

Year	State-Owned	Collective-[1] Owned	Individual-Owned	Other Ownership
1978	78% (114.4)	22% (110.6)[2]		
1979	78 (108.9)	22 (108.6)		
1980	76 (105.6)	24 (119.2)		
1981	75 (102.5)	25 (109.0)	.1 (234.6)	.6 (131.6)
1982	74 (107.1)	25 (109.5)	.1 (179.0)	.7 (127.7)
1983	73 (109.4)	26 (115.5)	.1 (220.6)	.8 (133.9)
1984	69 (108.9)	30 (134.9)	.2 (197.5)	1.0 (156.8)
1985	65 (112.9)	32 (132.7)	1.9 (1189.6)	1.2 (139.5)
1986	62 (106.2)	34 (118.0)	2.8 (167.6)	1.5 (134.2)
1987	60 (111.3)	35 (123.2)	3.6 (156.6)	2.0 (166.4)
1988	57 (112.6)	36 (128.2)	4.3 (147.3)	2.7 (161.5)
1989	56 (103.9)	36 (110.5)	4.8 (123.8)	3.4 (142.7)
1990	55 (103.0)	36 (109.0)	5.4 (121.1)	4.4 (139.3)
1991	53 (108.6)	36 (118.4)	5.4 (125.3)	4.4 (150.1)
1992	48 (112.4)	38 (133.3)	6.8 (147.0)	7.1 (164.8)
1993	47 (105.7)	34 (135.0)	8.0 (166.2)	11.1 (192.5)
1994	37 (106.5)	38 (124.9)	10.1 (156.3)	14.8 (174.3)
1995	34 (108.2)	37 (115.2)	12.9 (151.5)	16.6 (137.2)
(Average)[3]	(8.2)	(19.8)	(132.3)	(50.2)

Source: State Statistical Bureau, *China Statistical Yearbook* (1996: 403), *Statistical Yearbook of China* (1993: 412-414).

Note: 1. Collective-owned enterprises include township, village, and joint-venture enterprises.
2. Percentage numbers are based on the total gross output values of industry (100%). Numbers in parentheses are indices of gross output value in each industrial sector, based on preceding year = 100.
3. Average numbers are calculated average annual increases of indices in each sector during the period of 1978 to 1995.

increases for animal rearing and aquatic products are almost twice those for farming and forestry activities.

Moreover, similar structural changes were also found in China's industrial sector. The data in Table 4.6 show that the share of state-operated industry declined steadily from 78 percent of GOVI in 1978 to about 34 percent of GOVI in 1995. The share of collective industry rose from 22 percent of GOVI in 1978 to about 37 percent in 1995. The collective industry includes township, village, and joint-venture enterprises. The structural changes in the industrial sector were especially noticeable when examining the increase of shares of individual-owned and other ownership enterprises. The share of individual-owned enterprises increased from 0.1 percent of GOVI in 1981 to about 13 percent of GOVI in 1995, while the share of other-ownership enterprises rose from 0.6 percent of GOVI in 1981 to about 17 percent of GOVI in 1995. It was in 1992 that the share of state-owned enterprises dropped to less than 50 percent of the GOVI. The share of state-owned enterprises today accounts for only about one-third of the overall GOVI.

The findings about structural changes in the industrial sector are supported by examining the calculated average annual increase of GOVI indices in the four types of enterprises (also in Table 4.6). During the period of 1978 to 1995, the average annual increase of GOVI indices were 8.2 percent for state-owned enterprises, 19.8 percent for collective-owned enterprises, 132.3 percent for individual-owned enterprises, and 50.2 percent for enterprises of other ownership. It is clear that during the reform years the collective, individual, and other enterprises outgrew the state-owned enterprises. The percentage increase in enterprises of individual-owned and other ownership are especially impressive.

The findings about structural changes in China's industry are similar to those reported in other studies (e.g., Field, 1992). For example, Field noticed that a change of industrial structure was based on their categories as the above-township or at- and below-township levels. The share of industries above the township level (consisting of state, county collective, urban street collective, and other) declined from 89 percent in 1980 to about 68 percent in 1990, while the share of industries at or below the township level (consisting of township, village, cooperative, and individual) increased from about 11 percent in 1980 to about 32 percent in 1990 (Field, 1992: 590). In addition, Field (1992: 591-592) indicated that the industrial growth after the reforms was dominated by three branches of heavy industry (machinery, building materials, and chemicals) and cultural goods. The branches with primary output of consumer goods (e.g., food, textiles, clothing, leather, and cultural goods) grew faster than their historic rate, while branches with a primary output of produced goods grew more slowly.[5]

Foreign Trade and Investment

To examine the impact of China's open-door policy, the evaluation of China's economic achievements during the reform years also focused on the analysis of China's foreign trade and investment. Data about China's foreign trade during the period of 1978 to 1995 are presented in Table 4.7. First, the total of foreign trade (the combination of export and import) increased dramatically during the reform years. The total trade increased from US $20.6 billion in 1978 to $280.9 billion in 1995, an increase of about 14 times.

Next, the increase of exports and imports are also reported in Table 4.7. Exports increased from US $9.8 billion in 1978 to $148.8 billion in 1995, an increase of about 15 times. Imports also increased from US $10.9 billion in 1978 to $132.1 billion in 1995, an increase of about 12 times. During those 18 years, China's trade balance changed significantly, ranging from $-14.9 billion of the trade deficit in 1985 to $16.7 billion of the trade surplus in 1995.

The increasing role of foreign trade in China's economy also can be found in the analysis of the ratio between exports and GNP. As also shown in Table 4.7, the export-GNP ratio rose from about 5 percent of GNP in 1978 to about 22 percent of GNP in 1995, an increase of more than 4 times. The data certainly indicate not only the effect of China's open-door reform policy but also the importance and contribution of exports to China's economy after the economic reforms.

Table 4.7
Foreign Trade, 1978-1995

Year	Total	Export[1]	Import[1]	Balance	Export/GNP[2]
1978	20.6	9.8	10.9	-1.1	0.05
1979	29.4	13.7	15.7	-2.0	0.05
1980	38.1	18.1	20.0	-1.9	0.06
1981	44.0	22.0	22.0	0	0.08
1982	41.6	22.3	19.3	3.0	0.08
1983	43.6	22.2	21.4	0.8	0.08
1984	53.6	26.1	27.4	-1.3	0.08
1985	69.6	27.4	42.3	-14.9	0.09
1986	73.9	30.9	42.9	-12.0	0.11
1987	82.7	39.4	43.2	-3.8	0.13
1988	102.8	47.5	55.3	-7.8	0.12
1989	111.6	52.5	59.1	-6.6	0.12
1990	115.4	62.1	53.4	8.7	0.16
1991	135.6	71.8	63.8	8.0	0.18
1992	165.5	84.9	80.6	4.3	0.18
1993	195.7	91.8	104.0	-12.2	0.15
1994	236.6	121.0	115.6	5.4	0.22
1995	280.9	148.8	132.1	16.7	0.22

Source: State Statistical Bureau, *China Statistical Yearbook* (1996: 580); *Statistical Yearbook of China* (1993: 633).

Note: 1. Based on the current prices in US$ billion.
2. Calculated ratios between export and GNP.

In addition to foreign trade, the open-door policy affected the performance of China's foreign loans and direct foreign investments. Based on the incomplete data summarized in Table 4.8, both values of foreign loans and direct foreign investments improved during the reform years. With regard to foreign loans, China achieved a total of $13.55 billion of contract loans and $10.69 billion of actual loans between

1979 and 1982, with an average annual amount of $3.39 billion and $2.67 billion, respectively. After the earlier years, both contract and actual loans increased between 1983 and 1995, from $1.51 billion to $11.29 billion and from $1.07 billion to $10.33 billion, respectively. Between 1983 and 1995, the increase of foreign loans by about 9.7 times for actual loans and 7.5 times for contract loans certainly indicated the success of the Chinese government in seeking loans from foreigners. The calculated rates between the actual and the contract values also indicated high rates of actual loans.

Table 4.8
Foreign Capital, 1978-1995[1]

Year	Foreign Loans Actual	Foreign Loans Contract	Foreign Loans Rate[2]	Direct Foreign Investment Actual	Direct Foreign Investment Contract	Direct Foreign Investment Rate[2]
1979-82	10.69	13.55	79%	1.17	6.01	19%
1983	1.07	1.51	71	0.64	1.73	37
1984	1.29	1.92	67	1.26	2.65	48
1985	2.69	3.53	76	1.66	5.93	28
1986	5.01	8.41	60	1.87	2.83	66
1987	5.81	7.82	74	2.31	3.71	62
1988	6.49	9.81	66	3.19	5.30	60
1989	6.29	5.19	121	3.39	5.60	61
1990	6.53	5.10	128	3.49	6.60	53
1991	6.89	7.16	96	4.37	11.98	36
1992	7.91	10.70	74	11.01	58.12	19
1993	11.19	11.31	99	27.52	111.44	25
1994	9.27	10.67	87	33.77	82.68	41
1995	10.33	11.29	91	37.52	91.28	41

Source: State Statistical Bureau, *China Statistical Yearbook* (1996: 597).
Note: 1. Based on the current prices in US$ billion.
2. Calculated ratios of the actual value to the contract value.

The impact of the open-door policy also can be examined by focusing on the data of direct foreign investment. As also shown in Table 4.8, between 1979 and 1982, the total contract direct foreign investment was $6.01 billion and the actual direct foreign investment was $1.17 billion, with an annual average of $1.5 billion and $0.3 billion, respectively. After the earlier years, both contract and actual numbers of direct foreign investments increased dramatically between 1983 to 1995, from $1.73 billion to $91.28 billion and from $0.64 billion to $37.52 billion, respectively. The data showed an increase of about 58.6 times for the actual direct foreign investment and about 52.8 times for the contract direct foreign investment. The calculated rates of the actual value to the contract values showed relatively high rates of the actual investment, ranging from the highest rate of 66 percent in 1986 to the lowest rate of 19 percent in 1992. Again, the open-door reform policy certainly had a positive impact on foreigners' confidence in China's economy and contributed huge amounts of capital to China's economic development.

In sum, the evaluation of China's economic indicators during the reform years showed that despite the pressure of rising inflation, the post-Mao economic reforms have improved China's overall economic performance in both domestic and international activities. The evaluation also revealed the impact of changing focuses and policies during each stage of the reform. Indeed, the economic reforms have resulted in not only rapid growth and expansion in major aspects of economic activities but also structural changes in China's agricultural, industrial, and foreign trade sectors. All of these indicate achievements and positive effects of the reform policies.

PROBLEMS OF ECONOMIC REFORMS

Despite the impressive record of economic performance, the post-Mao economic reforms have also produced some negative effects on China's economy and society. The negative effects are reflected in major problems or obstacles that emerged during the reform years. They include, for example, the overheating economy; the rise of inflation and national deficits; the shortage of raw materials; the inadequacy of infrastructure (e.g., telecommunication and transportation); the problem of unemployment (especially in the urban areas with the increased population moving in from the country side); the imbalance of regional development between China's coastal and interior areas; the rise of income inequality between China's urban and rural areas and between the newly rich and the majority of the population; the deterioration of environment and resource protection; the problem of labor relations and working conditions; the pervasiveness of corruption, crimes, and unhealthy tendencies; and the unrest and dissatisfaction of China's minorities (e.g., *Beijing Review* 1993-1994; Jiang, 1995; Shanor & Shanor, 1995).[6] Directly or indirectly related to economic reforms, the existence and extension of these problems will certainly affect the continuing development of economic reforms in the short run and challenge the stability of Chinese society and the power and control of the government in the long run.

Recognizing the broad nature of many problems, this section will analyze four major problems that are considered critical to China's economic development (Lieberthal, 1995; Liou, 1998). The four problems are high inflation, regional and income inequality, environmental protection, and corruption and social unrest. Directly related to economic activities, the first two issues of inflation and regional and income inequality address the economic stabilization and distribution functions of Chinese government, respectively. While not directly related to economic issues, the last two issues are also important to economic development. The issue of environmental protection is related to the regulatory function of the government and concerns about the negative impact of economic development on the natural resources and environment. The issue of corruption and social unrest has to do with the changing social environment of China's society, which will certainly affect the future development of economic reforms.

Inflation

The rise of inflationary pressure during the reform years was addressed briefly in the previous analysis of China's macroeconomic performance. As explained, China has experienced continuous sharp rises in prices, with an average annual increase of retail price of 7.5 percent between 1978 and 1995. While this is better than the average inflation rate found in developing countries (about 20.95 percent between 1960 and 1985; see Li, 1989: 664), the inflation rate was considered very high and unacceptable to the Chinese people because of the nature of Chinese society during the pre-reform years (1949-1978). For about 30 years, the Chinese people lived in a society where the state controlled every aspect of their economic (and noneconomic) life. They were used to artificially low prices that depended on heavy state subsidies for virtually everything related to daily life (e.g., food, housing, cooking fuel). In other words, during the pre-reform years, China fundamentally froze prices within the economic plan and achieved a level of almost complete price stability (Yabuki, 1995: 125).

The increase of inflation during the reform years was related to both economic growth and reform policies. In general, inflationary pressure is usually associated with rapid economic growth because inflation is considered as one of the side effects of economic growth, due to changes and imbalances of total supply and demand. This kind of inflation, named "growth-related inflation," is common to any market economy and is not considered a policy mistake.

In addition to growth-related inflation, inflation in China was caused by two interrelated policy factors: changes in the economic structure and mistakes associated with the formulation and implementation of economic policies (Li, 1989; Li, 1994). This type of inflation, named "policy-change inflation," consisted of both structural problems and policy mistakes. First, the structural problems have to do with some inherent conflicts that relate to the introduction of a new system. One example of the structural problems was the introduction of the two-track system, especially the dual-price system in China's price reform. The two-track system brought the problem of price conflicts because one part of economic activities is based on the free price of the market, while the other part is controlled and regulated by the state. The relationship between the dual-price system and inflation was noticed in the case of the rise of urban food prices (Naughton, 1995a: 247-249). The increasing cost of urban food was related not to state-controlled prices of some foods (e.g., grains) but to the rise of the prices of foods that are based on the market (e.g., nonstaple foods, including vegetables, poultry, eggs, and meat). It was the large increase in nonstaple food prices that eventually led to increases in overall prices.

Next, the policy mistakes of inflation refer to two interrelated issues: the expansion of excess aggregate demand and the lack of macro-control mechanisms (Chang, 1984; Chow, 1994; Li, 1989; Yeh, 1992). On the one hand, the expansion of excess aggregate demand has to do with the overextended investment by state-owned enterprises during the reform years. For example, Li (1989: 657) estimated that between 1983 and 1987, the annual growth rate in capital investment and in total wages was greater than that of national income and that about two-thirds of the capital investment was made by state-owned enterprises. The overinvestment situation among state-owned enterprises resulted from a problem of soft budget constraint (Kornai, 1980) that was common to enterprise management in the central planning system. The soft-budget constraint refers to the situation that under the central planning system, state-owned enterprises and public organizations do not face any budgetary pressure on their operations because their resources depend primarily on administrative authorities and distributions.

On the other hand, the overinvestment situation was also affected by the lack of macro-control mechanisms. The lack of macro-control mechanisms refers to the fact that China had lost its traditional control mechanisms on the one hand and lacked a new one on the other. Traditionally, the central planning committee controlled inflation by ordering local governments and state enterprises to reduce investment spending and control consumption funds. During the reform process, the central government has lost this close control mechanism by giving more autonomy to local governments and enterprises (i.e., the decentralization policy). One example of this was the central government's loss of control over the money supply. Local officials have used their power to influence local bank branches to lend funds beyond their prescribed quotas.

Because of a lack of new control mechanisms, China, while moving to a market economy, has not established sound financial and monetary systems that are common in Western market economies. In other words, the problem refers to the fact that China did not have a modern financial system (e.g., tax system) to control aggregate supply and demand and that the Peoples' Bank of China did not have the independent authority to formulate and implement monetary policy to adjust business spending. As explained earlier, the macro-control problem was recognized by the Chinese leaders and addressed in their reform policies of macroeconomic structures emphasized in the 1990s.

The consequences of inflation are severe. It will not only destroy economic growth and destabilize the economy but also reduce enterprise efficiency and intensify unfair distribution of resources and income. Especially, sharp and continued inflation caused strong resentment from citizens and resulted in political and social instability. For example, the people's dissatisfaction with continuing inflation was considered one of the major reasons for the large demonstration in Beijing in 1989. As indicated in Table 4.3 of the previous analysis, retail prices rose 18.5 percent in 1988 and 17.8 percent in 1989, two of the highest rates in the 18 years of the reform.

Despite the discussions about the causes and consequences of inflation, the record showed that the Chinese leaders were very concerned about inflation and were able to control it (Chow, 1994). For example, after the high inflation rates in 1988 and 1989, the Chinese government was able to reduce the retail price indices from 18 percent in 1989 to about 3 to 5 percent in the early 1990s. The government achieved this through both administrative and economic means (e.g., controlling credit amounts of regional banks and raising interest rates) during the period of the slowdown of economic reforms. Inflation, however, rose again after 1993 along with the rapid growth after the reassurance of economic reform in 1992. In addition to using the administrative and economic means emphasized before, the Chinese leaders have also introduced financial reform and, especially, banking reforms to address the structural issue related to inflation. It is clear that along with the rapid economic growth, the leaders need to continue to pay attention to the issue of inflation in future development.[7]

Regional and Income Inequality

Another challenging issue that emerged during the period of China's economic reform has been the unequal distribution of resources and incomes between coastal and interior regions as well as between urban and rural areas since the beginning of the reforms. With regard to the issue of regional inequality, the adoption of the open-door policy and especially the emphasis on the coastal areas development strategy clearly showed that China has adopted an uneven, imbalanced regional development strategy. The uneven strategy allows differential development among the regions and grants preferential policies to the coastal region so that it might develop faster and become the engine of growth for the country. The new policy and strategy are totally different from the traditional, balanced development policy and the interior-oriented strategy.[8]

The results of the new development policy and strategy are that both domestic and international economic activities in the coastal region have increased more than those in the interior (the combination of the central and western regions) region since the early 1980s (Lyons, 1991; Tsui, 1991; Yang, 1990). As discussed and analyzed in Chapter 5, China's coastal region has grown faster than the interior region in terms of such economic measures as gross output value of industry, total investment in fixed assets, domestic trade of retail sales, and foreign capital actually used. The differences in development speed has resulted in the increase of regional gaps and disparities as reflected in people's living standards. Again, people in the coastal region experienced higher rates of increase in their per capita national income and per capita consumption than those of the residents in the interior region.

Besides the interior-coastal inequalities, there have been increases in inequalities between China's rural and urban areas since the economic reforms in 1978 (Tsui, 1993). Also addressed in Chapter 5, the income disparity between urban and rural areas changed along with the economic reforms. While both groups increased their incomes during the economic reforms, the analyses show that net incomes increased more among urban households (7.4 times) than those of farmers (6.9 times). The ratios of urban to farmer incomes fluctuated, ranging from 2.37 in 1978, to 1.72 in 1985, and to 2.54 in 1993. The fluctuation of the ratios again shows a U-type relationship and reveals the impact of the process of agricultural and industrial reforms.

The concerns about income inequality also focused on the inequalities within China's urban and rural areas (Khan, Griffin, Riskin & Zhao, 1992; Ma 1994). Studies have found that inequality in the distribution of income in the rural area is higher than that in the urban area. The reasons for the increasing inequality in the distribution of income in rural China have to do with wages and incomes from different types of enterprises (including those of private entrepreneurs). On the other hand, China's urban inequality is less than rural inequality because most urban residents work for some kind of public enterprises and government agencies, which emphasize egalitarianism in their wage structures.

The increasing regional and income inequality may result in not only regional conflicts but also potential disintegration in China (Goodman, 1994; Holloway, 1995). The leaders of the interior provinces are asking equal or special treatment and assistance from the central government. The leaders of the coastal provinces are moving away from the central policies and toward China's rich overseas regions such as Hong Kong and Taiwan. The outcome of the regional conflicts may be the political disintegration of China. The issue becomes further complicated if the inequalities and dissatisfaction increases among China's minorities, especially the Muslims and Tibetans. For them, the rise of new, independent states along the Chinese borders since the breakup of the Soviet Union has already resulted in increasing nationalistic desires and activities in some boarder provinces (e.g., Tibet and Xinjiang) (Shanor & Shanor, 1995).

Environmental Protection

Rapid economic growth and development have also brought problems to China's natural resources and environment. The environmental problems existed before the reform years and became one of the serious policy issues after the reform. The environmental problems resulted from two interrelated factors. On the one hand, the deterioration of China's environment has to do with the country's objective condition of a large population and limited useful land (especially farmland). The ratio of farmland to population deteriorated because of population growth and declining arable land before the reform years. During the period of 1957 through 1977, per capita arable land fell from 2.59 *mou* (0.18 hectares) to 1.57 *mou* (0.1 hectares); the net loss of arable land was 180 million *mou* (12 million hectares) (Prybyla, 1982: 1215).

On the other hand, China's environmental problems also related to the past development policy and experience (Prybyla, 1981; Lieberthal, 1995). The emphasis on heavy industry during Mao's era caused a basic problem because heavy industry in general tends to consume more resources than does light industry. The central planning system also generated problems because, under the system, industrial ministries and enterprise managers focused on the achievement of physical output targets and gave little attention to the efficiency of using environmental resources. Moreover, several policies and movements initiated to increase land cultivation resulted in the blind pursuit of grain cultivation at the expense of damaging the land in terms of reducing productivity and increasing soil erosion. Finally, the impact of politics on economic policy negatively affected the environment because of the attack on professionals by nonprofessionals in issues such as land terracing, hill leveling, and grassland management (e.g., the blind emulation of the *Dazhai* model).

The environmental problems have worsened since the start of the reforms. Despite some positive effects of the reforms on the environment (e.g., encouraging the efficiency of using resources), the post-Mao reforms have accelerated the deterioration of China's environment. The success of the reforms in promoting China's overall economic growth has resulted in a consumer society that produces increasing levels of consumption, waste, and pollution. In the case of air pollution, for example, some 10,500 billion cubic meters of waste gas were discharged in the country (not including the township industrial waste) in 1992. The amount of sulphur dioxide discharge is rising annually (a total of 16.85 million tons in 1992), causing a wide precipitation of acid rain (in about 30 percent of China's total territory) (*Beijing Review*, 1995c: 6; Liao, 1993: 12-16).

In the case of water pollution, the official report indicated that the national discharge of waste water was 36.65 billion tons in 1992 (23.39 billion tons from the discharge of industrial waste water). Water pollution in many towns and cities became very serious. For example, about 85.7 percent of monitoring projects of urban rivers showed water quality below standard. Lakes are contaminated by minerals such as nitrogen and phosphorus. The direct negative impact of water pollution on the fish population is also evident. A survey of 15 provinces, autonomous regions, and municipalities indicated that the country faces extinction of fish in its 2,800 kilometer length of 29 rivers, and water quality in 25,000 kilometers of rivers was not up to fishery standards. Heavy pollution resulted in 45.5 million kg of dead fish in 327,000 hectares of national freshwater fish farms (Liao, 1993: 12-13).

In addition, it was noticed that land abuses and illegal allocation of land have been mounting in China since the reforms. For example, officials estimated that overexploitation reduced China's arable land by 400,000 hectares in 1993. More than 6,660,000 hectares of grassland revert to desert every year. Again, the land problem resulted from both human errors and natural forces. On the human error side, for example, the number of development zones increased from 117 in 1991 to more than 2,700 in 1992, with 80 percent of the zones built on agricultural lands. The problem is that while the allocated development zones cover an area of 15,321 square km, only 2 percent is under construction. On the natural side, about 1.79 million square meters of land have been washed away by floods and 1.88 million square km by wind erosion. The estimated direct economic losses caused by the damage of wind and sand reached as high as 4.5 billion yuan annually (*Beijing Review*, 1995c: 6; Liao, 1993: 14).

The concern of the environmental problems becomes one of China's major public policies. To deal with the environmental problems, the Chinese government has adopted numerous environmental laws and regulations as well as established environmental agencies and bureaus at the central (e.g., Environmental Commission, National Environmental Protection Administration) and local levels. In addition, the government has also built up a cadre of experts on environmental issues and actively participated in international environmental activities.

Studies of China's environmental policy and management indicated that problems of environmental protection in China are not laws and policies but implementation issues (Boxer, 1989; Chan & Wong, 1994; Chan, Wong, Cheung & Lo, 1995; Ross, 1984). They noticed that China has promoted environmental protection as a major national concern and has developed numerous laws, regulations, administrative policies, education, and propaganda. The implementation problems occurred because of the inability of the government to coordinate and balance economic development and environmental protection from a long-term perspective because of the continuing emphasis on short-term growth. As commonly known, environmental problems are not locally bounded and tend to cross the administrative boundaries of local authorities. The decentralization of decision-making power and the increase in the local economic activities associated with the economic reform policies, however, have weakened the effectiveness of centrally developed plans and programs.[9]

Corruption and Social Unrest

Besides the deterioration of the environment and resources, the economic reforms have also led to major problems of the pervasiveness of corruption and the rise of crimes and unhealthy tendencies in China's society. First, it should be noted that the issue of corruption existed before the reform era and was seriously criticized by Chinese leaders during the pre-reform social movements (e.g., the Three-Anti campaign in the 1950s and the Socialist Education Movement in the 1960s) (Harding, 1981). The economic reforms have increased the level of corruption (in terms of both scope and frequency) because of their impact on the redistribution of economic power (Liu, 1983; Lo, 1993; Myers, 1989; Sands, 1990; Sun, 1991). While it is difficult to estimate the overall level of corruption, Chinese officials have continuously reported increasing numbers of corruption cases (e.g., more than 95,000 cases in 1994, *Beijing Review*, 1995a: 6) and numbers of officials prosecuted and executed because of embezzlement and accepting bribes (*Beijing Review*, 1993b).

The causes of corruption are related not only to problems of China's political, social, and economic systems but also to effects of the reform policies. The system problems include factors such as the dominance and control of the Party and the lack of external monitoring mechanisms (e.g., the media, the legislature, and the court) in China's political system; the problems of the central planning economic system (e.g., stresses and dislocation problems in different regions and sectors); and the pervasiveness and acceptance of informal network activities (e.g., *Guanxi*) in China's cultural, social, and ideological traditions (Liu, 1983).

The negative effects of the economic reforms, however, have been identified as major reasons for the recent increase of corruption (Lieberthal, 1995; Liu, 1983; Lo, 1993; Ma, 1989; Rocca, 1992; Sands, 1990; Sun 1991). The problems of economic reforms have to do with both policy failures and leadership issues. First, with regard to policy failures, the economic reforms provided opportunities for some officials to expand and abuse power for their own interests. For example, the structural loopholes created by the dual-price policy have allowed many local leaders and enterprise managers to gain advantages for their organizations and themselves by manipulating their resources and production because of the differences between the official and the market prices. In addition, the reform policies of decentralization of decision-making power and separation of economic management from government administration have also weakened traditional control mechanisms. The control problem became even more serious because of the lack of viable substitutes (i.e., the rule of law) during the economic transition period.

Next, the wide spread of corruption also stemmed from leadership mistakes in reform policies and promotion of values. The former has to do with the situation that, to maintain political support for economic reforms, Deng Xiaoping has permitted some top officials to help their families during the reform process. Many offspring of top officials *(taizidang)* became heads of newly formed trading companies and used their connections to gain inside information, secure scare goods and licences, and protect themselves from legal retribution (Lieberthal, 1995: 268). The value problems occurred because the leaders promoted values such as "to get rich is glorious" and "some people should become rich first." Contrary to Mao's plain living and equal treatment, these values have promoted materialism in the Chinese society and provided incentives for officials (and everyone) to use all kinds of opportunities to gain additional income.

The pervasion of corruption has resulted in severe social and economic effects. The negative consequences of corruption consist of, for example, enhancing social inequality between the small group of newly rich and the majority of the public; causing inflation and price disorder because of the officials' manipulation of resources; contributing to the values crisis and moral erosion because the corrupted became rich based not on their contribution to the society but on their position; and promoting a culture of corruption in the organization and the society (Liu, 1983; Sun, 1991). In addition, corruption also caused the rise of social tensions because the general public dislikes the fact that the corrupted Chinese use the money for their conspicuous consumption and luxurious lifestyle. Researchers (e.g., Mason, 1994; Sun 1991) have argued that it was the corruption issue that linked the interests of students, workers, and the public in their protest against the party and the authority in the Tiananmen Square incident of 1989.[10]

Finally, along with improved economic conditions and rising living standards, the reform years also witnessed an increase in crimes and social unrest in Chinese society (Myers, 1989; Perry, 1993). Some of the crimes are closely related to the problem of corruption and other types of economic crimes, including, for example, offenses committed by an institutional agent (e.g., departmentalism, localism, waste of resources), by the cadres (e.g., bribery and blackmail), and by the generally poor (e.g., theft and appropriation of public property, absenteeism) (Myers, 1989; Zafanoli, 1985).

Moreover, the problem of social unrest refers to the deterioration in the quality of life due to the rise in crime rates (e.g., murders, robberies, kidnappings, rapes, thefts, drug trafficking) and other indicators of social life (e.g., divorce rates, suicides). Many secret societies and native-place gangs materialized in amazing numbers to serve as the organizational nuclei for some of these crimes. In 1993, for example, the police crushed 150,000 domestic criminal gangs, involving 570,000 offenders, a 24 percent growth since 1992 (*Beijing Review*, 1994: 5). Especially, some of these groups have established ties with powerful crime syndicates in Hong Kong, Macao, and Taiwan. The Chinese society today is very different from that in Mao's years in terms of social life and crimes.

Again, the problem of social unrest has been related to the impact of economic growth and the lack of control mechanisms since the reforms (Kaye, 1994c; Kuhn, 1994a, 1994b; Wang, 1993). The issue of economic growth refers to the increase of material-oriented drive in the society during the reform years. Materialism and commercialism have become popular and replaced the traditional Confucian value system and the socialist norm system. Without necessary skills, education, and opportunities, some people, especially young men and women, will resort to illegal means to make easy money in order to satisfy their desires for new and expensive lifestyles (e.g., clothes and entertainment).

The issue of control mechanisms has to do with the breakdown of the traditional social control system. For example, work units used to perform many police functions such as disciplining employees convicted of crimes. In urban areas, the police-supervised street committees used to watch the comings and goings on the block and enforce the hukou household registration system. These kinds of social control systems have been seriously damaged or destroyed because the economic reforms have increased openness and free movement in the society and the pervasiveness of commercial activities.

The issue of social unrest becomes even more serious when we consider the public's perception of the effectiveness of crime control. It was noticed that people are concerned about the corrupt behavior of some justice and law enforcement officials and have a very negative view of some of legal officials (Kuhn, 1994a). Concern about corrupt legal officials is supported by some official reports. For example, in his report to the annual session of the National People's Congress in 1995, Zhang Siqing, China's top procurator, admitted that a growing number of corruption and bribery cases has involved judicial and law-enforcement officials (*Beijing Review*, 1995b: 6).[11]

DISCUSSION AND CONCLUSION

This chapter provided a comprehensive evaluation of China's post-Mao economic reforms. The evaluation covered both achievements and problems of the reforms. On the side of achievements, the evaluation analyzed major economic indicators during the reform years and found some excellent records in almost every aspect of China's economy, including overall growth, national and per-capita income, agricultural and industrial output, and foreign trade and investment. On the side of problems, the present evaluation also indicated several issues that emerged and worsened during the reform years and may affect the future development of the reforms. These problem issues include, for example, the continued pressure of inflation, the increasing income inequality in various regions and groups, the deterioration of environment and resources, the pervasiveness of bureaucratic corruption, and the rise of crimes and social unrest.

The findings of the present evaluation certainly offered needed information for both supporters and opponents of China's economic reforms. Emphasizing the positive side of achievements, the supporters would conclude that the reforms have achieved their goals of changing the economic structure and system, improving economic growth and modernization, and increasing people's incomes and living standards. While agreeing with the growth records, the opponents would argue that the reforms have not fundamentally resolved past problems of the inefficient and irrational system of production, distribution, and consumption and that the reforms have produced some new problems of economic uncertainty, inequality, and dissatisfaction.

Understanding the arguments of both sides, the author believes that China's post-Mao economic reforms have been very successful when considering the history of China's past development and the experience of other postsocialist states. Unlike the experience of Mao's development, the economic reforms since 1978 have been peaceful and stable, without sudden changes in development policies and strategies and major struggles in the internal political power relations (except the Tiananmen Square incident). The economic reforms have not only produced positive economic results but also changed the attitude of the Chinese from past required ideological struggles to embracing modern economic competition. The impact of economic reforms have extended to noneconomic activities, and the Chinese society today is more open and dynamic than it used to be.

The records of Chinese reforms are even more outstanding when comparing them with those of other postsocialist countries. Sharing a similar centrally planning system, many of the countries were more advanced and developed than China before the late 1970s. Today, however, many of them are in the throes of economic bankruptcy and system collapse. Many people in these countries live in a situation worse than they were in before. In addition, some of the countries are involved in civil war and other armed incidents. Many of these countries are actually learning from China's development experience.

The problems of China's economic reforms are real and should be handled properly. The existence and expansion of these problems stem mainly from some friction associated with changes between the old and new systems during the transition period. Many of the problems will have a negative impact on China's further development. The next three chapters will address three of the most important issues that occurred during the reforms: regional and income inequality, the administrative problem and reform, and state-society relations. These issues cover three policy areas emphasized in the literature of economic development, including the equal distribution of social incomes, the effectiveness of a public management system, and the stability of political and social conditions (e.g., Haggard & Webb, 1993; Rondinelli & Montgomery, 1990; Summers & Thomas, 1993; Todaro, 1985). The analysis of these issues will certainly help policy makers and researchers to further understand the management of China's economic reforms.

NOTES

1. The present analysis of China's macroeconomic performance was based on China's

official statistics. Many researchers have noticed some problems with the official statistics (e.g., Yeh, 1992). In preparing the GNP data, for example, the author found different GNP values and indices presented in the 1994 and 1996 statistical yearbooks. The decision was made to use the latest figures and to include missing figures from the earlier versions of the statistical yearbooks.

2. The data about China's national income covered only the period of 1978 to 1993 because the 1996 statistical yearbook did not provide information about it. The author decided to report the national income data for the purpose of comparing the data of the 1978-1993 period with the income data of the 1949-1977 period (see Table 2.2, presented in Chapter 2).

3. The selection of the urban unemployment rate and the retail price index was based on the availability and completeness of the data for the research period. The outcome of inflation would be similar if the consumer price index were used.

4. For more information about the floating population issue, see the discussion of changes in social mobility in Chapter 7.

5. In addition to changes in total output and structure, many studies of the impact of economic reforms on Chinese industry also addressed the issue of productivity. Some argued that despite the growth of output, the productivity of state enterprises did not improve during the reform years. For more information about this issue, see, for example, Chen et al., (1988), Field (1992), Jefferson and Xu (1991), and Wu (1995).

6. Many problems and obstacles emerged along with the process of economic reforms. For a brief discussion about some of the problems, see, for example, Shanor and Shanor (1995: 6-9).

7. The issue of inflation is very important to the evaluation of Chinese economic reforms. For more information and analysis of China's inflation problem, see, for example, Chow (1994: 91-97, Chapter 9), Y. Li (1989), T. Li (1994), Yabuki (1995: 123-136, Chapter 12), and Yeh (1992: 532-542).

8. For more information and analysis about China's regional development policy and strategy, see Chapter 6 about changes in regional development.

9. For more information about China's environmental problems, policy, and management, see, for example, Boxer (1989); Chan and Wong (1994); Chan, Wong, Cheung, and Lo (1995); Glaeser (1987); Lieberthal (1995: 276-291, Chapter 10); and Ross (1984).

10. For more information about China's corruption issue, see, for example, Lieberthal (1995), Liu (1983), T. W. Lo (1993), Ma (1989), Rocca (1992), Sands (1990), and Sun (1991).

11. For more information about the social unrest in post-Mao China, see discussions in Chapter 7 about the changes in state-society relations.

CHAPTER 5

Changes in Regional Development

INTRODUCTION

Post-Mao economic reforms have successfully improved China's economic performance since the beginning of the reforms in 1978. During the period of 1978 to 1995, the Chinese economy achieved high growth rates in almost every aspect of economic indicators, including an average annual increase of 9.8 percent in gross national product (GNP), 8.3 percent in per-capita GNP, 6.6 percent in gross output value of agriculture, and 15.0 percent in gross output value of industry. Especially, as one of the major reform measures, the open door policy has promoted China's economic relationship with foreign countries and increased foreign trade and investment activities. Again, from 1978 to 1995, China's export increased from about 5 percent of its GNP to about 22 percent of the GNP, and the amount of foreign direct investment jumped from less than 1 billion to more than 37 billion U.S. dollars.[1]

The outstanding economic performance in post-Mao China has to do with some changes in China's economic system that were introduced during the reform years. Since 1978, the economic system has transformed from a centrally planned administrative command system to a market socialism with Chinese characteristics (Deng, 1984; Zhao, 1987). In the traditional system, resources allocation was controlled not by the market but by the state. That is, resources were first centralized in the state agencies and then redistributed to different sectors of the society to maximize social goods according to the state plan. The state was responsible for patterns of investment and regional development in China.

The present Chinese economic system is characterized as a two-tier plan and market system (Byrd, 1987), where both planning and market coexist to guide economic resources and operations. In other words, the economic reforms have added some market mechanisms and activities in the Chinese economic system at the expense of reducing some state planning mechanisms and activities. One of the major effects of the two-tier system is the uneven development approach and outcomes in China's different economic sectors and regions. Those sectors and regions influenced by the new market activities have experienced more rapid development and improvement than those still controlled by the state activities. One of the typical examples of the operation of the two-tier system and the uneven development approaches is the policy of regional development emphasized in post-Mao China.

The issue of post-Mao regional development has become increasingly popular and important among researchers of China's economic reforms (e.g., Goodman, 1994; Kaye 1995a; Lee, 1994, 1995; Lyons, 1991; Tsui, 1991, 1993; Yang, 1990, 1991; Yang & Wei, 1996; Zweig, 1995). The interest in and emphasis on the regional development studies resulted from not only the concern about the direct relationship between post-Mao reform policies and regional economic growth but also the concern about the impact of regional development and growth on China's future development. Specifically, interest in studies of the reform policies and regional growth issue is related to the issue of China's increasing regional inequalities and autonomy that are associated with the economic reforms.

The issue of regional and income inequalities is especially important to the future fate of the reforms. As indicated in the review of the economic development literature, one of the major policies emphasized in the success of economic development is the social equity policy (Haggard & Webb, 1993; Rondinelli & Montgomery, 1990; Summers & Thomas, 1993). The social equity policy attempts to reduce the social adversity imposed by various inequalities (e.g., regional, class, or ethnic) and to affect the distribution of income resulting from economic growth. With regard to the Chinese experience, the emphasis on the impact of regional development has to do with the issue of whether China will stay united or break up because of increasing inequalities and regionalism.

This chapter attempts to examine the issue of regional development in the post-Mao economic reform years. The chapter begins with an overview of China's regional development policy before and after the reform years. Identifying major changes in the regional development policy, the chapter then provides comprehensive analyses to evaluate the impact of the new regional development policy. Based on the official statistical data, the analyses compare economic activities (e.g., gross output value of agriculture and industry, total investment, domestic trade and foreign investment) among China's regions (the coastal, the central, and the western) and provinces. In addition, the chapter addresses some new challenge issues that are related to China's regional development, including income inequalities between regions and provinces, inequalities between and within urban and rural areas, and policy concerns between the central and regional leaders. The chapter concludes with discussions about the implication of the changes and concerns in regional development, especially the issue of economic integration within Greater China and the issue of increasing regionalism and the possibility of political disintegration in China.

CHANGES IN THE REGIONAL DEVELOPMENT POLICY

The post-Mao economic reforms have fundamentally changed the orientation and principle of China's traditional development policy and strategies. The traditional development policy was a balanced-oriented development policy, which focused on balancing economic growth and development among different regions in China. Under the balanced-oriented policy, the development strategy emphasized various interior-oriented development programs in order to correct the traditional imbalance between the coastal and the interior regions. Since introducing economic reforms in the late 1970s, Chinese leaders have gradually changed the traditional balanced-development policy and interior-oriented development strategy to a new coastal-oriented imbalanced development policy and strategy.

Traditional Development Policy

Traditional regional development in China was imbalanced between the country's interior and coastal regions. The imbalanced development stemmed from such economic and geographical factors as the long distance between the industrial production area (mainly in the coastal region) and the raw material supply areas (mainly in the interior region). From the market consideration, the imbalance also was related to the fact that there is more concentration of human and financial resources in the eastern, coastal region than in the western, interior region.

While enjoying many economic advantages, traditional coastal development suffered from one major problem of vulnerability, based on the consideration of national defense and security. The problem of vulnerability was experienced during World War II, when the Japanese intruded and occupied most of China's eastern and coastal areas. The occupancy of Japanese in the industrialized coastal area caused a serious survival problem for the national government, which was forced to retreat to the western, interior area. The issue of national security was further emphasized as one of the major considerations of regional development policy during Maoist China, especially when the relationship between China and the Soviet Union worsened and the involvement of the United States in Vietnam was intense.

The balanced regional development policy during the Maoist era was based on the consideration of political and military factors. The purpose of the balanced development was to achieve the goal of self-reliance (or self-sufficiency) in each of China's regions. In other words, to protect against intrusion and to prepare for wars, every province in China should develop its own production capacities in industry and agriculture. The production units in these areas might be small but must be complete. The self-reliance policy was further stressed and promoted when Chinese leaders divided the country into three fronts along the coastal, central, and western regions. The policy of three fronts was especially related to the balanced regional development because most of the industrial construction and major enterprises and research institutions were located in various western and interior provinces in the third front (e.g., Sichuan, Gansu, and Shaanxi) (Yang, 1990).

To achieve a balanced development and to mitigate the difference between the coastal and the interior regions, the Chinese government emphasized and adopted a centrally directed investment in the interior region before the post-Mao reforms. In his study of China's regional development, Yang (1990: 235) estimated that, between 1953 and 1980, the Chinese government distributed about 60 percent of the country's investment in fixed assets in the interior region. The investment in the interior region ranged from 56 percent in the First Five-Year Plan (1953-1957), to 60 percent in the Second Five-Year Plan (1958-1962), to 71 percent in the Third Five-Year Plan (1966-1970), and finally to 61 percent and 55 percent in the Fourth (1971-1975) and Fifth (1976-1980) Five-Year Plans, respectively.

The direct allocation of resources to the interior region was made through China's central planning system, using state-fixed prices and differential revenue sharing rates (Lyons, 1987; Riskin, 1987; Yang, 1991). Under this system, the central government, on the one hand, tended to underprice raw materials and overprice manufactured goods. On the other hand, the government taxed the manufacturing industries at higher rates and then redistributed resources from the coastal region to the interior region through the allocation of investment funds. In other words, among the large share of revenue collected by the central government, a disproportionate amount was raised from richer provinces in the eastern coastal region. The result of this redistributive investment was that the interior region's gain was at the expense of the coastal. For example, in 1972, the rich and industrial coastal areas of Shanghai and Liaoning were allowed to keep their revenues only about 10 percent and 18 percent, respectively. On the other hand, the poor, interior provinces such as Xinjiang, Qinghai, Tibet, Gansu, and Guizhou not only were permitted to retain all their revenues but also received additional central subsidies.[2]

While emphasizing political and military considerations, the interior-oriented balanced development policy was inefficient from the economic point of view. Despite the tremendous resources invested, the interior region continued to be outproduced by the coastal region. The balanced development policy indeed improved the equity distribution of China's industrial facilities and development among regions. But the expense of this even distribution was the problem of inefficiency because the Chinese economy would have grown more rapidly if the investment was made based on efficiency. Several Chinese economists criticized the balanced regional development policy under Mao as disregarding the basic idea of comparative advantage, consuming excessive amounts of input, causing a serious disproportion in investment at the expense of light industry and services, and retarding technological progress (Dong, 1988; Xue, 1982; Yang, 1990).

The New Regional Development Policy

To promote economic efficiency, the post-Mao reform leaders have gradually replaced the traditional balanced development policy and the interior-oriented strategy with a new, uneven, and coastal-oriented development policy. The uneven development policy allows differential development among different regions and especially gives preferential policies to the coastal region. The reformers believe that the faster development of the coastal region will become the engine of China's growth and eventually lead to development in other regions. The new, uneven development policy was clearly emphasized in China's Sixth (1981-1985) and Seventh (1986-1990) Five-Year Plans. Especially, the leaders have introduced several specific reform policy measures that gradually have changed China's regional development to the uneven and coastal-oriented development approach. Two of the policy measures that started in 1978 are especially important in encouraging local and regional economic development and growth.

The first policy measure introduced in the post-Mao regional development was the decentralization of decision-making power and economic management. The decentralization of decision making and management to local governments was not new to the Chinese people. Various decentralizing measures were introduced in the past, both in the leftist economic programs (e.g., the Great Leap Forward or the Learn from Dazhai campaigns) and in the more pragmatic economic policies that followed leftist failures (e.g., economic readjustment). The difference between the traditional decentralization policy and the new decentralization reform lies in the issue of market. Under Mao, decentralization meant autarky or self-reliance; while under Deng, decentralization refers to market decentralization, in which each area and unit produces to best advantage within an interdependent market network (Womack & Zhao, 1994). Especially, the new decentralization policy recognized that local government officials (cadres and enterprise managers) have the authority to make decisions about productivity-related issues based on consideration of their local conditions. The decentralized approach was emphasized in both the agricultural reform activities (e.g., the contract-responsibility system) and the industrial reform activities (e.g., the separation of enterprise management from administrative management).

The second policy measure that contributed to post-Mao China's regional development was the adoption of the open-door policy (*Kaifang Zhengce*) in the late 1970s. In December 1978, the Third Plenary Session of the Eleventh Central Committee of the Chinese Communist Party announced that China would actively expand economic cooperation with other countries and adopt the world's advanced technology and equipment. To implement the open-door policy, the Chinese government formulated its new "Laws of the People's Republic of China on Joint Venture Using Chinese and Foreign Investment" on July 8, 1979. Specifically, the open-door policy attempted not only to attract and absorb foreign technology and capital but also to introduce and promote Chinese products into the world market (Tzeng, 1991). The adoption of the open-door policy is critical to China's economic development because it indicates a fundamental change in China's past economic development principle of self-reliance. The increases of foreign trade and capital certainly provide some Chinese local governments that benefited from their geographic locations with alternative sources to assist their economic development. These localities include such coastal and border provinces as Guangdong, Fujian, Jiangsu, Shandong, Liaoning Xinjiang, and Yunan.

One of the major components in China's open-door policy has been the emphasis on the coastal development strategy (Tzeng, 1991). Since its emphasis in 1978, the development of China's coastal areas has lasted more than a decade and extended from several isolated cities to most areas of the eastern, coastal region. The development process started from the opening of four special economic zones in Shenzhen, Zhuhai, Shantou (in Guangdong province) and Xiamen (in Fujian province) in 1979. Then, in 1984, the State Council announced the openness of 14 coastal cities and Hainan Island to foreign investment. The 14 cities range from Dalian (in Liaoning province) in the north to Beihai (in Guangxi province) in the south (Weihai, in Shandong province, was later added to give a total of 15). Coastal development was then extended to the three deltaic areas of the Zhujiang, South Fujian, and the Changjiang. Finally, the coastal development strategy was formally adopted by the

Fourth Meeting of the Political Bureau of the Party on February 6, 1988. The 11 open coastal provinces, ranging from Liaoning province to Guangxi province and comprising a total of 288 *xian* (counties), were allowed to open up and develop. In the same year, Hainan Island was upgraded to provincial status. Later, the Chinese government added the Pudong development project in Shanghai, which further promotes development in the coastal areas.

The coastal development strategy is basically a two-tier combination of import-led growth and export-led expansion (Tzeng, 1991: 277). The import-led growth attempts to strengthen China's capability for obtaining advanced technology and capital, while the export-led expansion is targeted to make China a global economic power. The major policy elements addressed in the coastal development strategy are (1) development of an export-oriented and labor intensive economy in the coastal areas, (2) emphasis on the two principles embodied in the slogans "putting both ends (sourcing and marketing) toward the global marketplace" and "importing more (raw materials) and exporting more (products)," (3) assistance to foreign enterprises in exercising their managerial authority with regard to their operation and profits and losses, and (4) development of township enterprises to promote the regions' urban and rural development. Local and regional governments in the coastal development areas have more authority and flexibility in setting their tax rates in order to attract investment. The result of the coast-oriented development strategy and policy is that both domestic and international investments in the coastal region have increased dramatically in the 1980s. The new, increased investments and the traditional superiority in technology, management, research and development in the coastal region have increased the region's share of the national growth since the mid-1980s.

EVALUATION OF REGIONAL DEVELOPMENT

To evaluate China's regional development during the reform years, this study examines regional economic development by focusing on the comparison of five economic indicators between China's three regions (the coastal, the central, and the western) in two different years (1985 and 1993). The indicators and years selected were based on the consideration of the importance and the availability of data. Measuring different aspects of economic performance, the five economic indicators are gross output value of agriculture (GOVA), gross output value of industry (GOVI), total investment in fixed assets, domestic trade, and foreign capital actually used. The year of 1985 was selected because it was the beginning of China's industrial reforms, which have had significant impact on China's regional development. Moreover, in 1985, the Chinese government adopted the strategy of three economic regions of the coastal (eastern), central, and western. The central and western regions (i.e., the interior region) encompass two-thirds of China's total territory and contains over half of the nation's total population.

With regard to agricultural and industrial activities, Table 5.1 and Table 5.2 provide information about GOVA and GOVI in different regions and provinces. First, Table 5.1 shows that the distribution of GOVA among three regions remained about the same between 1985 and 1993. The GOVA in the coastal region decreased from

50 percent to 49 percent of the total GOVA, while the central region decreased from 32.85 percent to 32.43 percent of the total and the western region increased from 16.82 percent to 18.50 percent of the total. The interior region, the combination of central and western regions, increased its share from 49 percent to 50 percent of the total GOVA.

Among the provinces, Jiangsu had the largest GOVA (10 percent of the national total) and Tibet had the smallest GOVA (about 0.2 percent of the national total) in 1985. In 1993, while Tibet remained the smallest GOVA province, Shandong became the largest GOVA province (about 9 percent of the national total). The calculated percentage changes showed that both the coastal and the central regions had decreased percentages of GOVA, while the western region had an increased percentage of GOVA. Both the largest decreased percentage (in Jiangsu) and the largest increased percentage (in Guangxi) are in the coastal region.

Next, the distribution of GOVI in Table 5.2 reveals a different pattern. Between 1985 and 1993, the coastal region increased its share by 7.7 percent (from 59.4 percent to 67.1 percent of the total GOVI), while both the central and the western regions decreased their shares by 5.3 percent (from 27.6 percent to 22.3 percent) and 2.4 percent (from 13 percent to 10.6 percent), respectively.[3] Clearly, the coastal region developed faster than the interior region in industrial activities after the industrial reform emphasized in 1985.

Among the provinces, Jiangsu had the largest GOVI in both 1985 (9.9 percent) and 1993 (12.8 percent), while Tibet had the smallest GOVI (about .01 percent) in both years. Especially, the calculated percentage changes revealed that most provinces in the central and western regions showed decreased percentage distributions of GOVI (except an increased percentage in Henan and zero percent increases in Qinghai and Tibet); while most provinces in the coastal region (except Beijing, Liaoning, Shanghai, and Tianjian) showed increased distributions of GOVI.

The data about total investment and domestic trade displayed in Table 5.3 and Table 5.4 also show a similar pattern, indicating an increased percentage in the coastal region at the expense of the decreased percentages in the interior region. Table 5.3 shows that, between 1985 and 1993, total investment in fixed assets increased from 50.1 percent to 61.7 percent in the coastal region and decreased from 29.4 percent to 21.5 percent in the central region and from 15.6 percent to 13 percent in the western region. Among the provinces, Guangdong had the largest percentage of total investment in both 1985 and 1993, while Tibet had the smallest percentage of total investment in both years. The calculated percentage changes indicate that Guangdong and Jiangsu have had the largest percentage increases of total investment, while Heilongjiang and Shanxi have had the largest percentage decreases.

Table 5.4 reveals that, between 1985 and 1993, the coastal region increased its total value of retail sales from 50 percent to 57 percent of the national total. On the other hand, the central and the western regions showed decreased percentages of total retail sales from 30.8 percent to 27.2 percent and from 15.8 percent to 14.1 percent, respectively. Among the provinces, Guangdong had the largest percentage of retail sales in both 1985 and 1993, while Tibet had the smallest percentage of retail sales in 1985.[4]

Table 5.1
Gross Output Value of Agriculture by Regions and Provinces, 1985 and 1993[1]

Region/Province	1985		1993		%Change
National	4580.32	(100%)	10995.53	(100%)	
Coastal	2305.13	(50.3)	5395.25	(49.1)	(-1.2)
Beijing	47.71	(1.0)	100.47	(.9)	(-.1)
Fujian	123.59	(2.7)	395.26	(3.6)	(.9)
Guangdong	332.94	(7.3)	899.03	(8.2)	(.9)
Guangxi	114.97	(2.5)	390.11	(3.5)	(1.0)
Hainan[2]	-		120.25	(1.1)	-
Hebei	244.57	(5.3)	511.29	(4.7)	(-.6)
Jiangsu	460.88	(10.1)	875.37	(8.0)	(-2.1)
Liaoning	172.15	(3.8)	442.70	(4.0)	(.2)
Shandong	414.36	(9.0)	994.25	(9.0)	(0)
Shanghai	68.88	(1.5)	96.20	(.9)	(-.6)
Tianjian	47.10	(1.0)	70.62	(.6)	(-.4)
Zhejiang	277.98	(6.1)	499.70	(4.5)	(-1.6)
Central	1504.81	(32.9)	3566.25	(32.4)	(-.5)
Anhui	230.19	(5.0)	519.12	(4.7)	(-.3)
Heilongjiang	126.26	(2.8)	330.60	(3.0)	(.2)
Henan	287.47	(6.3)	671.69	(6.1)	(-.2)
Hubei	226.52	(5.0)	501.17	(4.6)	(-.4)
Hunan	224.78	(5.0)	563.47	(5.1)	(.1)
Inner Mongolia	76.39	(1.7)	220.80	(2.0)	(.3)
Jiangxi	131.80	(2.9)	360.11	(3.3)	(.4)
Jilin	98.86	(2.2)	243.95	(2.2)	(0)
Shanxi	102.54	(2.2)	155.34	(1.4)	(-.8)
Western	770.38	(16.8)	2034.04	(18.5)	(1.7)
Gansu	52.80	(1.2)	140.42	(1.3)	(.1)
Guizhou	76.41	(1.7)	201.40	(1.8)	(.1)
Ningxia	13.05	(.3)	31.89	(.3)	(0)
Qinghai	13.10	(.3)	31.00	(.3)	(0)
Shaanxi	97.88	(2.1)	250.49	(2.3)	(.2)
Sichuan	352.47	(7.7)	876.37	(8.0)	(.3)
Tibet	10.68	(.2)	23.06	(.2)	(0)
Xinjiang	60.39	(1.3)	198.20	(1.8)	(.5)
Yunan	93.60	(2.0)	281.21	(2.6)	(.6)

Source: State Statistical Bureau, *Statistical Yearbook of China* (1986: 35); (1994: 330).
Note: 1. Values are based on current prices, RMB 100 million.
2. The province of Hainan was established in 1988. Prior to 1988, it belonged to the province of Guangdong.

Table 5.2
Gross Output Value of Industry by Regions and Provinces, 1985 and 1993[1]

Region/Province	1985		1993		%Change
National	8755.64	(100%)	52691.99	(100%)[2]	
Coastal	5200.23	(59.4)	37239.17	(67.1)	(7.7)
Beijing	324.39	(3.7)	1513.60	(2.7)	(-1.0)
Fujian	148.59	(1.7)	1547.77	(2.8)	(1.1)
Guangdong	490.16	(5.6)	5237.38	(9.4)	(3.8)
Guangxi	132.31	(1.5)	905.92	(1.6)	(.1)
Hainan	-		128.14	(.2)	-
Hebei	358.59	(4.1)	2623.98	(4.7)	(.6)
Jiangsu	862.53	(9.9)	7096.45	(12.8)	(2.9)
Liaoning	716.83	(8.2)	3510.78	(6.3)	(-1.9)
Shandong	603.85	(6.9)	5970.09	(10.8)	(3.9)
Shanghai	825.23	(9.4)	3327.85	(6.0)	(-3.4)
Tianjian	291.19	(3.3)	1404.84	(2.5)	(-.8)
Zhejiang	446.56	(5.1)	3972.37	(7.2)	(2.1)
Central	2414.78	(27.6)	12403.93	(22.3)	(-5.3)
Anhui	244.73	(2.8)	1558.15	(2.8)	(0)
Heilongjiang	380.01	(4.3)	1394.35	(2.5)	(-1.8)
Henan	355.15	(4.1)	2444.37	(4.4)	(.3)
Hubei	433.02	(4.9)	1983.20	(3.6)	(-1.3)
Hunan	288.34	(3.3)	1438.92	(2.6)	(-.7)
Inner Mongolia	107.48	(1.2)	520.01	(.9)	(-.3)
Jiangxi	163.80	(1.9)	936.36	(1.7)	(-.2)
Jilin	243.78	(2.8)	1033.25	(1.9)	(-.9)
Shanxi	198.47	(2.3)	1095.32	(2.0)	(-.3)
Western	1140.63	(13.0)	5878.93	(10.6)	(-2.4)
Gansu	122.42	(1.4)	501.60	(.9)	(-.5)
Guizhou	91.04	(1.0)	381.26	(.7)	(-.3)
Ningxia	23.25	(.3)	119.64	(.2)	(-.1)
Qinghai	21.80	(.2)	94.30	(.2)	(0)
Shaanxi	173.46	(2.0)	813.60	(1.5)	(-.5)
Sichuan	491.98	(5.6)	2825.92	(5.1)	(-.5)
Tibet	1.69	(.01)	4.14	(.01)	(0)
Xinjiang	83.63	(1.0)	448.40	(.8)	(-.2)
Yunan	131.36	(1.5)	690.07	(1.2)	(-.3)

Source: State Statistical Bureau, *Statistical Yearbook of China* (1986: 35); (1994: 376).

Note: 1. Values are based on current prices.

2. The gross output value of all regions (55522.03) does not equal the value of national total (52691.99) because the national value has been adjusted. The percentage figures are based on the total region value of 55522.03.

Table 5.3
Total Investment in Fixed Assets by Regions and Provinces, 1985 and 1993[1]

Region/Province	1985		1993		%Change
National	2543.19	(100%)	12457.88	(100%)	
Coastal	1274.83	(50.1)	7688.78	(61.7)	(11.6)
Beijing	94.52	(3.7)	418.81	(3.4)	(-.3)
Fujian	54.99	(2.1)	370.96	(3.0)	(.9)
Guangdong	196.59	(7.7)	1637.33	(13.1)	(5.4)
Guangxi	42.07	(1.7)	272.24	(2.2)	(.5)
Hainan	-		166.66	(1.3)	-
Hebei	113.11	(4.4)	452.44	(3.6)	(-.8)
Jiangsu	149.97	(5.9)	1117.16	(9.0)	(3.1)
Liaoning	139.02	(5.5)	710.92	(5.7)	(.2)
Shandong	193.42	(7.6)	892.08	(7.2)	(-.4)
Shanghai	118.76	(4.7)	642.38	(5.2)	(.5)
Tianjian	66.94	(2.6)	225.66	(1.8)	(-.8)
Zhejiang	105.44	(4.1)	782.14	(6.3)	(2.2)
Central	746.75	(29.4)	2684.15	(21.5)	(-7.9)
Anhui	80.52	(3.2)	290.52	(2.3)	(-.9)
Heilongjiang	110.52	(4.3)	330.55	(2.7)	(-1.6)
Henan	126.90	(5.0)	464.17	(3.7)	(-1.3)
Hubei	101.64	(4.0)	388.21	(3.1)	(-.9)
Hunan	80.78	(3.2)	324.58	(2.6)	(-.6)
Inner Mongolia	51.20	(2.0)	206.63	(1.7)	(-.3)
Jiangxi	43.73	(1.7)	196.25	(1.6)	(-.1)
Jilin	62.90	(2.5)	248.29	(2.0)	(-.5)
Shanxi	88.56	(3.5)	234.95	(1.9)	(-1.6)
Western	395.97	(15.6)	1620.88	(13.0)	(-2.6)
Gansu	32.61	(1.3)	97.49	(.8)	(-.5)
Guizhou	33.13	(1.3)	102.48	(.8)	(-.5)
Ningxia	12.51	(.5)	44.14	(.4)	(-.1)
Qinghai	16.13	(.6)	46.08	(.4)	(-.2)
Shaanxi	56.94	(2.2)	215.11	(1.7)	(-.5)
Sichuan	144.65	(5.7)	580.57	(4.7)	(-1.0)
Tibet	7.09	(.3)	18.26	(.1)	(-.2)
Xinjiang	44.55	(1.8)	254.33	(2.0)	(.2)
Yunan	48.36	(1.9)	262.42	(2.1)	(.2)
Non-region	125.62	(4.9)	464.08	(3.7)	(-1.2)

Source: State Statistical Bureau, *Statistical Yearbook of China* (1986: 367); (1994: 142).
Note: 1. Values are based on current prices, RMB 100 million.

Table 5.4
Domestic Trade by Regions and Provinces: Total Value of Retail Sales[1], 1985 and 1993

Region/Province	1985		1993		%Change
National	4305.00	(100%)	13592.60	(100%)[2]	
Coastal	2153.68	(50.0)	7741.66	(57.0)	(7.0)
Beijing	127.90	(3.0)	549.42	(4.0)	(1.0)
Fujian	107.09	(2.5)	420.07	(3.1)	(.6)
Guangdong	343.19	(8.0)	1399.70	(10.1)	(2.1)
Guangxi	101.12	(2.3)	337.20	(2.5)	(.2)
Hainan	-		70.19	(0.5)	-
Hebei	204.45	(4.7)	577.08	(4.2)	(-.5)
Jiangsu	307.68	(7.1)	1040.42	(7.7)	(.6)
Liaoning	231.53	(5.4)	720.77	(5.3)	(-.1)
Shandong	280.79	(6.5)	993.84	(7.3)	(.8)
Shanghai	183.16	(4.3)	651.07	(4.8)	(.5)
Tianjian	68.95	(1.6)	227.45	(1.7)	(.1)
Zhejiang	197.82	(4.6)	754.45	(5.6)	(1.0)
Central	1327.27	(30.8)	3695.34	(27.2)	(-3.6)
Anhui	143.81	(3.3)	391.70	(2.9)	(-.4)
Heilongjiang	172.61	(4.0)	490.57	(3.6)	(-.4)
Henan	220.49	(5.1)	594.56	(4.4)	(-.7)
Hubei	205.82	(4.8)	556.54	(4.1)	(-.7)
Hunan	177.30	(4.1)	539.19	(4.0)	(-.1)
Inner Mongolia	82.70	(1.9)	211.02	(1.6)	(-.3)
Jiangxi	98.33	(2.3)	279.55	(2.1)	(-.2)
Jilin	124.09	(2.9)	357.49	(2.6)	(-.3)
Shanxi	102.12	(2.4)	274.72	(2.0)	(-.4)
Western	681.04	(15.8)	1915.92	(14.1)	(-1.7)
Gansu	58.45	(1.4)	161.88	(1.2)	(-.2)
Guizhou	57.17	(1.3)	131.19	(1.0)	(-.3)
Ningxia	15.29	(.4)	42.78	(.3)	(-.1)
Qinghai	17.63	(.4)	41.69	(.3)	(-.1)
Shaanxi	91.90	(2.1)	269.37	(2.0)	(-.1)
Sichuan	274.30	(6.3)	807.97	(5.9)	(-.4)
Tibet	11.00	(.3)	-		-
Xinjiang	62.10	(1.4)	182.15	(1.3)	(-.1)
Yunan	93.20	(2.2)	278.89	(2.1)	(-.1)

Source: State Statistical Bureau, *Statistical Yearbook of China* (1986: 450); (1994: 496).
Note: 1. Values are based on current prices, RMB 100 million.
2. The sum of all regions is less than the national total because some regions do not have complete data.

The calculated percentage changes revealed that provinces in both the central and the western regions showed some reduced percentages of retail sales between the two years.

Moreover, the data about foreign capital used (including both foreign loans and foreign direct investment) provided additional information about China's post-Mao regional development. As listed in Table 5.5, it is clear that foreign capital changed the investment pattern by moving from the central government at the ministry level to the regional level. Between 1985 and 1993, the foreign capital used at the ministry level dropped about 41.8 percent (from 64.2 percent to 22.4 percent), while the foreign capital used at the regional level increased 41.8 percent (from 35.8 percent to 77.6 percent).

Next, among the three regions, the coastal region dominates the amount of foreign capital used at the regional level, despite a drop from 90.1 percent to 87.9 percent. The central region increased its share of the regional foreign capital used from 5.6 percent to 8.7 percent, while the western region decreased its share from 4.3 percent to 3.4 percent of the regional total.

Among the provinces, Guangdong had the largest percentage of foreign capital used in both years. But the calculated percentage changes show that Jiangsu had the largest percentage increase of foreign capital used (6.2 percent) between 1985 and 1993, while Guangdong had the largest percentage decrease of foreign capital used (13.6 percent).

Finally, the summary table (Table 5.6) of major economic indicators provides comparisons of the above economic indicators between the coastal and the interior (the combination of the central and the western) regions. The data clearly show some changes in and effects of the changes on China's regional development policy from a balanced development approach to an uneven development approach. In 1985 (after seven years of the economic reform), China's coastal region and interior region are still in a comparable situation, an indicator of the traditional balanced development strategy. Both GOVA and total investment are almost equally distributed (50 percent) between the coastal and the interior regions. The GOVI data showed that despite China's past efforts to balance the industrial development between regions (i.e., the interior-oriented development strategy), the coastal region still showed a better percentage of industrial activities (59 percent of the total GOVI) than that in the interior region (41 percent of the total).

After the economic reform, especially the industrial reform introduced in 1985, the coastal region experienced major increases in its shares of the country's GOVI, total investment in fixed assets, domestic trade in retail sales, and foreign capital (including both foreign loans and direct foreign investments) used. The coastal region showed an increase of 7.7 percent in its share of GOVI (from 59.4 percent to 67.1 percent), an increase of 11.6 percent in its share of total investment in fixed assets (from 50.1 percent to 61.7 percent), an increase of 7 percent in its share of domestic trade in retail sales (from 50 percent to 57 percent), and an increase of 35.9 percent in foreign capital actually used (from 32.3 percent to 68.2 percent).

The interior region, on the other hand, experienced major decreases in the above-mentioned GOVI, total investment in fixed assets, and domestic trade in retail

Table 5.5
Foreign Capital Actually Used by Regions and Provinces[1], 1985 and 1993

Region/Province	1985		1993		%Change
National	446211	(100%)	3895972	(100%)	
Ministry	286298	(64.2)	872142	(22.4)	(-41.8)
Regional	159913	(35.8)	3023321	(77.6)	(41.8)
Coastal	144005	(90.1)	2656562	(87.9)	(-2.2)
Beijing	11628	(7.3)	81731	(2.7)	(-4.6)
Fujian	17109	(10.7)	290599	(9.6)	(-1.1)
Guangdong	73885	(46.2)	984313	(32.6)	(-13.6)
Guangxi	3073	(1.9)	89756	(3.0)	(1.1)
Hainan	-		74832	(2.5)	-
Hebei	1050	(.7)	39654	(1.3)	(.6)
Jiangsu	5111	(3.2)	284371	(9.4)	(6.2)
Liaoning	2458	(1.5)	139693	(4.6)	(3.1)
Shandong	6201	(3.9)	188267	(6.2)	(2.3)
Shanghai	10938	(6.8)	317803	(10.5)	(3.7)
Tianjian	6379	(4.0)	62368	(2.1)	(-1.9)
Zhejiang	6173	(3.9)	103175	(3.4)	(-.5)
Central	9014	(5.6)	264183	(8.7)	(3.1)
Anhui	303	(.2)	25764	(.9)	(.7)
Heilongjiang	657	(.4)	23232	(.8)	(.4)
Henan	1029	(.6)	30491	(1.0)	(.4)
Hubei	2078	(1.3)	55467	(1.8)	(.5)
Hunan	3097	(1.9)	61716	(2.0)	(.1)
Inner Mongolia	262	(.2)	8526	(.3)	(.1)
Jiangxi	1049	(.7)	22817	(.8)	(.1)
Jilin	487	(.3)	27527	(.9)	(.6)
Shanxi	52	(.03)	8643	(.3)	(.3)
Western	6894	(4.3)	102576	(3.4)	(-.9)
Gansu	57	(.03)	1195	(.04)	(.01)
Guizhou	978	(.6)	4294	(.1)	(-.5)
Ningxia	28	(.02)	1190	(.03)	(.01)
Qinghai	15	(.001)	324	(.01)	(.009)
Shaanxi	1555	(.1)	23430	(.8)	(.7)
Sichuan	3007	(1.9)	57141	(1.9)	(0)
Tibet	-		-		-
Xinjiang	1091	(.7)	5300	(.2)	(-.5)
Yunan	163	(.1)	9702	(.3)	(.2)

Source: State Statistical Bureau, *Statistical Yearbook of China* (1986: 501-502); (1994: 530).
Note: 1. Values are based on current prices, US $10,000.

sales at the expense of the increases in the costal region. The interior region showed a small increase of 1 percent in the country's GOVA (from 49.7 percent to 50.9 percent) and an increase of 5.8 percent in foreign capital used (from 3.6 percent to 9.4 percent). The change in the GOVA may be related to the more industrial-oriented development activities in the coastal region, while the increase of foreign capital shows the impact of the open door policy, which successfully attracts foreign loans and direct investments not only in the costal region but also in the interior region.

Table 5.6
Comparison of Five Major Indicators between the Coastal and the Interior Regions, 1985 and 1993

Indicator	Year	Coastal	Interior
Gross Output	1985	50.3%	49.7%
Value-Agriculture	1993	49.1	50.9
Gross Output	1985	59.4%	40.6%
Value-Industry	1993	67.1	32.9
Total investment[1]	1985	50.1%	45.0%
in Fixed Assets	1993	61.7	34.5
Domestic Trade[2]	1985	50.0%	46.6%
Retail Sales	1993	57.0	41.3
Foreign Capital[3]	1985	32.3%	3.6%
Actually Used	1993	68.2	9.4

Source: See previous tables.
Note: 1. The percentages of total investment do not include investment percentages outside these regions (4.9 percent in 1985 and 3.7 percent in 1993).
2. The percentages are not equal to 100 percent because of missing data.
3. The percentages are not equal to 100 percent because of the percentages at the ministry level (64.2 percent in 1985 and 22.4 percent in 1993) were not listed.

CHALLENGE ISSUES RELATED TO THE REGIONAL DEVELOPMENT

The economic indicators evaluated in the previous section certainly provide empirical evidence to support two major findings about China's regional developments. First, it is clear that the post-Mao economic reforms have had positive effects on China's regional development because of the improved economic growth and development in all Chinese regions and provinces. The findings here are consistent with those reported about the improvement of China's macroeconomic performance in the previous chapter (Chapter 5). Second, the regional growth and development records have shown some levels of difference between various regions and provinces. The eastern coastal region and provinces have grown faster than those in the central and western regions. The findings here support the effectiveness of China's post-Mao unbalanced regional development policy, which offered preferential measures and strategies in the coastal region.

Unequal development between China's regions has brought some challenging issues to Chinese policy makers. Three of the issues are important and discussed here, including the rising income inequality among regions, the inequality between rural and urban areas, and different concerns between the interior and the coastal regions.

Income Inequality among Regions

Since the economic reform in 1978, the coastal-oriented uneven development policy has resulted in increasing wealth for people and provinces in the coastal region. The rapid growth of the coastal region caused an important issue of regional inequality. The inequality issue refers to not only the increasing economic activities in the coastal region as discussed earlier but also the increasing income gap between peoples in the regions. In other words, while sharing the outcome of the overall economic reform policies, the people and provinces in the interior region have fallen behind those in the coastal region in terms of general economic growth and individual income. While the previous section evaluated development records, the present section will analyze the issue of income inequality among China's three regions.

To examine income inequality among the three regions, the study collected and analyzed the data of China's per-capita national income and consumption between 1984 and 1992. First, Table 5.7 shows the distribution of per-capita national income among regions and provinces. In 1984, while the per-capita national income for the whole nation was 547 yuan, the average per-capita national incomes for the three regions are 1,003 yuan for the coastal, 535 yuan for the central, and 429 yuan for the western. In other words, the per-capita national income for the central region was about half (53 percent) of the income of the coastal region, and the per-capita national income for the western region was less than half (43 percent) of the income of the coastal region. In 1992, while the per-capita national income increased to 1,736 yuan, the average per capita national incomes for the three regions are 2,852 yuan for the western, 1,415 yuan for the central, and 1,247 yuan for the western. Again, the per-capita national income for the central region was about half (50 percent) of the income of the coastal region, and the per-capita national income for the western region is less than half (44 percent) of the income of the coastal region.

Among provinces, the largest per-capita national income is in Shanghai, with 2,832 yuan in 1984 and 6,840 yuan in 1992; while the smallest per-capita national income is in Guizhou, with 322 yuan in 1984 and 823 yuan in 1992. The differences between the largest and the smallest per-capita national income in 1984 (2,832 yuan to 322 yuan) and 1992 (6,840 yuan to 823 yuan) were 8.80 times and 8.31 times, respectively. Finally, the calculated ratio increases among provinces between 1992 and 1984 showed that seven provinces (Guangdong, Fujian, Zhejiang, Guangxi, Jiangsu, Xinjiang, and Yunan) had ratio increases above the national average of 3.17. It is important to notice that the first five provinces are costal provinces, while the last two provinces are border provinces.

Next, Table 5.8 reveals the distribution of per-capita consumption among regions and provinces. In 1984, while the national average per-capita consumption was 330 yuan, the average per-capita consumption for the three regions were 449 yuan for the coastal, 347 yuan for the central, and 314 yuan for the western. The average per-capita consumptions in the central and the western regions were about 77 percent and in the coastal region 70 percent. In 1992, while the national per-capita consumption increased to 1,148 yuan, the average per-capita consumptions for the three regions were 1,283 yuan for the coastal, 828 yuan for the central, and 798 yuan for the western. The average per-capita consumption in the central region is about 65 percent of the consumption in the coastal region, and the average per-capita consumption in the western region is about 62 percent of the consumption in the coastal region. The percentage differences between two years and three regions indicate a change of the consumption pattern, with the increase in per-capita consumption larger in the coastal region than in the other regions.

Among the provinces, the largest per-capita consumption was in Shanghai in both 1984 and 1992, while the smallest per-capita consumption was in Henan in 1984 and in Guizou in 1992. The differences between the largest and the smallest per-capita consumption increased from 2.99 times in 1984 (729 yuan in Shanghai and 244 yuan in Henan) to 4.93 times in 1992 (2704 yuan in Shanghai and 549 yuan in Guizhou), indicating the increasing consumption gap among provinces. The calculated ratio increases between 1992 and 1984 show that Shanghai and Guangdong (both in the coastal region) had ratio increases larger than the national ratio increase of 3.48.

The issue of income inequality was further studied in the comparison of per-capita national income and consumption between the coastal and the interior regions. As shown in Table 5.9, both per-capita national income and per-capita consumption increased in the coastal and interior regions because of the success of China's post-Mao economic reforms. Between 1984 and 1992, the per-capita national income in the coastal region increased about 2.84 times (from 1,003 yuan to 2,852 yuan), which is a little higher than the increase of 2.76 times in the interior region (from 482 yuan to 1,331 yuan). Similarly, per-capita consumption also increased among the coastal and interior regions. The former achieved an increase of 2.86 times (from 449 yuan to 1,283 yuan), while the latter showed an increase of 2.46 times (from 331 yuan to 813 yuan).

Table 5.9 also reveals that the income and consumption gap between the coastal and interior regions increased between 1984 and 1992. Based on the calculated ratio between the two regions (interior/coastal), the income gap between the interior and the coastal regions increased about 2 percent (from 48 percent in 1984 to 46 percent in 1992). Similarly, the consumption gap between the two regions increased about 11 percent (from 74 percent in 1984 to 63 percent in 1992). Both data showed that people in the interior region are falling behind the people in the coastal region with regard to their income and consumption.

Table 5.7
Per-Capita National Income by Regions and Provinces,[1] 1984 and 1992

Region/Province		1984	1992	1992/1984
National		547	1736	3.17
Coastal		1003	2852	2.84
	Beijing	1661	4868	2.93
	Fujian	481	1923	4.00
	Guangdong	644	2795	4.34
	Guangxi	337	1115	3.31
	Hainan	-	1668	-
	Hebei	514	1515	2.95
	Jiangsu	756	2448	3.24
	Liaoning	969	2660	2.75
	Shandong	625	1962	3.14
	Shanghai	2832	6840	2.42
	Tianjian	1523	3930	2.58
	Zhejiang	693	2500	3.61
Middle		535	1415	2.64
	Anhui	433	1151	2.66
	Heilongjiang	804	1997	2.48
	Henan	400	1154	2.89
	Hubei	602	1502	2.50
	Hunan	446	1240	2.78
	Inner Mongolia	485	1386	2.86
	Jiangxi	414	1198	2.89
	Jilin	645	1749	2.71
	Shanxi	585	1362	2.33
Western		429	1247	2.91
	Gansu	412	1158	2.81
	Guizhou	322	823	2.56
	Ningxia	450	1255	2.79
	Qinghai	485	1348	2.78
	Shaanxi	410	1179	2.88
	Sichuan	399	1157	2.90
	Tibet	462	1258	2.72
	Xinjiang	553	1878	3.40
	Yunan	365	1168	3.20

Source: State Statistical Bureau, *Statistical Yearbook of China* (1986: 44); (1994: 38); World Bank (1994: 181).

Note: 1. Per-capita figures are based on current prices, yuan.

Table 5.8
Per-Capita Consumption by Regions and Provinces,[1] 1984 and 1992

Region/Province		1984	1992	1992/1984
National Total		330	1148	3.48
Coastal		449	1283	2.86
	Beijing	698	1513	2.17
	Fujian	337	1124	3.34
	Guangdong	408	1420	3.48
	Guangxi	265	709	2.68
	Hainan	-	1051	-
	Hebei	289	795	2.75
	Jiangsu	397	1043	2.63
	Liaoning	488	1402	2.87
	Shandong	338	841	2.49
	Shanghai	729	2704	3.71
	Tianjian	622	1634	2.63
	Zhejiang	365	1159	3.18
Central		347	828	2.39
	Anhui	286	667	2.33
	Heilongjiang	446	1126	2.52
	Henan	244	571	2.34
	Hubei	386	848	2.20
	Hunan	311	810	2.60
	Inner Mongolia	370	844	2.28
	Jiangxi	311	752	2.42
	Jilin	464	1074	2.31
	Shanxi	308	757	2.46
Western		314	798	2.54
	Gansu	249	689	2.77
	Guizhou	258	549	2.13
	Ningxia	322	764	2.37
	Qinghai	371	966	2.60
	Shaanxi	297	712	2.40
	Sichuan	288	757	2.63
	Tibet	359	903	2.52
	Xinjiang	410	1098	2.68
	Yunan	270	748	2.77

Source: State Statistical Bureau, *Statistical Yearbook of China* (1986: 558); (1994: 256).
Note: 1. Values are based on current prices, yuan.

Table 5.9
Comparison of Per-Capita National Income and Consumption between the Coastal and Interior Regions,[1] 1984 and 1992

Indicator	Year	Coastal	Interior	Ratio (I/C)
Per capita	1984	1003	482	48%
National Income	1992	2852	1331	46%
	(92/84)	(2.84)	(2.76)	
Per capita	1984	449	331	74%
Consumption	1992	1283	813	63%
	(92/84)	(2.86)	(2.46)	

Source: See previous tables.
Note: 1. Values of per capita national income and consumption are based on current prices, yuan.

Table 5.10
Comparison of Annual Per-Capita Net Income and Consumption between Rural and Urban Residents, in selected years

Year	Income[1]			Consumption		
	Rural	Urban	Ratio[2]	Rural	Urban	Ratio
1978	134	316	2.37	132	383	2.90
1980	191	439	2.29	173	468	2.71
1985	398	685	1.72	324	727	2.24
1990	686	1387	2.02	524	1477	2.82
1992	784	1826	2.33	650	2032	3.13
1993	922	2337	2.54	774	2480	3.20

Source: State Statistical Bureau, *Statistical Yearbook of China* (1994: 255).
Note: 1. Both values of per-capita net income and consumption are based on current prices, yuan.
2. Both ratio numbers are based on the calculation of urban data to the rural.

Inequalities between Rural and Urban Areas

The issue of unequal regional development was further complicated when relating it to inequalities between China's rural and urban areas. To understand the difference between the rural and urban areas, this study provided a simple comparison of annual per-capita net income and consumption between farmers and urban residents. Again, based on the official Chinese statistical data, Table 5.10 shows income and consumption distributions between rural and urban residents in the selected six years. With regard to income distribution, it is clear that the ratios between urban residents and rural residents started as 2.37 times in 1978, decreased to 1.72 times in 1985, and increased to 2.54 times in 1993. This U-type distribution may reveal the impact of China's economic reform policies. In other words, the income ratios decreased after the 1978 reform, especially during the stage of the rural-agricultural reform (1978 to 1984). The ratios, however, increased again after the urban-industrial reform (since 1985).[5] Comparisons of consumption between urban and rural residents revealed a similar U-type distribution pattern. The consumption ratio between urban and rural residents started as 2.90 times in 1978, decreased to 2.24 times in 1985, and increased to 3.20 in 1993.

In addition to the inequality between urban and rural areas, several studies have also examined inequality within China's urban and rural areas since the economic reforms. For example, using the Gini ratio as the principal indicator of inequality, Khan, Griffin, Riskin, and Zhao (1992) found that inequality in income distribution in the rural area (i.e., the Gini ratio of 0.34) is higher than that in the urban area (the Gini ratio of 0.23). They noticed that the income inequality in rural China has increased since the early 1980s and that the most disequalizing component of rural income is wages from different types of enterprises. While rural inequality is less than in most of the developing countries of Asia, they reported that the inequality is greater than in Taiwan and South Korea. Moreover, they found that urban inequality in China is lower than rural inequality, which is different from the experience of most developing countries. In other words, China's urban inequality is smaller than that of other developing countries in Asia. The high degree of equality in China's urban area may be related to the extreme egalitarianism of the wage structure in public enterprises, because most of the urban residents work for some type of government agencies and public enterprises.

The issue of urban and rural inequality was also mentioned and examined in Ma's (1994) study of China's income inequality in the 1980s. Ma analyzed regional inequality by using three different indicators: (1) the coefficient of variation (i.e., the ratio of the standard deviation to the mean of the average income levels of the various), (2) the Gini coefficient (i.e., the degree of deviation, from a completely equal distribution of zero to the greatest inequality of one), and (3) the Lorenz index (i.e., the ratio of the income share of the top quintile of the sample population to that of the bottom quintile). The three indicators analyzed provided findings that are consistent with those found in the analysis of this chapter and the study of Khan and colleagues.

Ma first reported that the coefficient for interprovince rural income started as 0.294 in 1978, decreased to 0.264 in 1983, and rose to 0.394 in 1989. Again, the observed U-Type distribution indicated that the earlier rural-agricultural reform programs have had an equalizing effect on regional distribution in the rural areas. With regard to the urban inequality, Ma found that the coefficient of variation rose from .11 in 1981 to about .18 in 1989. Similarly, the coefficient distribution in this study indicated that the interprovince differential is much smaller for urban than for rural incomes. Next, Ma reported that the Gini coefficients for rural China rose from 0.21 in 1978 to 0.30 in 1988 and that the Gini coefficients for urban China also rose, though the overall level of inequality is much lower (the Gini coefficient ranging around 0.1) than in rural China. Finally, Ma showed that the Lorenz indices in rural areas rose between 1978 (ranging from 1.99 in Hunan to 3.39 in Beijing) to 1985 (ranging from 2.50 in Hunan to 4.30 in Xingjing). The data here indicated that in rural China the poor became poorer and the rich became richer. The Lorenz indices for urban China also rose from 1.69 in 1981 to 1.84 in 1989. Again, the Lorenz indices in urban areas are much lower than those in rural areas because of the high concentration of public employees in the urban areas under a somewhat unified salary scale.

In sum, the previous findings about the differences of economic development and income inequality are certainly related to various policy measures introduced in the agricultural and industrial reforms as well as the change from the traditional balanced development strategy to the new, uneven development strategy. The results are that the coastal area has developed faster than the central and western regions, that the income gap between regions has increased among the regions, and that the income inequalities within rural and urban areas have also risen.

Concerns between the Interior and the Coastal Regions

To deal with the disparity and inequality, the leaders of the interior regions have worked very hard to improve economic development in their regions. These leaders first tried to identify problems and reasons for the low rate of development in their regions. The problems they identified include both objective and subjective factors. The objective factors refer to such issues as underdeveloped communications and remoteness from the world market, while the subjective factors have to do with issues such as the lack of market consciousness, the deep-rooted idea of stressing farming, and the neglect of commerce (Han, 1993). The interior leaders further emphasized various strategies to promote regional development. The strategies considered include, for example, emphasizing the growth of collective, private, individual, and joint-venture enterprises; increasing value-added products in line with resource layouts; providing more funding support to township enterprises (e.g., expanding bank-loan scale); and encouraging foreign businesses to invest in mature projects with solid backgrounds (Han, 1993).

Moreover, the leaders of the central and the western provinces also used each annual session of the National People's Congress as an important occasion to ask central leaders to speed up the development of their regions. These leaders are especially interested in two types of central assistance. First, they ask for more funds and programs from the central government, including, for example, tax assistance, special funds, and a program for east-west cooperation in rural enterprise development. Second, the leaders seek the extension of many preferential policies from the coastal region to the interior region. The preferential policies suggested focus on the authorization to establish special development zones, which provide lower tax rates and tax exemptions to attract different kinds of investment (e.g., the opening of the border economic cooperation zones in 1992) (Yang, 1990; Yang & Wei, 1996).

While the central and western regions are trying hard to improve their regional development, the eastern coastal region is in the process of moving away from the central government after becoming richer and wealthier (Kaye, 1995a, 1995b). It has been noticed that the coastal region is increasingly challenging the dominance of the central government and redefining many central policies to fit its own interests. The coastal region found that the central government in Beijing cannot help the region's further development because of both financial and ideological problems. Instead, the region is moving away from inland China toward some richer and more developed offshore areas in the Overseas Chinese (Hong Kong, Taiwan). For example, people in the coastal provinces of Guangdong and Fujian are more interested in developing economic relations with Hong Kong and Taiwan because of their common ethnicity and dialects.[6]

Demands from the interior region and challenges from the coastal region resulted in a difficult problem for China's central government, one especially related to the central government's lack of financial capability for macroeconomic control. The state revenue has declined from 26 percent of gross domestic product (GDP) to less than 12 percent of GDP since the beginning of the reform (Kaye, 1995a). The decline has to do with China's financial system. The past financial system was based on the system of negotiating revenue contracts between the central and the provincial governments. The newly implemented tax system emphasizes fiscal recentralization and allows the central government to have its own tax collectors and its own revenue base in the form of value-added and consumption taxes. But the new system has not achieved its expected outcomes because of the increasing amount of nontax revenue sources (ad hoc fees) and outright bribes in the local government (Kaye, 1994a, 1994b).

These problems of income inequalities and conflicting interests among China's regions, inequalities between and within the rural and urban areas, as well as different policy concerns between the central and provincial governments may have some negative effects on China's future development. Many researchers have already warned about increasing crimes and unhealthy tendencies in Chinese society during the reform era (Ma, 1989; Myers, 1989; Perry, 1993) and potential political struggles within the Chinese Communist Party in the post-Deng era (Bachman, 1996). The increasing inequalities in China's regions and the new challenging problems associated with unequal development may produce tension in China's ethnic groups and in various social classes. Especially, the rising wealth and autonomy of some regions may also raise the possibility of China's political disintegration.

DISCUSSION AND CONCLUSION

The foregoing examination of China's post-Mao regional development analyzed the change of development policy and strategies, the impact of regional development on China's regions and provinces, and the challenge issues related to the new regional development. The regional development policy has changed from the traditional balanced approach to the new uneven approach. The uneven development policy emphasized the importance of developing China's eastern, coastal region. The coastal oriented development policy was related to China's open-door policy, which promoted such development strategies as special economic development zones in the coastal region. Local governments in the coastal region development areas enjoyed the advantages of preferential policies that gave them more authority to arrange special activities to attract foreign investments.

The new regional development policy has resulted in increasing economic differences among China's three regions. The coastal region and provinces have grown faster than the central and western regions. The comparisons of economic indicators of gross output value of agriculture and industry, total investment in fixed assets, and domestic trade and foreign investment showed that all of the regions have improved their economic performance and that some of the improvements in the coastal region are made at the cost of a decrease in the central and western regions.

The growing differences in China's regional development are also related to three challenge issues that may affect the country's future development. The regional development differences directly affect the Chinese people's income inequality between the coastal and the interior regions. Compared with those in the interior regions, people in the coastal region have enjoyed a higher level of per-capita income and consumption. The issue of income inequality becomes further complicated when we relate it to the inequality between and within China's urban and rural areas. While inequality increased within China's urban and rural areas, it is the rural society that has experienced increasing large degrees of income inequality since the post-Mao economic reforms. The results of uneven development and income inequality brought policy problems to Chinese leaders. Local leaders in both the coastal and the interior regions are pushing policies that promote the interests of their regions. While the leaders in the interior regions ask for equal treatment and additional assistance from the central government, the leaders in the coastal region are interested not in the central policy but in further development and connection with the richer overseas Chinese areas such as Hong Kong and Taiwan.

The success of China's post-Mao economic reforms and the changes in regional development have had both positive and negative impacts on China's future development. On the positive side, researchers (e.g., Ash & Kueh, 1993; Chang, 1995) noticed that the improvements in China's economy and especially the increasing connections between China's coastal region and the overseas Chinese have promoted economic integration within Greater China. On the negative side, researchers (e.g., Chang, 1992; Goodman, 1994; Yang & Wei, 1996) are also concerned about the possibility of political disintegration or breakup in China because of the increasing inequalities and differences among China's regions.

The issue of economic integration within Greater China refers to the increasing economic activities, especially trade and investment, between Southern China and Hong Kong and Taiwan. Many studies (e.g., Ash & Kueh, 1993; Chang, 1995) already have reported that trade and investment between China and Hong Kong as well as between China and Taiwan have increased tremendously since the post-Mao economic reforms. The increased trade and investment in the areas are especially related to the connection between Guangdong and Hong Kong as well as between Fujian and Taiwan.

The increased economic activities and connections between these regions stem from three major factors. First, it is certainly the implementation of China's open-door policy that allows foreigners, especially the overseas Chinese, to participate in the development of these regions. Second, the impressive development records in Guangdong and Fujian provinces are also related to geographical location and similarly cultural and linguistic backgrounds. Third, the huge investments from Hong Kong and Taiwan to China have to do with their own worsening investment environment at home, caused by shortages of land and cheap labor as well as increasing government regulation activities (e.g., pollution control, employees' safety).

The increasing economic interdependence between Southern China (Guangdong and Fujian), Hong Kong, and Taiwan may have great implications for China's future development (Chang, 1995; Shambaugh, 1995). In the short run, the area of Southern China has become the most prosperous region in China and has enjoyed one of the highest growth records in Asia. In the long run, if the current economic conditions and political stability remain unchanged, the development of Greater China, including Hong Kong, Taiwan, and all provinces of China, will become the fastest-growing region in the world and move the economic condition of Greater China closer to the level of United States and Japan.[7]

The increasing economic differences among China's regions may also result in rising regionalism in the short run and the possibility of political disintegration in China in the long run if the current political and economic conditions change (Goodman & Segal, 1994; Holloway, 1995; Kaye, 1995a, 1995b; Yang & Wei, 1996). Rising regionalism in China has to do with the increase of local political autonomy during the post-Mao reform years. Especially, three key reform initiatives have encouraged local political autonomy. They include (1) the decentralization of economic management and decision-making from the central to the local governments, (2) the development of a more market-oriented and market-determined economy that changes resource allocation from the central government to the highly localized markets, and (3) the open-door policy that provides foreign trade and capital to local governments for alternative sources of economic development (Goodman, 1994: 4-5).

The decentralization of economic management and decision making are especially important because the decentralization policy in the reform years is different from the decentralization policy in the Maoist era (Womack & Zhao, 1994). As discussed in the early part of this chapter, the decentralization policy addressed in the Maoist era meant autarkic self-sufficiency, which focused on economic and political security because of the shortage of goods. The decentralization policy emphasized in the reform years has been related to market decentralization, which not only abandoned the idea of self-sufficiency but also encouraged local governments and producers to respond to market opportunities based on their own conditions. The outcome of this market opportunity is an increase of localism among regions and the possibility of conflicts among them because of different market demands, protection, and expansion.[8]

Rising regionalism is evidenced in the fact that many Chinese provinces have developed their own economic trading partners with various external regions and countries. These include the relationships between the province of Guangdong and Hong Kong, between the province of Fujian and Taiwan, between the province of Shandong and South Korea, between provinces in Northeast China and the Russian Far East, between the province of Xinjiang and the Turkic republics of the former Soviet Union, and between the province of Yunnan and Burma and Thailand.

Rising regionalism and increasing inequality have caused debates about the issue of China's potential disintegration (Goodman, 1994; Holloway, 1995; Yang & Wei, 1996). The argument for possible disintegration suggests that the major factor behind it is the lack of an institutional framework for managing social and political tensions. Especially, in the post-Deng years, disintegration would be related to such conditions as the loss of control by the central government over the provinces, the struggle for dominance and power between factions within the Party's leadership, and the split of the armed forces along regional lines (Holloway, 1995: 15).

Recognizing the arguments for disintegration, others (e.g., Yang & Wei, 1996: 475) suggest that it is unlikely that China will break up because the Chinese leaders have adopted policy measures (i.e., fiscal and tax reforms) to institutionalize relations between the central and the local governments, to alleviate regional disparities and grievances, and to encourage interregional cooperation. In addition, they (Goodman, 1994: 3-4; Holloway, 1995: 15) maintain that the argument about political disintegration (because of regional economic growth and inequality) is based only on economic determination and is too simple to explain the current condition in China. They noticed that the different views among China's leaders have shrunk and can be resolved in reasonably civilized frameworks. Despite tensions between the central government and the provinces, they recognize that the Party still controls the appointment of senior provincial leaders, that there are no major organizations outside the current Party-state system to promote interests and wishes of a province or region, and that central and local leaders frequently work together to promote specific policy initiatives.[9]

In sum, this chapter provides information about China's regional development during the post-Mao reform years. The success of the new development policy is evidenced in the overall improvement of economic performance among all regions. But the faster growth and development in the eastern, coastal region and provinces have resulted in increasing problems of inequality and regionalism. To promote economic integration within Greater China and to avoid political disintegration, it is very important for Chinese leaders to develop policies to strengthen development in the interior region, to control regional development in the coastal region, to promote cooperation not confrontation among regions and provinces, and to maintain political and social stability.

NOTES

1. For more information about China's post-Mao economic performance, see the evaluation of economic performance in Chapter 4 of this book.

2. For more information about China's regional development during the Mao era see, for example, Lyons (1987), Riskin (1987, especially Chapter 9 about the self-reliance policy), and Yang (1990: 233-241).

3. The national GOVI (52,691.99) does not equal the total regional GOVI (55,522.03) because the national value has been adjusted (see State Statistical Bureau, 1994: 376).

4. The national total number value of retail sales (13,592.60) does not equal the regional total value because of incomplete data in some regions (see State Statistical Bureau, 1994: 496).

5. It is important to notice that the official income data about urban residents may be lower than the real income because urban residents also receive various subsidies (e.g., rental, price, and welfare benefits). For more information see, for example, Ma (1994: 21).

6. For more information about the increasing economic connection between China, Hong Kong, and Taiwan, see, for example, Chang (1995), Ash and Kueh (1993).

7. The discussions about the issue of Greater China here are limited to China's regional economic development. For more information about the concept, development, and potential problems of the issue of Greater China see, for example, Harding (1993), a symposium edited by Shambaugh (1993), and later a book edited by Shambaugh (1995).

8. For information about differences between Mao's decentralization policy and the decentralization policy emphasized in the post-Mao reform years see, for example, Womack and Zhao (1994: 143-144).

9. Goodman (1994) argued that the relationship between China's central and local governments is better interpreted in terms of increasing negotiation than in terms of conflicts leading to political disintegration. For more information about the debates regarding the issue of increasing regionalism and disintegration see, for example, Goodman (1994), Holloway (1995), Yang and Wei (1996), and an edited book by Goodman and Segal (1994).

CHAPTER 6

Changes in the Administrative System

INTRODUCTION

To promote China's modernization and development, the post-Mao Chinese leaders since 1978 have gradually reformed the country's administrative system. The reform leaders emphasized the movement of Four Modernizations (i.e., modernizing agriculture, industry, science and technology, and national defense) in the late 1970s and recognized the need to reform the administrative system to achieve the modernization. Deng Xiaoping (1984) clearly pointed out that China's modernization requires necessary changes in both the structure and the forms of management, not only in industrial and agricultural enterprises but also in state administration agencies that supervise these enterprises.

China's administrative reforms are critical to its economic development because of the nature of the Chinese system (Cabestan, 1992; Prybyla, 1982, 1989). Like all traditional communist countries, China is run by a gigantic bureaucracy which is characterized as a type of centrally administrative command planning system. The central administrative system directly controls many of the country's economic activities through its vertical information flows and centralized coordination. In addition to formulating economic policies and activities, the administrative system also owns many production units and controls the implementation of the policies.

The huge administrative system in China suffered from many bureaucratic problems and dysfunctions. For example, the system was run not by competitively recruited civil servants but by cadres recommended by Chinese Communist Party organizations. The cadres, on the one hand, did not possess knowledge and expertise that are necessary for managing the economic development. On the other hand, they were politically committed and heavily involved in political and ideological campaigns and struggles. The problems of the traditional cadre system has been considered by the reform leaders as one of the major impediments to the success of China's economic reform and development. To improve China's economic performance, the leaders concluded that economic modernization and development depend on a rational and efficient bureaucracy (Burns, 1983) and that economic reforms and administrative reforms are inseparable (Cabestan, 1992; Falkenheim, 1980).

The topic of administrative (or bureaucratic) reforms has become very popular in the studies of China's post-Mao development. Studies of administrative reforms have examined various aspects of the reform movement. For example, most of the studies focused on the analysis of the background, the process, and the problem of establishing a new civil service system in China (e.g., Aufrecht & Li, 1995; Bing, 1992; Burns, 1983, 1989; Cabestan, 1992; Chow, 1991; Lam & Chan, 1995; Li, 1990; Liou, 1997; Manion, 1985). Other studies reviewed the overall scope of administrative reforms and addressed the difficulties and the implications associated with the reforms (e.g., Burns, 1993; Falkenheim, 1980; Li, 1993; Ma, 1990; Tsao & Worthley, 1995; You, 1986; Zhou, 1995).

The examination of China's administrative reforms is also based on the consideration and suggestion of the economic development literature. In their studies of lessons of successful development, many researchers (e.g., Haggard & Webb, 1993; Rondinelli & Montgomery, 1990; Summers & Thomas, 1993) indicate the importance of a public management system to economic development. They suggest policies to reform the public management system to create an effective government structure and procedures to deliver public services, regulate activities affecting the public health and safety, and extend the protection of laws to citizens. They recognize the important contribution of the well-trained public employees, competent and disciplined, to implement reform and development policies.

This chapter attempts to provide an overall examination of China's administrative reforms in the post-Mao development years. Specifically, the chapter offers a comprehensive analysis of the administrative reforms by summarizing major changes of the reform activities and examining critical issues related to the future fate of the reforms. The chapter begins with a review of the background of the administrative reforms, including the problems of China's traditional administrative system and the motives of the administrative reforms. The chapter then focuses on the introduction of key reform measures that have been developed, including (1) decentralization of decision-making power, (2) separation of economic enterprises from administrative agencies, (3) establishment of a civil service system, (4) simplification of administrative structures, and (5) professionalization of public administration activities. In addition, the chapter addresses major challenging issues and problems of the administrative reforms, including bureaucratic attitudes and support, the role of the Party, and political and economic conditions. Finally, the chapter concludes with summaries and discussions of some policy implications of the administrative reforms.

BACKGROUND OF ADMINISTRATIVE REFORMS

To understand China's administrative reform during the post-Mao era, we need first to examine the background of the reforms. Three interrelated issues are important for this background examination: (1) the development of China's administrative system, (2) the problems of the administrative system, and (3) the motives of the administrative reforms. The first issue addresses the development and characteristics of the Chinese administrative system. The second issue is related to bureaucratic dysfunctions, public maladministration, or bureau pathologies as explained by Caiden (1991). The third issue has to do with how the post-Mao reform leaders decided to initiate the reforms after considering their political and economic interests.

Development of the Administrative System

Since the establishment of the People's Republic of China in 1949, the Chinese Communist Party has gradually established a huge and complex administrative (i.e., the cadre and bureaucratic) system.[1] Like all the traditional communist countries, the Chinese administrative system plays a major role in the operation of the redistributive socialist economy (Szelenyi, 1978). In other words, the administrative system not only manages the allocation of resources and implements state policies but also serves as the only stable institutional linkage between the state and society. The role of linking the state and society is important because the administrative system is considered the organizational weapon of the Party in exerting state control over the society (Selznick, 1952).

In this party-controlled unitary state, the power of policy making has been traditionally shared among a relatively small number of cadres who occupy important Party and state positions. On the Party side, they are members of the Politburo and its standing committees. The members commonly consult a small circle of semiretired Party elders on critical policy and personnel issues (Lieberthal & Oksenberg, 1988; Hamron, 1992). On the state side, the State Council and its ministries, commissions, bureaus, and offices are responsible for planning and managing a centrally planned economy.

The administrative units below the central level include some provinces, autonomous regions, and centrally administered cities (Beijing, Tianjin, and Shanghai). These units are headed by governors or mayors and are also responsible for managing the planned economy. Similarly, administrative units below the provincial level consist of counties, municipalities, and towns. These units are responsible for implementing the central policy and managing local affairs. Party committees and secretaries coexist with the administrative hierarchy and are responsible for coordinating and supervising the administrative units.

It was estimated that in the late 1970s, China's huge administrative system consisted of about 20 million administrative officials and accounted for about 6 percent of total national budgetary expenditures (not counting fringe benefits and other intangibles) (e.g., Burns, 1983; Prybyla, 1982). These figures may understate the overall picture because they did not include ordinary party members, the army, and basic level cadres (e.g., rural brigade and team officials or urban residence committee members).

The huge administrative system consists of three types of organizations (or work units, *danwei*) with different power and status (Zhou, 1995). They include (1) governmental agencies (*zhenfu jiguan*) that are involved in the process of policy making and implementation, including ministries, commissions and bureaus and offices at various levels of the Party and state bureaucracies; (2) public organizations (*shiye danwei*) that are related to nonprofit public services, including educational and research institutions as well as organizations in the medical, publishing, broadcasting, and entertainment sectors; and (3) industrial organizations (*qiye danwei*) that are enterprises in both the public and the private sectors, including manufacturing, processing, and other production firms. Among the three types, governmental agencies have the authority to supervise public and industrial organizations because they are at the center of the redistribution system. Public organizations have higher social economic status than industrial organizations because they belong to the state sector.

Within the administrative system, there are three general types of jobs that possess different power and positions (Zhou, 1995). They consist of (1) administrators (*xingzheng ganbu*) who perform administrative duties and tasks, including the manager of the firm, the director of the bureau, the president of the university, and the like; (2) technocrats (*jishu ganbu*) who possess different kinds of professional expertise; and (3) politicrats (*zhenggong ganbu*) who are responsible for ensuring the implementation of the Party-state policy and are under the direct control of the higher-level Party organization rather than the administrative office, including Party secretaries in the workplace, other cadres in charge of political education in universities, or Party group leaders on the shop floor.

The development of the Chinese administrative system has been related to and influenced by the Party's organizational heritage (Harding, 1981). They include, for example (1) China's long history of bureaucratic government, (2) the Leninist-Stalinist Soviet system, and (3) the Party's own administrative experience between 1927 and 1949. Despite their rich theoretical and practical sources, the three sets of organizational heritage had complex and ambiguous problems and did not provide Chinese leaders clear guidance about how to develop a sound administrative system that would promote the country's development.[2]

The administrative system that developed has shown many positive aspects in its overall performance in the past. For example, Harding (1981: 357) noticed that the Party has been able to establish a complex system that has effectively controlled a large and diverse nation. The system has promoted a reasonably high rate of economic development and created an impressive record of social welfare and economic equality. Especially, Chinese leaders have been very sensitive to any bureaucratic problems and have devoted considerable time and attention to solving these problems.

Problems of the Administrative System

Despite its positive activities, the Chinese administrative system has also experienced many negative bureaucratic problems (Burns, 1983; Chow, 1993; Harding, 1981). For example, Harding (1981: 344-357) identified and discussed these problems in terms of lack of commitment of Party and state officials to socialist doctrine; low zeal and poor morale among Party and state cadres; inadequate skills and knowledge among most of the cadres; waste and inefficient activities (e.g., overstaffing, poor coordination, and excessive administrative costs); as well as the corrupt behavior of the cadres (e.g., acquiring special privileges, graft, embezzlement, and bribery).[3]

In addition, it is important to note that Chinese leaders and cadres also openly admitted the existence of many bureaucratic problems in the system. Based on critiques by Chinese leaders (e.g., Mao's Twenty Manifestations of Bureaucracy, Hua's comments), for example, Burns (1983: 694) provided a comprehensive list of bureaucratic problems: authoritarianism, routinism, elitism, corruption, shirking responsibility, deceit, laziness, talentlessness, formalism, red tape, nepotism, seeking special privilege, overstaffing, duplication, ineffective, overcentralization, and a weak, ineffective cadre system. Some of these problems (e.g., unresponsiveness, lack of innovation, inefficiency, and corruption) have also been recognized by many cadres in Chow's (1993) field interviews and studies.

Many researchers have identified different factors and offered some explanations of the sources of China's bureaucratic problems. For example, Harding (1981: 358-359) recognized that some of the bureaucratic problems (e.g., inefficiency, corruption, and arrogance) are inherent in the management of large bureaucracies because these bureaucratic pathologies cannot be totally avoided and eliminated (Almond & Powell, 1978: 279). Some other problems are related to China's historical traditions (e.g., problems of elitism, abuse of power, and corruption) and its level of economic development (e.g., problems of lack of trained and skilled officials). Especially, many of the problems are related to the Party's organizational theory and control techniques. For example, such organizational techniques as indoctrination, ratification, and mass campaigns tend to produce problems of stifling conformity and reluctance to take risks or independent initiatives.

These sources of China's bureaucratic problems have also been supported by other researchers that provided similar explanations. For example, Burns (1983) related the bureaucratic problems to three sources: traditional official rules prior to 1949, scarcity of material resources, and structural defects in the management and personnel systems of state and Party organizations (e.g., life tenure, inadequate recruitment, performance and retention criteria, and lack of an administrative responsibility system). Based on Heady's (1984) theory about the study of administrative systems, Chow (1993) identified three interrelated areas that are associated with China's bureaucratic problems, including environmental (e.g., political turmoil and centralization); behavioral (e.g., prevalence of a corruption norm and prevalence of the norm of reciprocity); and organizational (e.g., lack of the norm of professionalism, lack of an objective performance appraisal system, and weak perverse reward/punishment system). Li (1993) also indicated that the clumsiness and bureaucratic problems are related to subjective and dogmatic elements in Marxism; the exclusiveness of China's historical heritage; and especially, the dictatorship of the party and the government that excludes criticisms.

Motives of the Administrative Reforms

Since 1949, the Chinese leaders have been very sensitive to the previously discussed bureaucratic problems and have adopted various organizational mechanisms to control them. These control mechanisms include four different approaches: radicalism, rationalization, external remedialism, and internal remedialism (Harding, 1981). Chinese leaders have tried all four approaches to deal with the bureaucratic problems. For example, they experimented with mechanisms in the area of rationalization, such as promulgating rules and regulations, establishing a complex network of audition and monitoring agencies in the mid-1950s, simplifying bureaucratic structures, and decentralizing economic management in the middle of the Cultural Revolution. The radical approach was emphasized in the Cultural Revolution years, when some leaders proposed the destruction of the bureaucracy and the establishment of a more participatory and less hierarchical form of system. The external remedial approach was noticed when the leaders used the mobilization of the masses to serve as organizational monitors, including, for example, the solicitation of criticism from intellectuals during the Hundred Flowers period. Finally, the internal remedial approach was evident in the leaders' continuing use of rectification campaigns in the New San-fan campaign of 1953, the movement to study the works of Mao in 1965-1966, and the proposals for rectification in 1975.[4]

Comparing the four approaches, Harding (1981) concluded that the Chinese leaders have relied more on internal remedialism and less on external remedialism. The common internal remedial measures used consist of recruitment of officials on the basis of their political standpoint, rectification and indoctrination of officials to maintain their ideological commitment, and the use of mass campaign techniques to carry out policy. The lesser emphasis on external remedialism has to do with the fact that the leaders distrust any form of supervision that is not controlled by the Party. The distrust of non-Party members and activities offers an explanation for why the Chinese have not developed independent legislatures, courts, interest groups, or news media.

Despite the problem of the control techniques, it was also noticed that most campaigns against bureaucratic problems before 1978 were mainly political in nature and related to the Party's internal political struggles. For example, Morgan (1981) argued that the bureaucratic problems were related to the legacy of China's socialist experience (especially the Cultural Revolution) and that control measures used in the earlier time (e.g., the rectification campaigns conducted through intensive media propaganda) were mainly political. Similarly, the leaders' original purposes of criticizing bureaucratic reforms during the post-Mao years were political in nature. Facing the increasing divisive politics within the central committee, the leaders intended to use the campaign against bureaucracy to restore party authority and to remove factionalism that was related to the Gang of Four.[5]

The campaign against bureaucratism had changed from political motives to administrative considerations by the end of 1978. Concerned about poor administrative performance, the post-Mao leaders admitted the existence of such serious problems as the avoidance of responsibility, corruption, bribery, waste, poor work style, and failure to practice democratic centralism (*Beijing Review*, 1980). To improve administrative capability and performance, the leaders started to emphasize problem-solving skills to be considered as one major criteria for a good cadre (*People's Daily*, 1978).

The emphasis on cadres' skills was directly related to the leaders' intention to revitalize and modernize China's economic system. The leaders recognized that the success of economic reforms and development depends on a rational administrative system that emphasizes expertise. Recognizing the cadres' advanced age and lack of skills, the official news media started to argue that selection of cadres would be based on such criteria as better education, professional competence, and younger age (*People's Daily*, 1980a, 1980b). Especially, Deng Xiaoping (1984) recognized the need for administrative reform and emphasized changes in the Party and state leadership system as well as administrative reforms in the streamlining of Party, army, and government organizations. Finally, to promote economic performance, the reform leaders also addressed the importance of decentralization of decision-making power in the early stages of administrative reforms (*Beijing Review*, 1980).

In sum, this review of the background of the Chinese administrative system introduced the development and problems of the system as well as the motives of the post-Mao administrative reform. Especially, China's recent administrative reforms resulted from the post-Mao leaders' interest in promoting economic performance and development. They recognized that an efficient administrative system is critical to China's economic reforms and that China's old cadre system was inefficient and showed many serious bureaucratic problems. The leaders began to introduce several policy measures to reform China's administrative system because they realized many of the bureaucratic problems are related to the Party's traditional recruitment, selection, promotion, and control mechanisms. For example, they understand that cadres are inefficient and unprofessional because in the past cadres were selected on the basis of class background rather than managerial ability, promoted on the basis of seniority and political considerations rather than job-related achievement, and enjoyed lifetime tenure regardless of performance.

REFORM MEASURES DEVELOPED AND IMPLEMENTED

Since the late 1970s, the Chinese leaders have developed and implemented a number of administrative reform measures designed to assist economic reforms and development. Based on official documents and many studies of administrative reforms (e.g., Burns, 1983, 1993; Falkenheim, 1980; Lee, 1984; Liu, 1993; Ma, 1990; Williams, 1993; You, 1986), key reform measures in five areas can be summarized: decentralization of decision-making power, separation of economic enterprises from administrative agencies, establishment of a civil service system, simplification of government structures and functions, and professionalization of public administration activities. The first two areas are closely related to each other and tied to China's economic reform strategies.[6] The last three areas are considered as specific changes in administrative activities. It should be noticed that some of the reform measures introduced are not new ideas but revised policies or suggestions of the earlier time. Also, the concerns and needs of administrative reforms have changed and evolved along with China's economic reforms and development. In other words, despite the early motives of administrative reforms to promote economic development, the success of economic reforms and development in the 1980s has produced additional needs and required different activities in China's administrative reforms.

Decentralization of Decision-making Power

One of the earlier policy measures in China's administrative reforms was the effort of the central government to decentralize decision-making powers to local administrative units. The purpose of this reform measure is to improve the quality of government decisions. The decentralized approach was noticed in both economic and administrative activities. Provincial, county, and village governments have more authority in issues relating not only to supervision and co-coordinating functions within their jurisdiction but also to local economic planning, resource management, and even foreign trade (Burns, 1993; Falkenheim, 1980; You, 1986).

Regarding economic activities, the decentralization of decision-making power to localities has been considered one of the major factors contributing to the earlier success of China's economic reforms (e.g., Prybyla, 1989; Perkins, 1988). For example, based on the successful experiments in the Province of Sichuan, the "contract-responsibility system" (CRS) was started in 1979 in rural areas to reform agriculture's collective sector. The CRS was designed to reduce the central state role in production decisions and to increase the scope of free market activities and local units' self-management. It asked peasants to contract to produce and sell to the state certain quantities of commodities at low official prices and allowed them to sell on the free market anything produced over the contracted amount (Koo, 1990). The successful experience of the CRS in rural, agricultural areas has led Chinese leaders to extend the concept of the system (i.e., set various management targets for profits, profit remittance and taxes) to urban, industrial areas in 1984. In addition, the decentralized approach was also noticed in China's open-door policy and activities. Beginning in 1978, for example, the leaders ended the Ministry of Foreign Trade's monopoly of foreign trade and authorized local governments and various state agencies to sign foreign trade agreements directly (Endean, 1991: 744; Kueh & Howe, 1984: 829). Similarly, when the government opened 14 coastal cities and Hainan Island (later Hainan Province) to foreign investment in 1984, local governments in these areas were also allowed to set up networks of their own foreign trade companies.

Decentralization of power was also noticed in China's administrative system. For example, after several years of experiments, the Chinese government decided to devolve management of financial revenue to provincial governments (Shirk, 1990: 230) in 1980. This reform measure increased the power of provincial governments because it allowed provincial governments to bargain over their remittances to the central government when they signed revenue-sharing contracts with the central. In addition, to assist local officials to implement reform policies, in 1984 the Party decentralized control of personnel administration by giving Party officials the power to appoint, remove, or discipline the officials immediately below them (Burns, 1987). To maintain political stability, the central authorities still keep the power to appoint key national positions (e.g., governors, ministers, CEOs of state enterprises) and stipulated numerous guidelines regarding political background, age, and educational level required for each lower-level position (Bing, 1992; Li, 1990).

Perception of the importance and need for decentralization of decision-making power has gradually changed during the reform years (Burns, 1993). The central leaders today do not emphasize this reform measure because they felt that decentralization power had already been given to local governments. After increasing their power to manage the economy, local government leaders, on the other hand, begin to question the need for the central government to control local organization structure and establishments. They argue that they should have the power to determine their administrative activities (e.g., streamlining government) according to their own local needs (Burns, 1993: 349-350).

Separation of Economic Enterprises from Administrative Agencies

As explained earlier, the Chinese administrative system includes many industrial organizations (*qiye danwei*). Governmental agencies not only owned many economic enterprises but also forced the mechanical adaptation of economic activities to administrative conveniences, channels, and systems. The result of this control system was the problem of overadministration, which confuses and disrupts the flow of economic materials and causes system-wide problems of inflexibility and nonaccountability (Falkenheim, 1980).

To overcome the situation, the reformers emphasized not only decentralization of decision-making power (especially decisions relating to economic activities) but also the separation of economic enterprises from government agencies. For example, the implementation of the CRS involves changes in local organizations and administrations (Perkins, 1988; You, 1986). The changes in rural, agricultural areas consist of the separation of economic units from the government; the merger of the people's commune with the government, the party committee, and the cooperative; and an increase in the linkage between the reward system and the work performed.

Similar changes have also been arranged in urban, industrial areas. Starting from October 1984, reform leaders emphasized the separation of government functions from enterprise management and property rights from operating rights. In other words, enterprises are separated from government bureaucracies and have become autonomous economic units. Especially, under the contract responsibility system, enterprises have authority to make decisions regarding resources control, levels of production, and prices of products. As autonomous units, enterprise managers are being asked to manage manpower allocation, resource use, production, and marketing in accordance with the rules of the market. The introduction of competition, especially the introduction of a bankruptcy law, is designed to move away from the guaranteed government bailout.

The Chinese leaders' intention to separate economic enterprises from administrative agencies has been further evidenced by their recent reform of state-owned enterprises. The goal for the reform of state-owned enterprises is to establish a modern enterprise system adapted to the requirements of a market economy. The requirements emphasized consist of clear definitions concerning property rights relationships and explicit obligations and responsibilities, separating enterprise management from government functions, and applying scientific management expertise (Li, 1995). Since 1992, a series of laws and provisions have been promulgated, including the Regulations on Transformation of Operational Mechanisms of Enterprises Owned by the Whole People, Regulations on the Supervision and Control of State-Owned Assets, and the Corporation Law. The proposed enterprise reforms are especially related to China's 14,400 large and medium-sized state-owned enterprises because many problems existed in their financial and social burdens (Wu, 1995).[7]

Establishment of a Civil Service System

To improve the quality of government decision-making, the reform leaders emphasized not only decentralization of decision-making power to those who have better information but also changes in the traditional administrative system. The leaders first introduced reform measures to solve some bureaucratic problems in their past cadre management practices. Then, the leaders implemented several new mechanisms in order to establish a rational and professional civil service system.

As discussed earlier, China's traditional administrative system suffered many bureaucratic problems that made the system inefficient and unprofessional. While some of the problems are common to any large and complex organization, many of China's bureaucratic problems resulted from its traditional cadre management practices. These practices include some questionable recruitment, performance evaluation, and reward methods. For example, the recruitment of cadres was based not on talent and merit through objective selection processes but on personal backgrounds and political qualifications through subjective selection processes controlled by the Party. Similarly, there were no scientific, objective methods to evaluate cadres' job performance. The reward system was based on an equalitarian pay model that was not related to job performance and provided no real incentives (or sanctions) for cadres.

The process of reforming the cadre system has lasted more than ten years and involves various stages. First, a retirement and pension system plan was established in 1982 to encourage aging cadres to retire with a generous pension and give up their positions to the younger generation of cadres. Then, in 1984, the Party gave officials the power to appoint, remove, or discipline the officials immediately below them, which indicates the decentralization of personnel management authority. Finally, policy makers decided to establish a civil service system separating civil servants from the rest of the cadre system.

The establishment of a civil service system started in 1984. The Central Organization Department of the Party and the former Ministry of Labor and Personnel tried to draft the Regulations on State Administrative Organ Personnel based on studies of China's own civil service system and those of other countries. In 1987, the Thirteenth Congress of the Party adopted proposals to establish a more competent and efficient civil service and administrative system, and the title of the Provisional Regulations on State Administrative Organ Personnel was changed to Provisional Regulations on State Civil Servants. For the first time, the Communist Chinese had accepted the concept of civil servants and substituted it for the Soviet-inspired concept of cadres. In 1988, the Ministry of Personnel was established (formerly the Ministry of Labor and Personnel) and was charged with the task of revising the Provisional Regulations on State Civil Servants and drafting other supporting legal documents (e.g., regulations on position classification, recruitment, examinations, performance appraisals, promotions, and superannuation of civil servants).

After a series of redrafts and experiments (Cabestan, 1992), the "Provisional Regulations on State Civil Servants" was officially adopted and went into effect on October 1, 1993. The new act consists of 18 chapters and addresses major personnel issues such as the duties of civil servants, job categories (15 grades), recruitment procedures, appraisal procedures, performance rewards, discipline, promotion and demotion policies, transfer, pay, resignation, and retirement. Despite its long process and some limitations, the establishment of a modern civil service has been considered by many researchers as one of the major achievements in China's post-Mao administrative reforms.[8]

Simplification of Government Structures and Functions

In addition to establishing a new civil service system, the Chinese government has also emphasized the importance of the simplification of government structures and functions. The simplification of government structures was designed to deal with such problems as organizational overlapping, unclear jurisdictions, and overstaffing. In addition, simplification also attempted to restructure the scope and functions of government in order to reduce the role of government in microeconomic management. In other words, following the principles of streamlining, unification, and efficiency, the structural reform measures involved merging agencies with similar or overlapping functions, abolishing those duplicate ones, and eliminating excessive sectoral commissions. The reform measures were intended to restructure government organizations to better manage the development of the socialist market economy and to reduce government management of economic enterprises (Burns, 1983, 1993; Lee, 1984; Wu, 1993; You, 1986).

The process of simplifying government structures has been closely related to some problems associated with the development of economic reforms (Burns, 1993). For example, one of the negative consequences of China's economic reforms has been an increase of government budget deficits. To reduce the budget deficits, the reform leaders attempted to streamline central and local governments in 1982 after the huge deficits in 1979 and 1980, and again in 1988 after the increasing deficits in 1986 and 1987. Similarly, after introducing market mechanisms in China's economic system, the leaders started to emphasize changing the functions of government and to reduce some traditional activities of central planning.

The simplification process involves downsizing government agencies to reduce costs and rationalizing government functions to eliminate duplication. First, the downsizing activities were emphasized in the organizational reforms of 1982, 1988, and 1993. For example, it was noticed that the government cut the number of State Council agencies from 100 to 61 and the number of employees from 51,000 to 30,000 in 1982 and reduced the number of ministries and commissions from 45 to 41, the number of directly subordinate bureaus from 22 to 19, and the number of State Council employees from about 50,000 to 44,000 (Burns, 1993). In 1993, the State Council's Organizational Reform Program attempted to cut the size of central government staff by some 20 percent and to reduce the number of departments from 86 to 59 and of nonpermanent administrative bodies from 85 to 26 (Wu, 1993; *Beijing Review*, 1993a). In addition, the government also plans to cut personnel at the provincial, prefectural, and county levels by about 20 percent.

Next, to eliminate duplication, the government has made several organizational arrangements to meet new needs of China's market economy. These include strengthening the capacity of agencies that are involved in macroeconomic management, including, for example the State Auditing Administration, the State Statistical Bureau, the State Administration for Industry and Commerce, and the State Administration of Taxation in the State Council. They also call for removing agencies involved in microeconomic management and changing them to economic enterprises, associations, or councils. The changes of administrative agencies to corporations include, for example, the change of the Ministry of Petroleum to the National Petroleum Corporation in 1988 and the change of the Ministries of Aeronautics and Space Industry to aeronautics and space industry corporations in 1993. The changes of administrative agencies to associations were evidenced in the 1993 proposal that the ministries of Light Industry and Textiles Industry will become associations or councils. Similar organizational rearrangements were also noted at the local levels.[9]

Professionalization of Public Administration Activities

To fully understand China's administrative reform, we also need to examine changes and efforts that are related to the study and dissemination of administrative theories and methods. The changes and efforts emphasized here include the establishment of the Chinese Public Administration Society (CPAS) in October 1988, the expansion of public administration education, and the provision of public administration training. All of these activities were designed to promote the professionalization of China's administrative system.

The CPAS plays an advisory and consultative role in promoting China's public administrative scientification, legalization, and modernization. It unites national research institutions with colleges and universities to improve administrative efficiency, administrative studies, and administrative reforms. The CPAS consists of 22 regional sections (at provincial levels, autonomous regions, and municipalities); 8 professional groups (e.g., National Teaching Research Association in Public Administration, China Youth Institute for Public Administration); and 48 units in colleges, schools, departments, tutorial and research offices, research centers, and institutes. The official journal of CPAS, "*China Public Administration*," published monthly in Chinese, is a comprehensive magazine in public administrative studies and provides a channel for practitioners and researchers to discuss their managerial experiences and research findings (Chinese Public Administration Society, 1993).

During the reform era, public administration studies and training expanded extensively. Public administration courses and departments have increased dramatically in major universities (e.g., Peiking, Fudan, Jilin, Zhoungshan, Wuhan, Lau Zhou, Zhen Zhou, and the People's University) since 1984. Thousands of public administration books have been published covering topics such as organization theory and behavior, public personnel management, decision making, policy science, local government management, history of management, city administration, social work administration, and the psychology of management (Li, 1993; Huang, 1993; Zhang, 1993).

Public administration training institutes have been established at the national and provincial levels. The National School of Public Administration is the supreme training center of the national civil service and provides training to high- and middle-ranking government officials. More than 20 institutes of public administration have been set up at the provincial level, with the goal of training local government officials. It is estimated that, since 1984, more than 2 million state cadres have received public administration training through a variety of channels: university education, television education programs, training classes, and night school (Huang, 1993). Recently, the Party has emphasized its "1996-2000 National Cadre Education and Training Program" to improve the quality of cadres (*Beijing Review*, 1996: 5). Focusing on both moral and competence issues, the program is designed to train cadres above the county level, especially younger cadres, to meet the demands of economic reform, opening up, and modernization.

Finally, the forgoing discussions of five administrative reform measures provide information about the scope and progress of China's administrative reforms. It is clear that the reform measures have covered the behavior, function, and structure of China's administrative system. Based on different needs, the reform measures were first experimented with at various locations and gradually implemented nationally. The reforms have lasted over a decade and extended from one sector to another.

CHALLENGING PROBLEMS OF ADMINISTRATIVE REFORMS

In spite of noticeable changes in policy, structure, and process, the Chinese administrative reforms have encountered several problems that may affect its effectiveness and future development. The major problems and challenging issues to these reforms include (1) bureaucratic attitudes and support, (2) the Party's role and position, and (3) economic and social conditions. The three issues are important in the evaluation of China's administrative reforms because as Caiden (1988) argued, administrative reforms are more likely to succeed if they have a high level of political support, are implemented in a system with high administrative capacity and bureaucratic support, and can mobilize popular participation in the process of implementation. While the first issue is related to the internal and micro aspect of China's administrative system, the last two issues deal with the external and macro level of the system.

Bureaucratic Attitudes and Support

Bureaucratic attitudes play a major role in the success or failure of future development. Bureaucrats will participate in the reform process, accept or suggest new reform ideas, and implement reform policies if they have positive attitudes toward the reforms. On the other hand, bureaucrats may refuse, formally or informally, reform ideas and selectively implement reform policies if they possess some negative attitudes toward the reforms.

With respect to China's administrative reforms, bureaucrats reveal both positive and negative attitudes toward reform measures. On the positive side, it has been noticed that China's local bureaucrats' perceptions, expectations, and enthusiasm about reform ideas (e.g., decentralization of decision-making power) are considered one of the major reasons for the earlier success of China's economic development (Chen et al., 1992; Waste, 1986). Positive attitudes were also evidenced in the implementation of other reform measures such as the separation of administrative agencies and economic enterprises. Enterprise managers are now in a better position to make their own managerial decisions and experience fewer interruptions by administrative agencies.

On the other hand, it has also been observed that some Chinese bureaucrats have shown some negative attitudes and behaviors in the process of reforms (e.g., Burns, 1993; Ma, 1990). For example, to deal with the professionalization requirement in the administrative reforms, some bureaucrats tend to inflate their qualifications by falsifying documents or taking shortcuts in education. Facing the government restructuring, some bureaucrats use the opportunity to separate enterprises from governments and take advantage to benefit themselves by either serving as consultants for companies or setting up shadow companies. Especially, some bureaucrats selectively implement or enforce new rules or policies as a tool to gain or strengthen their power and control. Negative attitudes are especially pervasive among bureaucrats who lost their traditional power and status due to organizational changes in the reform process.

One major negative outcome of bureaucrats' attitudes is the issue of bureaucratic corruption. As discussed previously, bureaucratic corruption existed before the reform era. For example, Harding (1981: 355-357) noticed that corruption was identified as a serious problem twice in China's development. First, during the San-fan campaign (the early 1950s), it was noticed that some urban cadres accepted bribes and favors from merchants and industrialists in return for favorable government action to resolve such problems as contract disputes, taxation difficulties, and supply shortages. Next, during the Socialist Education Movement (the early 1960s), some rural cadres used their official positions to gain extra goods and money for themselves and their families.

Bureaucratic corruption, however, has become a serious issue in terms of both scope and frequency since the implementation of the reform policies. For example, according to official reports, China uncovered 95,000 cases of corruption from January to November 1994 and recovered economic losses of up to 1.7 billion yuan (*Beijing Review*, 1995a, 1995b). In addition, it is believed that the Shougan affair (the arrest of Zhou Guanwu and Zhou Beifang, the executives of the Capital Iron & Steel Corporation) and the removal of Chen Xitong (the former Beijing Party chief) have extended the corruption issue from the provincial to the national level (Huus, 1995).

Some causes and consequences of corruption have to do with the administrative system and the reform policies (Liu, 1983; Sun, 1991). Regarding causes of corruption, for example, they include such factors as the rise of materialism, the increasing income gap between government and nongovernment employees, the weakening of traditional control mechanisms, and the lack of viable substitutes (i.e., the rule of the law). Clearly, most of the causative factors are related to the changes of administrative structures and process, which provide opportunities for corrupt activities. The consequences of corruption not only affect the quality and effectiveness of China's administrative system but also produce negative activities in the society, including enhancing social inequality, devaluating merit and knowledge, contributing value crisis and morale erosion, and promoting a negative psychology of equality (i.e., a culture of corruption).

Role and Position of the Party

In addition to the problem of bureaucratic attitudes, China's administrative reforms also face one challenging issue about the relationship between the Party and the administrative system. Some researchers (e.g., You, 1986) have noticed China's intention to separate government bureaucracies from Party bureaucracies and differentiate power and function between the two. Many researchers (e.g., Lam & Chan, 1995; Li, 1990; Liou, 1997) have raised the issue of the politics-administration dichotomy and questioned the true separation of the party and the government.

There has never been a clear-cut line between Party leaders and government bureaucrats in China's administrative system. Party leaders at all levels are administrative officials at the same time; and in order to be a successful bureaucrat, one has to become a Party member first. In addition, China explicitly renounces the principle of political neutrality. The Party's control of the administration is demonstrated in several ways. First, the Party controls all the appointments of political civil servants through the Party committees within the People's Congress. Second, the Party controls the key personnel of the administration and career civil servants through the regulation indicating that all candidates have to be screened according to application requirements (emphasizing political and moral standing) before they can take part in the civil service examination. Specifically, Chinese civil servants have to adhere to the Four Cardinal Principles (i.e., adherence to the leadership of the Party, the dictatorship of the proletariat, the guidance of Marxism-Leninism and Mao Zedong Thought, and the socialist road) and carry out politics formulated by the Party (Bing, 1992; Li, 1993).

Moreover, the influence of the Party on China's administrative reforms has also been related to political disputes and struggles among top leaders within the Party. For example, in their study of China's civil service system, Lam and Chan (1995, 1996) argued that the process of introducing a civil service system in China has not been just a technical endeavor and that the process has been influenced by the political arguments, especially, over the Party's power. They noticed that there are major differences in the proposal in Zhao Ziyang's Report to the Thirteenth Congress in 1987 and the promulgation of the Provisional Regulations on State Civil Servants in 1993, including the civil service system and the party-government relationship; stability versus liveliness (*shengji*) and vitality (*huoli*); and distinctiveness of the civil service.

Economic and Social Conditions

As well as political issues, China's administrative reforms also encounter problems of economic and social conditions. First, on the economic side, effective administrative reforms need a sound economy to support reform measures. For example, when implementing the downsizing and streamlining process, we need to consider not only the capacity of the economy to absorb redundant staff but also the cycles of economic expansion in China. Burns (1993) noticed that China's 1988-1989 restructuring attempt failed in part because it was followed by a contraction of the economy to curb overheating and high rates of inflation. Manion (1992) also argued that the cadre retirement policy may bring additional burdens on China's treasury because it called for the two million retirees to receive pensions at 100 percent of their salary level just before they retired.

Next, on social conditions, China's administrative reforms may face problems because of increasing crime and disorder in the society. Along with improved economic conditions, the reform era also has witnessed an increase in crimes and unhealthy tendencies (Perry, 1993; Myers, 1989). Kaye (1994c) described the situation as "disorder under Heaven" because of the social chaos related to economic reforms and growth. The situation of social unrest may affect administrative reforms, especially in the case of bureaucratic corruption. Many Chinese today do not like the growing amount of bureaucratic corruption and abuse of power. In fact, one of the major reasons for the 1989 Tiananmen Square incident is the protest of the public and the students against bureaucratic corruption (Mason, 1994: Sun, 1991).

Finally, China's administrative reforms also encounter problems of low morale among cadres because of changing social conditions. Since the success of economic reforms, the Chinese society has become more material-oriented and the Chinese people are more interested in making money and becoming rich. The changing social conditions affect administrative reforms because, on the one hand, many talented young people do not want to work for the government because of its low wages and associated social status. On the other hand, the government is losing its talented, experienced employees because many are leaving their official positions to work for the private, joint-venture companies for better pay. All of this may have long-term effects on the quality of government policy making, implementation, and services.

DISCUSSION AND CONCLUSION

The previous examination covered three major aspects of China's post-Mao administrative reforms: background, scope, and challenge problems. The administrative system before the reform years could be described as a huge and complex organization with such bureaucratic problems as inefficiency, ineffectiveness, inflexibility, nonaccountability, and lack of innovation and incentive. Considering China's economic and political environment, the post-Mao leaders started the administrative reforms to promote economic development because they recognized the importance of the administrative system to economic development. Since 1978, the key reform measures developed are decentralization of the decision-making power, separation of economic enterprises from government agencies, establishment of a civil service system, simplification of administrative structures, and professionalization of public administration activities. While providing some significant changes, the post-Mao administrative reforms have also encountered several problems, including bureaucratic attitudes and support, the role of the Party, and the changing social and economic condition. All of these problems may affect the further development of the administrative reforms.

The examination of China's administrative reforms revealed several major characteristics. First, the approach of the reforms is pragmatic, realistic, and incremental. Based on the principle of "practice is the sole criterion of truth," Chinese reformers have emphasized the strategy of experimentation with regard to almost all of the reform policies. For example, the contract responsibility system, which decentralized economic authority, was first experimented with at the provincial level and then adopted nationally. Similarly, the Provisional Regulations on State Civil Servants, which outlined major components of the civil service system, was also experimented with in various provinces before its adoption nationally in 1993. Based on the results and experience of the experimental studies, the leaders have gradually moved reform measures from the local to the national level and from one sector to another. The gradual process has lasted over a decade (e.g., from 1984 to 1993 in the case of civil service reforms).

The scope of the reforms has been comprehensive in nature. They cover not only micro functional and structural issues but also macro system and process issues. The former issues include, for example, reforming personnel management (i.e., establishing a modern civil service system) and simplifying agency structures (downsizing and reorganizing the administrative agency). The latter consist of the change of the decision-making process (i.e., the decentralizing approach), the revision of the economic management system (i.e., the separation of economic enterprises from government agencies), and the provision of a professional support system (i.e., the professional public administration society, education, and training). The comprehensive nature of the reforms certainly have reshaped the whole administrative system.

Moreover, China's reforms have been unique because they emphasize both learning of Western experience and consideration of the Chinese situation. Reformers have tried to balance the two and establish a system with Chinese characteristics. On the positive side, this approach will adjust Western experiences into internal, local systems and make changes and reforms more smooth and acceptable. On the negative side, the combination approach will not resolve some fundamental problems of the administrative system, such as the role of the Party in the reforms and the political neutrality issue.

Despite these characteristics, it is difficult to offer a clear conclusion about China's administrative reforms. There is no doubt that China has successfully promoted its economic development and achieved excellent macroeconomic performance (e.g., Chen et al., 1992; Liou, 1996; Perkins, 1994; Yusuf, 1994).[10] Much of this economic success has to do with the improvement of the administrative system and the support of thousands of administrators at the national and local levels. The reform measures of decentralizing decision-making power and separating of enterprise units from administrative agencies are especially important to the economic successes.

The improvement of economic conditions alone does not provide strong enough evidence to support the overall success of the administrative reforms. The major concerns involve two interrelated issues. The first issue is the fundamental structural and attitudinal problems of China's administrative system. While the reforms attempt to rationalize, formalize, and legalize the system, the structural problems of party intervention and the attitudinal problems of informal networks (*guanxi*) still exist and dominate the daily operation of the system. Researchers of administrative reforms (e.g., Caiden, 1982, 1988; Caiden & Siedentopf, 1982) indicate that the key to improved public management lies in changing administrative cultures. Reform measures such as changing laws, overhauling organizations, and employing education and training will not work unless the attitude, behavior, and conduct of public employees change significantly. The pervasiveness of bureaucratic corruption indicates that the reform measures introduced have not overcome both problems. In terms of administrative efficiency, democracy, and legalization, there is still more work to be done, and China is just at the beginning of the process.

The second issue has to do with the lack of an independent and powerful external control and monitoring system. Despite many changes that occurred during the reform years, the Chinese society today still does not have a powerful legislative body, an independent press, and autonomous civil and professional organizations.[11] The lack of an independent external control system implies that the Chinese administrative system in the near future will continue to depend on its traditional internal control mechanisms (Harding, 1981). The traditional control approach may not be as effective as it used to be because Chinese society has become more open and complex and because the Chinese people have more opportunities to access different information sources and become more independent in their attitudes and behaviors.

In sum, the future development of China's administrative reforms depends on its economic and political environment. The success of economic reform and development will require more fundamental changes in China's administrative system. To assure the success of administrative reforms, Chinese leaders need to consider serious issues and changes in China's political system. One important issue has to do with the Party-state relationship. There is no doubt that the Party has played a major and dominant role in China's development. But, according to the development experience of newly industrialized countries, it is unavoidable that the dominant party will face political challenges after the improvement of social and economic conditions. The arrangement of an appropriate relationship between the Party and the state will certainly further test the wisdom and will of the Chinese leaders and people.

NOTES

1. The term "administrative system" has been related to other terms such as the bureaucratic or cadre system or organization. Similarly, other terms, such as cadre or bureaucratic reforms, have been used to describe China's administrative reforms. Except in the case of criticizing the traditional cadre system, the term administrative system and reform will be consistently used in this chapter.

2. For example, Chinese leaders criticized some characteristics of the traditional Confucian officials (e.g., arbitrary, corrupt, and divorced from the day-to-day life of the people), questioned some features of the Soviet heritage (e.g., the violence and terror practiced under

Stalin and the Soviet system's tendencies toward excessive centralism, rigid routine, and strict specialization), and questioned the fitness of their past rural experience to the new task of nationwide management and development. For more information about the ambiguity and contradiction see Harding (1981: 17-31).

3. For more information about the bureaucratic problems, see Harding's (1981: 344-357) discussion of bureaucracy as an administrative problem in the concluding chapter.

4. Harding (1981: 331) concluded that the Chinese experience suggested that we should also consider five additional categories, including regularized external remedialism, regularized internal remedialism, open-door rectification, radical external remedialism, and radical internal remedialism. For more information about the theoretical development and practical experience of China's organizational control mechanisms see Harding (1981), especially the chapter about politics of bureaucracy (pp. 17-31) and discussions in the concluding chapter (pp. 329-359).

5. For more information about the post-Mao political condition before 1978, see the discussion of political environment in the late 1970s in Chapter 2 of this book.

6. See information in Chapter 3 about economic reform measures introduced since 1978.

7. For more information about the official arguments of China's state-owned enterprises see, for example, Geng (1994) and Wu (1995).

8. For more information about the process of designing a new civil service system and the achievements and limitations of the proposed civil service system see, for example, Aufrecht and Li (1995), Bing (1992), Burns (1983, 1989, 1993), Chow (1991), Huang (1993), Lam and Chan (1995, 1996), Li (1990), Liou (1997), and Tsao and Worthley (1995).

9. For information about Chinese government structural and institutional changes see, for example, Burns (1993: 351-354) and Lee (1984).

10. For more information about the achievements of China's economic reforms, see the evaluation of economic reforms in Chapter 4.

11. During the reform years, we have observed some signs of independent activities in the National People's Congress and the increasing numbers of professional and civil organizations. These activities and organizations, however, are still limited in their control of government. For more information, see changes in China's society in Chapter 7.

CHAPTER 7

Changes in State-Society Relations

INTRODUCTION

Since 1978, the post-Mao Chinese leaders have developed and implemented various reform policies to promote China's modernization and development. As reviewed in the previous chapters, these reform policies have certainly improved China's macroeconomic performance and the Chinese people's living standards. In addition to economic activities, the post-Mao reforms have also had direct or indirect effects on other aspects of Chinese society. This chapter attempts to examine the general impact of economic reforms on Chinese society. Especially, the chapter focuses on changes in China's state-society relations since the beginning of the reforms.

The study of state-society relations is important in understanding not only the environment of the economic reforms but also the impact of the reforms on the environment. First, as reviewed in the literature of economic development, researchers (Haggard and Webb, 1993; Rondinelli and Montgomery, 1990; Summers and Thomas, 1993) indicated the stable political and social environment as one of the major factors that are associated with the success of reform and development. They maintained that the stable environment will allow policy makers to formulate and implement policies and structures to achieve development goals. In addition, our interest in state-society relations is directly related to the impact of the reforms on the social environment, because China's political environment has been relatively stable during the reform years.

The study of China's state-society relations has also been recognized by many researchers as a new model of studying Chinese politics (Perry, 1994).[1] The new model focuses on studies of neither the state nor the society in isolation, but rather the interaction between the two (Harding, 1994). In other words, researchers interpret changes, both causes and consequences, in Chinese politics as a product of interactions between the state apparatus and society at large (Nee & Mozingo, 1983). The major research question raised in the study of state-society relations is whether the post-Mao economic reforms are producing a significant change in the relative power of state-society relations.

The study of state-society relations is important to China's future development because of possible outcomes and consequences associated with changes in the state and society relations (Lieberthal, 1995: 293). For example, it is important to notice that the downfall of communist regimes in Eastern Europe and the Soviet Union between 1989 and 1991 was based on the initiative of the people living there, which was the outcome of their political and economic reforms. How do the Chinese economic reforms change the nature of the traditional tie that connects the society to the state? Especially, for many Chinese observers, the Tiananmen mass movement in April-June 1989 provided a clear signal that the reforms have indeed promoted democratic ideas and activities as well as the development of some forms of social groups that were not noticed in Maoist China.

While focusing on the issue of state-society relations, researchers have produced different conclusions about the possible consequences of the economic reforms. Some researchers (e.g., White, 1993) argue that the economic reforms have resulted in a basic contradiction between economic transformation and political immobility and that the social and political changes associated with economic reforms will undermine the legitimacy of the previous state-socialist polity and accelerate its political breakdown. Others (e.g., Solinger, 1993) contend that economic reforms have blurred and softened, rather than sharpened, the separation of state and society and that the reforms have not yet led to the emergence of civil society and any immediate changes in the existing system.

Recognizing the different arguments about China's state-society relations, this chapter will examine the impact of post-Mao economic reforms on Chinese society in general. The chapter first provides an overview of China's state-society relations before the post-Mao reforms. The chapter then offers some detailed analyses regarding changes in state-society relations that stem from the economic reforms. Specifically, the analyses focus on six major areas: (1) changes in rural areas, (2) changes in urban areas, (3) changes in social mobility, (4) changes in individual and social ideology, (5) changes in social control and stability, and (6) changes in the legal system.

The study of changes in the rural and urban areas is related to the rural, agricultural reforms and the urban, industrial reforms that were examined in Chapter 3. The study of changes in social mobility and ideology is due to the fact that along with the process of economic reforms, Chinese society has become more open and free in terms of individual beliefs, behaviors, and travel activities. The study of social control and the legal system is concerned with the issue of domestic control because of some crimes and unhealthy tendencies associated with the economic reforms. After studying these changes, the chapter concludes with summaries and discussions about critical issues that are related to these changes.

STATE-SOCIETY RELATIONS BEFORE THE REFORM YEARS

Before the post-Mao reforms, Chinese state-society relations could be categorized as a state-dominated society, that is, the existence of a strong state and a weak society. The Communist Party-state controlled almost all aspects of social life among the Chinese people. The Party-state control over the society functioned mainly through a huge and complex administrative structure, various monitoring policies and systems, and continued political and ideological struggles. Focusing on the impact of economic reforms, the present study of state-society relations before the reform years will not cover every issue of the relations. Instead, the study addresses life and conditions among rural peasants, urban residents, and the intellectuals. Additionally, it also describes the overall attitudes of the general public in the society.[2]

Before the reform years, the major policies used in China's countryside were the *hukou* resident-registration system, the food allocation system, and the work-point system. Under the registration system, every rural resident had to belong to a production brigade and a people's commune. The system strictly inhibited people's geographical mobility, especially from the villages to the cities. For rural peasants, they were required to engage in agricultural activities and produce agricultural products according to the state plan. A small group of local cadres provided political, economic, and cultural leadership in each village. These cadres had to implement state allocation policies and fulfill state demands for grains and other services (e.g., labor forces for public works). The rural villages during the Mao era were basically isolated and separated from China's urban areas.

Similarly, the resident registration system also required every urban resident to belong to a unit (*danwei*). Most urban residents worked for different units such as government agencies (*zhenfu danwei*), public organizations (*shiye danwei*), and industrial organizations (*Qiye danwei*). These work units were very important to urban residents because they provided jobs, houses, health care, and other social welfare benefits. In addition, the urban residents were encouraged to participate in state-sponsored political organizations such as the women's federation, youth leagues, trade unions, and residents' committees to promote their interests. Both the work units and political organizations were closely related to the Party organs and controlled by the Party committees and cadres.

The role of intellectuals in the Chinese society had been seriously challenged and damaged during Mao's era. In traditional Chinese society, intellectuals, both Confucian scholars in the past and Westernized scholars in modern times, enjoyed a special social status. Providing a societywide balancing force (Pye, 1991), intellectuals were allowed to criticize the government's policies to promote state interests. The special status and balancing role of the intellectuals were basically destroyed in the Maoist era. For example, intellectuals did not trust the Chinese authority and became mindless supporters of the official policy after the Hundred Flowers and Antirightist campaigns in 1957. During the campaigns, the intellectuals were punished for their suggestions and critiques, even though they had first been requested by the authorities. Especially, these intellectuals were further humiliated during the Cultural Revolution, and many of them suffered both physical and psychological abuse.

The result of total state control over society in Mao's China was a highly homogeneous society, characterized by dull conformity: people wearing similar blue Mao jackets, having similar hair styles (even among women), riding on the same brand of bicycle, receiving similar low salaries from state-owned factories, spending and consuming foods and other goods according to ration coupons or quotas controlled by the government (Chen, 1998; Lieberthal, 1995). There was no business advertising or any other commercial activities in most of the cities.

The general public attitudes before the reform years were unstable and violent, anti-intellectual and anticonsumer, isolated within Chinese society and outside world activities (Lieberthal, 1995: 296-297). It was unstable and violent because continuous political and class struggles taught the Chinese people that violence is perfectly acceptable for the purpose of ideological purification. It was anti-intellectual because, influenced by the official policy, the public felt that it was better to be a worker or farmer than an intellectual. It was anticonsumer because officials emphasized plain living and basic egalitarianism and criticized anyone who pursued personal gain. It was isolated within the Chinese society because the registration system and the personnel system allowed no one to escape from their work units and communes without permission. Finally, long-term isolation from world activities made the Chinese people distrust foreigners and believe that most of them wanted to exploit the Chinese.

CHANGES IN RURAL AREAS

The post-Mao reforms introduced not only policy changes in the agricultural prices but also structural changes in production methods (Chen, 1998). The policy changes consisted of, for example, increasing state procurement prices for agricultural products and reducing grain procurement quotas. The production changes included, for example, allowing more household production activities and granting communes autonomy in making decisions over production, distribution, and management. Especially, the government gradually introduced the Household Responsibility System: first, leasing land for household farming (*fentian dangan*) and second, setting quotas of agricultural production on a household basis (*baochan daohu*).[3]

The implementation of the Household Responsibility System has made significant changes in China's rural society. The new system not only promoted agricultural productivity but also changed social structures in the rural areas. Under the responsibility system, peasants have more freedom to make their farming decisions and to sell their products in free markets for flexible prices after the contract quotas are fulfilled. By the end of 1984, most of China's cultivated land had been contracted to individual households. People's communes were abolished, and their functions were divided between local townships for governmental operations and local economic committees for economic management. In other words, through the responsibility system, Chinese peasants have been liberalized from the state control regarding their economic activities.

Moreover, the rapid development of Township and Village Enterprises (TVEs) in China's rural areas has brought further changes to both the peasant's life and the social structure.[4] The TVEs have not only helped the rural areas to solve the problem of surplus labor that resulted from the reform but also provided additional sources of income for individual households and communities. Local governments are especially interested in developing TVEs because the profits associated with them became the primary source of extra budgetary revenues. In addition to the improvement in the peasant's living standards, one of the negative outcomes of the changes in China's rural society has been the increasing income gap between the new wealthiest households and the general public. In general, the wealthiest households consisted of two types of people (Unger, 1994). The first type includes some cadres and their relatives, who became rich by converting official positions into sources of revenue. The second type includes some rich peasant individuals or households who made money quickly through specialized agricultural production or diversification into local trade and transportation (Kelliher, 1991).

CHANGES IN URBAN AREAS

The post-Mao reforms have also introduced major changes in China's urban society. The changes were especially related to the industrial reforms that have been implemented gradually since the late 1970s. The government first decentralized the control of enterprises to enterprise managers and allowed these enterprises to share profits and control daily operational issues. Next, the government gradually created markets for inputs and outputs of certain goods and reduced its control in urban services. Finally, enterprise managers were required to behave according to the market rules after the government introduced mechanisms that emphasized competition. These include, for example, the introduction of the bankruptcy law and the management contract system, as well as the abolition of the guaranteed bailout.[5]

The reform measures introduced in the industrial sector affected urban residents, both workers and managers, in two ways. First, both workers and managers welcomed the opportunity to share enterprises' profits. The bonus system was introduced to help managers reward better work performance. The system, however, was found to be ineffective in the link between individual worker performance and material rewards because of the coalition established between workers and managers (World Bank, 1990). The coalition refers to a condition that, on the one hand, workers were able to arrange the rotation of bonuses with one another, and on the other hand, managers would like to satisfy workers' demand in order to increase their own wages and benefits.

Next, the reform provided managers the power to punish workers who show such work problems as absenteeism, tardiness, low quality, and wasted materials. The manager's power to dismiss workers, however, was still limited because of the absence of a labor market. Workers were able to unite to resist the manager's power. The conflict between managers and workers was also related to the situation when the managers occasionally employed temporary workers to fulfill the demand work. This conflict may cause some serious labor problems if different wages and benefits are arranged for temporary workers.

In sum, the life of urban residents changed significantly during the reform years. The urban society in the late Mao's era was relatively homogenous, made up of a great mass of wage workers in well-protected state or quasi-state sectors. The industrial reforms have transformed the past stable and equatable work environment to a new unstable and competitive work situation. Some workers have left their government jobs either to work for private, joint-venture companies or to start their own business. A few of them have been very successful and became a new class of private entrepreneurs (Young, 1994). The success of several state-owned enterprises also gave rise to a growing number of rich enterprise managers. Both successful private entrepreneurs and enterprise managers became a new rich class in the urban area. The income gap between the general public and the new rich class has also increased, even though the gap is smaller than that in the rural area.[6]

CHANGES IN SOCIAL MOBILITY

In addition to the changes within China's rural and urban areas, the post-Mao reforms have also brought a major change regarding the connection between the two areas. The change is especially related to the large and increasing numbers of people moving from the rural to the urban areas, that is, to the rural-to-urban migration. The increase of the rural-urban mobility is related to several factors (Chan, 1996: Li, 1992; Wu, 1994). First, the dramatic rise in productivity in the countryside has made tens of millions of rural laborers redundant. Second, the high growth of industrial and commercial activities in the urban areas has created many job opportunities for rural peasants. Moreover, the increase in mobility also resulted from the changes in the government's policy toward migration. The economic reforms have weakened much of the traditional administrative control of social and economic changes (i.e., the *hukou* system; the street committee) for the purpose of promoting economic growth. Relaxation of migration and employment controls were officially recognized in 1983 in some provinces and later extended to nationwide in 1985 (Solinger, 1985; *People's Daily*, 1985).[7] The system was further eroded by Deng Xiaoping's 1992 summons to unbridled economic growth. That call mobilized an army of nearly 100 million migrant laborers pouring into the cities in search of work.

The result of this removal of traditional control mechanisms is that in the present Chinese society, there are an estimated 100-150 million people on the move at any time (Ferdinand, 1996). The "floating population" refers to people staying in places for which they do not have permanent household registration status, which include people hunting for jobs, away on official business, visiting relatives, on holiday, and the like (Li, 1994: 65-72; Solinger, 1995: 127-146). In addition, the situation of the rural to urban migration includes both intraprovincial and interprovincial moves. While the former refers to individuals moving from rural to urban areas within the same province, the latter has to do with individuals moving from inland provinces to the cities in the coastal provinces.

The migrant workers have had both a positive and negative impact on China's economy (Gilley, 1996; Kuhn & Kaye, 1994). On the positive side, the migrant workers are the lifeblood of China's economic boom. The workers contributed to the construction work in major cities and provided baby-sitting and house cleaning for urbanites, which in turn allowed city dwellers to do extra jobs in the industrial and professional workforce. The migrants' incomes are usually much lower than what a duly registered city-dweller gets paid but more than twice the earnings of their counterparts back home. Thus, the migrants actually provide a bridge between the rich cities and the poor hinterland because their remittances allow relatives at home to improve their standard of living. In addition, after many years of hard work in the city, many migrants take their savings back home to set up small businesses and create much-needed jobs in the rural villages.

On the negative side, it is very common that not all the migrants can find some kind of employment. Some of them turn to trading to make ends meet. Some estimates suggest that 60 percent of all street markets in China are run by migrants or vagrants (Ferdinand, 1996). Especially, migrants tend to group themselves into ad hoc ghettoes according to their place of origin and profession to provide mutual support and assistance. One example of these groups is "Zhejiang village" in Beijing. Most of its residents come from southern Zhejiang province and concentrate in the garment trades. Moreover, an estimate 10 to 30 percent of the migrants get dragged into the spreading urban criminal underworld (Kuhn & Kaye, 1994: 27). Its activities include crimes such as prostitution, illicit trading of foreign currencies and state-controlled commodities, producing fake products, and drug trafficking and robbery.

The relationship between urban residents and migrants has worsened. The urban residents blame the migrants for a host of ills, such as overstretched city services and rising crime. The migrants, on the other hand, feel unfairly or unequally treated by the natives of the cities. They complain that the established residents look down on them and discriminate against them. For example, the migrants are not allowed to buy property in the cities or send their children to city schools.

In sum, the increasing migration from China's rural areas to urban areas have fundamentally changed the traditionally separated rural and urban societies. The migrants, on the one hand, have provided needed human resources for most of the low-level jobs in the urban areas and mitigated the income gap between rural and urban areas. The migrants, on the other hand, have also brought new problems of crime and unhealthy economic activities. The control of the floating population has become increasingly difficult because of the collapse of the traditional administrative control system. The floating population may contribute to short-term economic prosperity at the expense of long-term social and political stability.

CHANGES IN INDIVIDUAL AND SOCIAL IDEOLOGY

The post-Mao reforms have caused many changes not only in the structural aspect of Chinese society but also in the ideological and attitudinal aspect of the society. The ideological and attitudinal changes include the demising role of the state in guiding daily life of the Chinese people, the rising materialism in the Chinese society, and the increasing perception of social inequality among most of the Chinese people (Ferdinand, 1996; Lieberthal, 1995; Shih, 1995). The outcome of these interrelated ideological changes have also had major impacts on Chinese society.

First, with regard to the role of the state, Chinese government no longer provides a moral compass for the general population. During the reform years, many traditional nonstate sources of moral authority have emerged in Chinese society. For example, there has been a resurgence of traditional religions such as Buddhism, Daoism, and Christianity. Unlike Mao's society, official political ideology has become increasingly irrelevant as a source for the future direction of society. The socialist norm of collective interests has been replaced by concern for self-interest and the importance of individualism.

The increased interest in individualism is especially important to Chinese society. In both traditional and socialist China, the rights and autonomy of individuals have been constantly denied by the state in order to maximize the benefit of the group and the government (Pye, 1991). During the post-Mao reform years, it has been noticed that many artistic and intellectual creative works (e.g., films) were produced for greater individual self-expression. In addition, it has been noticed that individuals are increasingly shaping their own identities less in terms of their family or *danwei* and more in terms of broad strata in society, such as workers, migrants, students, and intellectuals (Pye, 1991: 464-465).

Next, along with the improvement of economic conditions, the post-Mao society also witnessed the rise of materialism and commercialism. In Mao's era, the leaders emphasized plain living and criticized anyone who pursued personal gain. To promote economic development, the post-Mao leaders used material incentives to spur greater effort. They claimed that to be rich is glorious and that spending on consumer goods is good for the economy. This emphasis on material incentives occurred at the same time as the Chinese society experienced the decline of the traditional Confucian value system and the loss of confidence and interest in the socialist norms of collective interest.

The rise of commercialism and the concern for business interests have affected not only the general public but also many government agencies. For the general public, it was noticed that many people left their stable government jobs and jumped into the sea of commerce to make money. The increased interest in making money among the general public was also evident in daily life where many basic services were not undertaken unless additional fees were provided. Many government agencies were doing their best to become involved in business activities to enrich themselves. For example, it is recognized that even the People's Liberation Army (PLA) has been involved in various business activities (e.g., dealings in arms, hotels, and traditional Chinese medicine) to supplement the official defense budget. The PLA's business activities have resulted in some negative problems, including both its internal control (e.g., corruption and conflict between units in different regions) and its external relations with civilian officials (e.g., disputes about the PLA's control of local land and resources as well as receiving special treatments such as tax breaks)(Bickford, 1994).

One of the major problems of the material-oriented drive is that not everyone has the knowledge and skills as well as the opportunity to make money and become rich. For example, the Chinese intellectuals believe that market opportunities are not available to them. Unlike government and party officials, most intellectuals do not have the power that would provide opportunities for them to make additional income (i.e., corruption). Unlike state workers, intellectuals receive a fixed salary and have little chance to earn bonuses on the job. They feel frustrated about the fact that many street vendors earn more money than do professors at leading universities. Similarly, with limited education and experience, a number of young people will resort to illegal means to make money. Thus, the emphasis on materialism in the society has also resulted in an increase in illegal activities among China's young people.

Finally, despite many improvements in people's standard of living, many Chinese people have perceived an increase in social inequality among them (Lieberthal, 1995: 308-309; White, 1991: 16). The unequal feeling is related to not only the income gap between the rich and the poor but also the general feeling of falling behind the advance of others. Many people expressed dissatisfaction over their personal status. They felt that too many others are acquiring wealth they do not deserve. The feeling of social inequality is easy to understand because of the homogeneous and egalitarian nature of Mao's society. The consequences of the inequality perceptions are a general lack of empathy for other groups and an increase of social hostilities and conflict. For example, the urban residents who frequently suffered the effects of food-price inflation resented the fact that certain elements of the peasantry are better off than they are. Especially, they showed negative attitudes toward migrants and blamed them for the increase in crime and the deterioration of their quality of life.

In sum, the reforms have resulted in major changes in China's individual and social ideology. The Chinese people today have no interest in the official political ideology, and the government is in no position to provide any moral and value guidance. Motivated by material incentives and business interests, most of the Chinese people are concerned about individual wealth and want to make money and become rich as soon as possible. In addition to the increasing income gap between the rich and the poor, many Chinese perceive various inequalities arising from the reforms, which have given rise to social hostilities and conflict.

CHANGES IN SOCIAL CONTROL AND STABILITY

The success of the economic reforms has made Chinese society more complex and fluid. The complexity refers to the structural and attitudinal changes in both rural and urban areas, while the fluidity has to do with the increased mobility between the rural and urban areas as well as between the interior and coastal regions. In addition, the process of the social changes has also caused a redistribution of social power from the state and toward individuals, households, and groups (White, 1991).

The increases in social complexity and fluidity as well as the distribution of social-economic power have resulted in problems of social control. Before the reform years, the Chinese Communist Party controlled the country (the government and the society) through various party and administrative mechanisms (e.g., the registration system, the street committee). In addition to their production function, for example, work units (*danwei*) also performed many police functions such as disciplining employees convicted of crimes. In both rural and urban areas, Party cadres supervised communes and work units with regard to the control and implementation of official Party policies and ideologies. The Party-controlled system worked well as long as there were no political struggles within the Party.

The problems of social control occurred during the process of economic reforms because many of the past control mechanisms have been removed for the purpose of increasing incentives and productivity. The control problems became a serious policy issue also, because of the changes in social mobility and changes in individual and social ideologies. People are more free in both their attitudes and their behaviors with regard to almost every aspect of life (except the political activities after the Tiananmen Incident). The control problems were further intensified by nonexistent or weak new control mechanisms. One example of the problem of social control is that the state has lost its control over society in China's single-child population policy. After the success of economic reforms, the peasants' households have the ability to resist state pressure and avoid or adjust to the related penalties (Croll, 1991). The outcome of this problem is that the Chinese population passed the 1.2 billion mark in early 1995, five years earlier than the date of 2000, which the government laid down in the early 1980s (Ferdinand, 1996).

The problems of social control were also evident in the rise of crime rates (e.g., murders, robberies, kidnappings, and drug trafficking) and other indicators of social life (e.g., divorce rates, suicides) in the Chinese society.[8] For example, as researchers (Ferdinand, 1996; Myers, 1989; Zafanoli, 1985) noticed, many of the increasing crimes were related to economic activities (e.g., more than 600,000 between 1982 and 1992), occurred in urban areas (about 40 percent of crime throughout the country), and committed by those migrants who were unable to find jobs in the urban areas (e.g., 80 percent of all criminal offences in Beijing in the early 1990s) (Ferdinand, 1996: 484).

In addition, some types of crimes have appeared in the Chinese society since the beginning of economic reforms. For example, drug-related crimes (drug-trafficking, -taking, and -planting) have grown rapidly since 1980, with the reopening of the border trade with Burma and the increasing trade with Hong Kong and Macao (Wang, 1993; Hong, 1995). In 1983, the Public Security Bureau only arrested 10 people for drug-related crimes and seized only 5 grams of drugs for the whole country. By 1993, officials cracked 26,000 drug-related cases, seizing 4,400 kilograms of heroin and 3,300 kilograms of opium (*Beijing Review*, 1994). Similarly, prostitution has also increased sharply. Between 1982 and 1992, more than 860,000 people were arrested for involvement in prostitution or committing indecent acts. A consequence of the increase in prostitution has been an increase in venereal disease, with an increase from only 3 people registered being infected with it in 1977 to more than 700,000 people in 1992 (Ferdinand, 1996: 485). Especially, China has also witnessed a rise in crimes committed by Chinese gangs. In 1993, officials crushed 150,000 domestic criminal gangs, involving 570,000 offenders (*Beijing Review*, 1994).

Another serious problem related to social control is the increasing prevalence of official corruption.[9] In 1994, for example, officials reported more than 95,000 cases of corruption and recovered up to 1.7 billion yuan (*Beijing Review*, 1995a). Especially, the level of official corruption has also risen, from the county and the provincial to the national level. For example, in spring 1995, the anticorruption movement reached the Party's highest levels with the removal of Chen Xitong, who was a member of the Politburo and the former Beijing Communist Party Chief (Ferdinand, 1996; Huus, 1995). Moreover, it was noticed that a growing number of corruption cases involved offenders from judicial and law-enforcement departments (*Beijing Review*, 1995b). Today, some Chinese feel that cops and robbers are of the same tribe (Kuhn, 1994a).

To deal with the problems of social control and stability, the Chinese leaders have continuously emphasized the importance of maintaining law and public order to ensure a better social environment for economic development. They urged that local Party and government officials work together with judicial departments to double their efforts to crack down on crimes. With regard to corruption, the leaders have enacted ethical codes for government officials and have actively prosecuted corruption cases. Without an independent legal and supervisory system, however, the overall effect of the government's campaign against crimes and corruption has been relatively limited.

CHANGES IN THE LEGAL SYSTEM

During the years of economic reforms, the Chinese government has also gradually reformed its legal system to provide needed institutional support for the economic development. One of the major supporters for reforming China's legal system was Deng Xiaoping, the reform leader. As a victim in the heyday of lawlessness (i.e., the Cultural Revolution), Deng (1984) openly criticized the traditional legal system as incomplete and changed whenever the leadership changed or the leaders changed their views. Emphasizing the importance of strengthening the legal system, Deng argued that socialist democracy and the socialist legal system are inseparable. That is, the socialist legal system should be based on socialist democracy and should promote and protect socialist democracy.

In his study of China's post-Mao legal system, Lo (1992: 654) identified five major principles of Deng's legal system: (1) there must be laws for people to follow; (2) the laws must be observed; (3) lawbreakers must be dealt with accordingly; (4) law enforcement must be strict; and (5) all persons are equal before the law. Especially, Deng (1984) pointed out the importance of the implementation of the law and suggested three criteria for evaluating law and the legal system: (1) its ability to foster improvements in people's material lives; (2) its ability to foster spiritual civilization in the sociocultural milieu; and (3) its capacity to promote democracy in political reform.

In response to Deng's call, the Chinese government has initiated a comprehensive and system-wide reform measure to build a new legal system. Following are the major reform activities that have been developed: (1) The massive legislative effort to cover major substantive law-criminal, civil, economic, and administrative (e.g., the promulgation of the Decision on Imposing Severe Punishment on Crimes Disrupting the Financial Order, the Law on Commercial Banks, the Insurance Law, the Education Law, and the amended Law on the Prevention and Treatment of Air Pollution in 1995). (2) The restoration and elaboration of law-related institutions such as the hierarchy of courts, arbitral tribunals and mediation committees, and the Ministry of Justice. (3) The restoration of a system of professional legal education, including a growing number of specialized law schools, a large number of law faculties within universities, an increasing number of law students and graduates, and a few more specialized institutes as centers for legal research. (4) An unprecedented campaign program of legal education covering primary and secondary schools as well as general propaganda work for the population at large. (5) Support of publishing a growing number of books and pamphlets, journals, legal newspapers and comments on new statutes, new textbooks, case reports, and procedural manuals. (6) The establishment of broad exchange relationships between Chinese and foreign law schools (e.g., the U.S.) to learn effective legislative techniques, lawyering skills, and law-teaching methods (Dicks, 1989; Edwards, 1984; Huang, 1996).[10]

Despite its comprehensive and sophisticated changes, the new legal system has failed to address one fundamental issue that significantly affects China's social and political system, that is the relationship between the law and the Party (Lo, 1992). Before the reform years, the Party dominated and controlled every aspect of Chinese society, including the law. Party policy was described as the soul of the people's democratic legal system, and the Party had a status higher than law. Specifically, during Mao's era, the law came in the person of Mao Zedong and later Mao's Little Red Book. Since 1978, the superior position of the Party over the law has shown some changes as Deng emphasized the highest authority of the law. But, in his Four Cardinal Principles, Deng still stressed the position of leadership of the Party. In fact, the phrase "leadership of the Party" was later inserted into the Preamble of China's 1982 Constitution. In other words, the highest law of the land was formally subordinated to a political party.

The relationship between the Party and the law was directly tested during the 1989 Tiananmen incident. From a legal point of view, there were several questionable issues related to the authority's action (Dicks, 1989; Lo, 1992). For example, people challenged the legality of charging students not merely as disrupters the socialist system but as counterrevolutionaries. In addition, the subsequent arrests and trials of the dissidents also showed the political influence of the procedural aspects of the criminal law. In other words, the Tiananmen incident revealed not only that the legal system cannot offer legal protection to those exercising their democratic rights but also that the Party continued its dominance over the law and the society.

The dominance of the Party over the law is also evidenced in the fact that the Party treats the law as a tool to enforce its own agenda. In practice, it is noticed that Chinese judges report to district Party politicians and law committees that routinely review and discuss major cases before they come to court. Judges become mere servants of the Party's will. In addition, Chinese judges follow a political, not an academic or professional, path to the bench because they generally start out as court clerks and are gradually promoted to assistant judges and to full judges if they prove willing to carry out Party orders. Thus, Chinese judges generally fail to meet a lawyer's qualifications because more than half of them are demobilized soldiers and officers (Forney, 1996).

Finally, it is also important to indicate some difficulties in developing a law-based society in China (Ferdinand, 1996: 488-490). First, there has been a lack of a developed legal tradition in China. The traditional Chinese value system emphasizes not the legal approach but the social norm and moral approach for resolving individual and social conflicts. Also, because of the experience of the political struggles during Mao's years, most Chinese people are still reluctant to file lawsuits against the authorities and governments for violations of civil or property rights. In addition, despite the government's efforts to build a new legal system, there is still a big mismatch between the needed legal infrastructure (e.g., formulating, writing, and approving new laws; training new lawyers; and establishing law firms) and the increasing pressures for a law-based regulation of society. In other words, in the near future, it is possible that the Chinese government will continue to rely upon harsh punishments and sometimes arbitrary justice to maintain social order (Ferdinand, 1996).

DISCUSSION AND CONCLUSION

The present analysis of the impact of the post-Mao economic reforms on China's state-society relations clearly reveals that the economic reforms indeed have brought many fundamental changes in China's society. Reform measures such as decentralization from the central to local governments, the contract responsibility system, and the separation of government administration and enterprise management have certainly changed the lives of peasants in the rural areas as well as the lives of workers and managers in the urban areas.

In the rural areas, the peasants have been liberalized by the reform measures because they are now allowed to make their own decisions about the production, management, and distribution of their agricultural activities. Cooperating with their local governments, some of the peasants have been involved in the development of TVEs and have increased their overall incomes. Similarly, workers and managers in the urban areas have also been affected by the reform measures and worked closely with each other to obtain additional bonuses and benefits from their work units. Again, some of them left their government jobs and worked for the growing private or joint-venture sector. Based on their relationship with the authorities, a few of them also started their own companies and were involved in domestic or international business activities. All of these changes indicate that the economic reforms have changed Chinese society by gradually reducing the size of directly state controlled economic activities on the one hand and increasing the size of some private-oriented market activities on the other.

While economic reforms have brought prosperity in the Chinese society, the increased resources and incomes, however, have not been fairly distributed among the Chinese people. The income gap between the new rich class and the general public has risen in both the rural and the urban areas. Influenced by the new material incentives, the general public is now using all kinds of methods, officially or unofficially, to make money and become rich (i.e., to become rich is glorious). Some jealous and negative attitudes have developed among those who feel they are falling behind because of a lack of relationships or opportunities. For some Chinese, this perception of inequality is especially difficult to accept because they were used to the past state-controlled system, which provided a poor but equitable environment.

To promote development, the post-Mao reform leaders have also removed the past monitoring and control system (i.e., the household registration system) and allowed Chinese people to move freely from the countryside to the city and from one province to another. While it is good for business activities, the free mobility situation has resulted in some social problems in Chinese society. Especially, among cities in the coastal areas, a large number of peasants have moved from their country homes to the city streets to find jobs and to make money. Despite the fact that they provide a cheap labor force, these new migrants also have caused additional problems and burdens for the city government in terms of social services and public safety.

Gradually, the relationship between the urban residents and the migrants has become worse, and conflict between the two has increased.

The rise of the material-oriented incentives and the decrease in the control system have resulted in an increase of crimes in the society. Being attracted by the luxurious Western lifestyle, some Chinese people, especially young men and women, became involved in crime activities because of their lack of knowledge, skills, and experience for well-paid formal jobs. The crime rate has increased, and the crime types have extended from theft and robbery to gang-related organized crimes such as prostitution and drug-trafficking. Making things worse are the increasing cases of official corruption, especially corruption among judicial and law enforcement agencies.

To deal with the increased social conflict and crimes, it is important for the Chinese government to control the society based on a modern legal system. In other words, if the Chinese society becomes more market-oriented, it is natural for the Chinese government to manage the society according to a well-established legal system, that is characterized as impartial and impersonal. Under this system, the law applies equally to all without exception, including the government and the Party. Indeed, the Chinese government has developed a new legal system and promulgated many laws and regulations in order to support the socialist market economy. Despite its comprehensive nature and rapid growth, the legal system developed during the economic reform years has failed to clarify the relationship between the law and the Party. After the experience of the Tiananmen incident, it is clear that in Chinese society, the Party still dominates and controls the law.

The forgoing analysis of the changes in China's state-society relations suggests an important role of the Party in the process of change. That is, in the process of decreasing state power and increasing individual and group activities in the society, the Chinese Communist Party still controls both the state and the society as well as the interaction between the two.

Despite its control over the state and the society, the Party itself has also experienced some changes during the process of economic reforms. In addition to the issue of corruption among its members, the Party has recently faced two major challenging problems (Ferdinand, 1996: 486-488). The first is the declining importance of ideology as a guide to action among Party members. Despite the official emphasis on the Four Principles, there has been a lack of commitment among Party members to the socialist ideology. Closely related to the ideological problem, the second challenging issue has been the increasing diversity of views and activities within the Party. For example, one of the vital signs of independent activities was a surprisingly low support for cabinet nominees and government bills at the National People's Congress in March 1995 (Kaye, 1995b). In the first instance, 36 percent of the deputies voted against the appointment of Jiang Chunyun as vice premier; in the second, 33 percent refused to support a new central-bank law. The consequence of the lack of ideological commitment and increasingly democratic activities is that the central Party leadership is no longer capable of providing sole direction for reforms or of ensuring unified, disciplined implementation of its decisions.

In sum, there is no question that Chinese society under the economic reforms has changed dramatically, from a dull-homogeneous society to an energetic and complex society characterized by different kinds of views and actions. Chinese society has become more complex in terms of both structure and attitudes as well as more fluid and dynamic in terms of both horizontal and vertical mobility. Chinese life has also changed greatly as individuals enjoy more freedom in terms of their work and leisure activities and their knowledge and information about the society and the world. On the other hand, the increased complexity and freedom have resulted in the problem of social control and stability because of the decline of the traditional control mechanisms and the lack of an effective new control system during this transition period.

The consequences of the changing state-society relations are critical to the future development of China. With regard to the impact of the changes, it is possible that some kind of social-disorder problems will continue to exist in Chinese society in the near future. It is unlikely that we will see changes overnight in the Chinese state such as those that occurred in former socialist countries in Eastern Europe and the Soviet Union. The key issue lies in the role of the Party. It is important for the Party to arrange and develop some kind of mechanisms to resolve conflicts between different faction groups, between the central and the local governments, between the coastal and the interior regions, and between the new rich class and the poor people. It is also necessary for the Party to gradually adjust its role in the society and to distinguish its functions and activities from those of the government.

NOTES

1. The following discussions of the current study of state-society relations are based on articles by Perry (1994) and Harding (1994).

2. For more information about state-society relations before the reform years, see Lieberthal (1995: 292-313, Chapter 11).

3. For more information about policy changes in rural society, see the discussion of the rural and agricultural reforms presented in Chapter 3.

4. Factors that contributed to the rapid growth of the rural industry include, for example, low taxes, high profits, available capital, and organizational diversity. For more information see Naughton (1995a: 149-157) and Byrd and Lin (1990, especially the chapter by Du Haiyan regarding causes of rapid rural industrial development).

5. For more information about the industrial reforms, see the discussion of the urban and industrial reforms presented in Chapter 3.

6. For the comparison of income gaps between the rural and the urban areas, see the analysis presented in Chapter 5.

7. For more information about changes in China's ***hukou*** system, see Chan (1996), Ferdinand (1996), and Wu (1994).

8. The issue of increasing crime rates was also discussed in Chapter 4 regarding some problems associated with economic reforms.

9. For more information on the corruption issue, see the discussion of reform problems in Chapter 4 and bureaucratic corruption in Chapter 6 as well as other studies such as: Liu (1983), Ma (1989), Rocca (1992), Root (1996), and Sands (1990).

10. For detailed information about the background and development of China's new legal system, see Dicks (1989), Edwards (1984), and Lo (1992).

CHAPTER 8

Conclusion: Lessons of Economic Reforms

China's post-Mao economic reforms have approached the second decade. To promote growth and development, the post-Mao Chinese leaders have implemented several reform policies and programs since the Third Plenary Session of the Eleventh Communist Party Central Committee in December 1978. These policies and programs have generated rapid and sustained economic growth, improved people's income and living standards, transformed the country's economy from a central-planning-command to a market-oriented system, and changed almost every other aspect of the Chinese society. The scope and impact of the economic reforms are indeed comprehensive and extensive.

As stated in the introductory chapter, this book was designed to examine the experience of China's post-Mao economic reforms and major issues associated with the reforms. Adopting the title of managing economic reform, the book focused on the role of the Chinese government in the process of economic development and reform. The introductory chapter reviewed previous research on the relationship between government and economic development and identified major public policies and key conditions associated with the success of development and reform. The experience of China's development and reform were explained in the next three chapters (Chapters 2, 3, and 4) of the book. These three chapters provided an evaluation of China's past development record, the stages and measures of post-Mao economic reforms, and the achievements and problems of the economic reforms. The following three chapters (Chapters 5, 6, and 7) focused on analyzing three major issues that emerged during the process of the reforms. The three chapters examined changes and issues in China's regional development, administrative reform, and state-society relations. Both the experience and issues of China's economic reforms are closely related to the development policies and critical conditions identified in the literature of managing economic development and reform.

The purpose of this conclusion chapter is to provide a retrospective and prospective assessment of China's post-Mao reform experience and development. The chapter begins with a summary of the process and outcome of economic reforms. It then provides a detailed analysis of major lessons and characteristics that are associated with the Chinese reforms. Finally, the chapter ends with discussions about the future development of economic reforms.

SUMMARY OF CHINA'S REFORM EXPERIENCE AND ISSUES

Economic development has been one of the major public policies in many developed, developing, and postsocialist countries. For the developed countries, economic development is directly related to the increase of their economic growth in some output and income measures. For the developing and the postsocialist countries, economic development means not only economic growth but also changes in their past political, social, and economic structures. In other words, economic development in these countries involves some reform policies and activities that require the involvement of government in the process of the development.

Issues in Managing Economic Development

The recent literature of economic development (Caporaso, 1982; Haggard & Webb, 1993; Rondinelli & Montgomery, 1990; Stern, 1991; Summers & Thomas, 1993) has in general supported the important and leading role of the government in economic growth and development. The functions of government provided in economic development include (1) economic management to promote growth, distribute incomes, and stabilize the economy; (2) industry and social regulation to balance growth and growth-related problems (e.g., pollution and labor disputes); and (3) general protection of the country's national security and social stability.

To achieve the goal of economic development, government needs to successfully formulate and implement such public policies as (1) economic growth to allocate economic resources and expand productive activities; (2) social equity to reduce various inequalities associated with economic growth; (3) international transaction to attract foreign investment and promote trade; and (4) public management to create and maintain an effective government structure and procedures to provide public services and implement policies.

Moreover, studies on the development experience of those successful developing countries have identified several important factors contributing to the development: (1) the importance of having a stable political and social environment; (2) the adoption of a flexible, pragmatic, and longitudinal development approach; (3) the appropriate integration of government and market activities (e.g., decentralizing and privatizing some government activities); and (4) the development of sound public and private institutions and infrastructures.

The Process of China's Economic Reforms

The review of China's development during Mao's years revealed some system and policy problems that resulted in the disappointing economic performance. For example, Chinese leaders adopted a central-planning economic system and a Soviet development model. Guided by the five-year national plan, the central system controlled all social resources through the nationalizing process and arranged resources distribution through different levels of government administration (vertical control) (Prybyla, 1982). The system limited the input from the local governments and restricted private economic activities. The Soviet development model emphasized a high rate of investment, especially in the heavy industry and military, and neglected investment in agricultural and consumer goods industries.

In addition to system problems, Chinese development in the past also suffered policy errors that were related to several political power struggles. The struggle and change between the two lines (Mao's revolutionary policy and non-Mao's revisionary policy) severely interrupted the process and effectiveness of national plans. Especially, the implementation of Mao's development ideas in several political movements (e.g., the Three-Anti movement and the Cultural Revolution) resulted in major negative effects on China's economic performance. The outcome of China's past development were inconsistent and below-the-target growth rates, low productivity in both agricultural and industrial sectors, chronic shortage of wanted goods, and low morale and incentives among peasants and workers. China in the late 1970s was basically a low-income country with an official per-capita gross national product of 375 yuan (about $250) in 1978. China's poor development and disappointing performance were especially noticeable when comparing them with the growth and development records of neighboring countries and regions (Japan, South Korea, Singapore, Hong Kong, and Taiwan).

To promote China's modernization and development, the post-Mao Chinese leaders have gradually formulated and implemented several policies and programs since 1978. The Third Plenum of the Eleventh Communist Party Central Committee in December 1978 made several policy decisions that support Deng Xiaoping's reform ideologies and programs. Emphasizing the philosophy of seeking truth from facts, the post-Mao leaders began their reforms first in China's rural-agricultural area because of the agricultural stagnation problem. The stagnation problem was caused by the government's industrial-oriented policy under the Soviet development model and by the peasants' lack of incentives under the people's commune system. To promote agricultural production, the reform leaders introduced both policy and institutional changes in China's rural, agricultural sector. The policy and institutional changes included, for example, opening up the labor and commodity market in rural areas, raising procurement prices of agricultural products, decentralizing production rights to local collectives, and gradually implementing the household responsibility system.

The success of the agricultural reforms provided the momentum for the leaders to expand reform policies and programs to China's urban, industrial area in their decision on reform of the economic structure in October 1984. The industrial reforms emphasized in the earlier time consisted of, for example, an expansion of enterprise autonomy (the decentralization of decision-making power to enterprise managers, the separation between government administration and enterprise management), the reduction of government allocations, the introduction of markets for the input and output of certain goods, the development of incentives and competition in enterprise management, and especially the reform of China's price system (the dual-price system).

The movement of China's economic reforms slowed down during the period of 1989 to 1991. Despite the positive changes in agricultural and industrial output and structure, the reform policies also produced problems such as high inflation rates, overinvestment, budgetary deficits, and widespread corruption. These problems caused further disagreements between the conservatives and the reformers on the pace and depth of economic reforms within the Party leadership. The inflation crisis in 1988 and the Tiananmen Square incident in 1989 resulted in the change of leadership in economic management and the beginning of hard-line dominance of economic policy.

The reform movement was regenerated and accelerated in 1992 after Deng Xiaoping's call for accelerating reform and opening-up policies in his trip to South China. The reform policies and programs emphasized in the 1990s have not only continued the reform activities in the rural, agricultural and urban, industrial areas but also focused on changing China's macroeconomic structures. The changes and proposals introduced in the macroeconomic structures have included, for example, reforming the exchange rate system, adjusting the fiscal system (the tax reform), reforming the banking system, emphasizing state-owned enterprises reform, reforming the social security system, and reforming the circulation system.

In addition to the agricultural and industrial reforms, Chinese leaders also emphasized the open-door policy in their reform movement. Unlike the traditional self-reliance development policy, the open-door policy was designed to encourage foreign investment, to import foreign technology, and to increase the integration of the Chinese economy into the international economy. Major policies and programs adopted in this area included, for example, increasing foreign trade and changing the foreign trade system, returning to the international development organizations (the World Bank and the IMF) and borrowing from these organizations, encouraging foreign investment (from joint ventures to wholly owned foreign-invested firms), and developing China's coastal areas (e.g., special economic zones).

Outcomes of the Economic Reforms

The evaluation of China's post-Mao economic reforms has revealed both positive and negative outcomes. On the positive side, the reforms have been very successful in generating rapid and sustained economic growth, increasing real income and living standards, improving output and structure of the agricultural and industrial sectors, and promoting foreign loans and investment. The reforms have gradually transformed China's economic system from a closed central-planning system to an open market-oriented system. The economic reforms have also had a profound impact on other aspects of Chinese society and reshaped the attitudes, expectations, and behavior of the Chinese people. Compared to the situation in Mao's years, Chinese society has become more open and commercialized, and the Chinese people have more freedom in their economic and social activities. Especially, all of the improvements and changes have been achieved peacefully without major political and social interruptions and uprisings. The Chinese reform achievements are outstanding even when compared to the reform experience of other transitional economies in Eastern Europe and the former Soviet Union.

Despite the overall success and positive records, China's economic reforms have also produced some negative outcomes in Chinese society. The negative outcomes include both economic and economic-related problems. The overheating economy has resulted in the rise of inflation and national deficits, the shortage of raw materials, and the inadequacy of the infrastructure. The change in economic and social structures has caused such problems as unemployment and a floating population, the imbalance of development between China's coastal and interior regions, and income inequalities between the urban and rural areas as well as between the few rich and the majority public. In addition, the economic reforms have also brought some economic-related problems such as the deterioration of the environment, the pervasiveness of corruption and crimes, and the unrest and dissatisfaction of China's minorities. Even without immediate and detrimental consequences or crises, the existence and expansion of these problems will certainly affect and challenge the future development of the reforms.

Challenge Issues in the Economic Reforms

With regard to the challenge problems, three major issues and changes were emphasized and analyzed in this book. The first issue has to do with China's regional development. The economic reforms have changed China's regional development policy from the traditional balanced approach to the new uneven approach. The new uneven development policy emphasized the importance of developing China's eastern, coastal region. The coastal preferential development policy has resulted in increasing economic differences between China's regions. The coastal region and provinces have grown faster than the interior region. Closely related to the differences of regional development, there have been increases of income gap (inequality) between people living in the coastal and in the interior regions as well as within the rural and urban societies. The differences in regional development may on the one hand promote the chance of economic integration within Greater China or may cause the political disintegration in China on the other.

The second issue related to China's future development is the reform of China's administrative (bureaucratic) system. China's traditional cadre system suffered from serious bureaucratic problems, such as unresponsiveness, lack of innovation and expertise, and inefficiency. Considering the bureaucratic problems impediments to economic development, Chinese leaders recognized that economic growth and modernization depend on a rational and efficient bureaucracy and that economic reforms and administrative reforms are inseparable. To assist economic reforms and development, Chinese leaders have developed and implemented several policy measures in their administrative system. Some key policies and programs are (1) the decentralization of decision-making powers to local economic and administrative units; (2) the separation of economic enterprises from administrative agencies and emphasis on enterprise autonomy and reform; (3) the establishment of a civil service system and adoption of the Provisional Regulations on State Civil Servants in 1993; (4) the simplification of government structures and functions (e.g., organizational rearrangements); and (5) the professionalization of public administration activities (including the establishment of the Chinese Public Administration Society in 1988 and the expansion of public administration education and training). The administrative reforms, however, have experienced such problems as the pervasiveness of bureaucratic corruption and the influence of the Party on the government.

The last challenge issue of state-society relations provided an evaluation of the impact of economic reforms on Chinese society in general. The evaluation especially focused on such areas as (1) changes in China's rural area (e.g., the liberalization of agricultural activities and the development of township and village enterprises); (2) changes in the urban area (e.g., the reduction of government activities, the increase of private commercial activities, and the emergence of a few rich managers and entrepreneurs); (3) changes in social mobility (e.g., the rural to urban migration and the problem of a floating population); (4) changes in individual and social ideology (e.g., the diminishing role of the state and official ideology, the rise of materialism, and the increased perception of inequality); (5) changes in social control and stability (e.g., the removal of the traditional control system, the lack or weakness of new control mechanisms, and the rise in crime rates); and (6) changes in China's legal system (e.g., the legislative effort to pass new laws, the restoration of law-related institutions, and the restoration of professional legal education). The changes in these areas have changed Chinese society from the past dull and homogeneous society to an energetic and complex society characterized by different kinds of views and actions. These changes have reduced the dominant role of the government in social activities and resulted in some problems of social disorder and unrest. The changes in China's state-society relations have not caused the collapse of communist regimes that occurred in former socialist countries in Eastern Europe and the Soviet Union.

In sum, based on the literature on economic development and reform, this book examined major management issues in China's post-Mao economic reforms. It is clear that the Chinese government has emphasized both economic growth (i.e., agricultural and industrial reforms) and international transaction policies (i.e., the open-door policy) during the reform process. Considering the importance of public management to economic development, the government has also introduced reform measures in China's traditional cadre system. The success of China's economic reforms, in terms of rapid economic growth and the rise in living standards, has provided evidence to support key factors and conditions of economic development, including a stable political and social environment, the pragmatic approach, and institutional development. The problems associated with Chinese reforms have also indicated the importance of reducing inequalities and controlling crime and corruption, which are emphasized in the development literature. The experience of China's post-Mao reforms certainly provides valuable lessons for policy makers and researchers who are interested in reforming their system to promote economic growth and development. The lessons of China's economic reforms are addressed in the next section.

LESSONS OF CHINA'S ECONOMIC REFORMS

The success of China's post-Mao economic reforms have attracted many researchers of economic development to identify characteristics and lessons of China's reforms (e.g., Chen, Jefferson & Singh, 1992; Rawski, 1995; Walder, 1995; White, 1995). The results of these studies, however, have been inconclusive and sometimes inconsistent with each other. For example, while some researchers (e.g., Chen, Jefferson & Singh, 1992) praised China's gradual and partial reforms as one of the major factors for the success of economic reforms, others (e.g., Prybyla, 1985, 1989) criticized these same reforms as a halfway approach and did not fundamentally resolve the problems of the past system.

Based on the literature on economic development and the analysis of the experience and issues of China's reforms, this book provides some major characteristics and lessons on China's economic reforms. The lessons consist of (1) the role of government-guided reform and development,(2) the nature of partial and gradual reforms, (3) the flexible and practical development approach, (4) the two-way development policy, (5) the strategy of decentralization and uneven development, (6) the kindred development model and Chinese social culture, (7) the contribution of a stable political and social environment, (8) the importance of administrative reform, (9) the balance of economic growth and social control, and (10) the need for monitoring and control mechanisms. These lessons are of course interrelated and represent both the achievements and problems of China's reforms.

The Role of Government-Guided Reform and Development

The first lesson of the Chinese economic development is the role of the Chinese government involved in the process of economic reforms and development. Two issues are important here. First, it should be noted that there is a close relationship between economic development and economic reforms. Recognizing fundamental problems of the past poor economic performance, China's development attempted not only to improve economic conditions (i.e., output, income, employment, and productivity) but also to change the country's economic structure from a central-planning system to a market-oriented system. In other words, China's post-Mao development is reform-oriented, and the motives and goals of the reforms are closely related to economic growth and development. Involving changes in almost every aspects of China's system, the reform-oriented development is considered more difficult and challenging than the past development experience in other developing countries.

Next, it is important to recognize the important role the Chinese government played in the process. Like all former communist countries, the Chinese government, especially the Chinese Communist Party, controls and dominates all the resources in China's society and all the activities in its people's lives. It is very natural that the government played a key role in initiating, formulating, and implementing all reform policies. As explained before, the Chinese government has never adopted the idea of the total elimination of government involvement in the economy or a democratic model of government like those of Western countries.

Similar to other East Asian countries, the Chinese government played a major role in guiding the country's economic reforms by incorporating their national planning with economic development policy (Huff, 1995; Park, 1990). But, differing from

China's previous planning experience, the post-Mao reformers promoted a revised role of government and separated the concept of ownership from the practice of management. The Chinese government has contributed to the success of reforms and development in terms of formulating and implementing economic growth, allowing the gradual development of market forces, promoting international economic transactions, helping facilitate fiscal stability, and providing a relatively safe and peaceful political and social environment for business and investment. The necessary and important role of government intervention in economic development and especially in economic transition has been recognized and accepted in recent studies of Chinese economic reforms (e.g., Nolan, 1994; Nolan & Ash, 1995; Yusuf, 1994).

The Nature of Partial and Gradual Reforms

One of the major characteristics of China's economic reform is its partial and gradual nature. The emphasis on partial and gradual reform in China is totally different from the adoption of shock therapy and mass privatization in economic reforms seen in Eastern Europe. Some researchers (e.g., Kornai, 1991; Prybyla, 1989; Wong, 1986) questioned the effectiveness of partial reform because of the incompatibility of market allocation with state ownership. They argued that transformation of the socialist economic system requires fundamental changes in institutions and ideas and that the partial reform brings some formerly suppressed disabilities into the open (e.g., inflation, income disparities) without the ability to master them (Prybyla, 1989).

Recognizing the difficulty of structural and system changes, the post-Mao leaders adopted a partial reform approach that has gradually adjusted China's economic system from a closed central-planning system to a more market-oriented system. The decision for the Chinese leaders to take a partial and gradual approach is based not on advice from Western economists but on China's past development experience. The leaders are aware of the painful experience that was related to Mao's big bang, revolutionary development policies (e.g., the Great Leap). They intentionally adopted the partial and gradual reform approach to reduce any risks and uncertainties that are associated with new reform ideas and policies.

The adoption of the contract responsibility system, the dual price system, and the special economic zones explained previously are some sample strategies in China's partial and gradual reforms. These strategies have helped the Chinese to gradually transform their collective-farming system to the individual household farming system, change their industrial enterprises from the total state control system to some joint ventures and independent private firms, reduce risks involved in the price reform, attract foreign investment, and open the Chinese market to the world. These strategies, however, have produced such problems as inefficiency and waste of resources because of incorrect sequences and delayed changes that are associated with partial reform (Fei & Reynolds, 1987; Prybyla, 1985).

The Flexible and Practical Development Approach

Closely related to the nature of partial and gradual reform, China's post-Mao economic reforms have also been described as flexible and practical in their development approach (e.g., Rawski, 1995; Walder, 1995). The flexible approach refers to the fact that there is no coherent or predetermined master blueprint for economic reforms and that China's post-Mao reforms have been criticized as having unsystematic and stop-and-go characteristics. The practical approach has to do with the pragmatism emphasized by the post-Mao reformers. The pragmatism philosophy is influenced by Deng Xiaoping's remarks about the cat and the mice (i.e., it does not matter what color the cat is as long as it catches the mice) and becomes the reform principle of "practice is the sole criterion of truth" (Pye, 1986; Solinger, 1981).

China's flexible and practical development approach is evidenced by a common pattern of policy development. Usually, a new policy or program will be tested first in selected local areas. After several years of experience, the policy or program will then be recommended and implemented nationwide based on the successful experience and record. This kind of policy development pattern was noticed in both the development of economic reform policies such as the contract-responsibility system and in the development of administrative reform policies such as the civil service system.

The adoption of the flexible and practical development approach again is based on the consideration of reducing risk, uncertainties, and negative effects associated with the new reform policies. The flexible approach, however, has resulted in some problems of widespread corruption and rise of cost because of unclear rules and fluid policy environment (Rawski, 1995). In other words, it is clear that by adopting the partial and gradual reforms and emphasizing the flexible and practical approach, Chinese leaders want to make sure about the effective and stable impact of any reform policies even at the expense of increased cost and inconveniences in the short run.

The Two-Way Development Policy

The fourth lesson of China's post-Mao economic reforms is the emphasis on a two-way development approach. The two-way development approach means that the reforms have simultaneously covered reform and development in both China's internal and external activities. As explained previously, Chinese leaders started the reforms by first emphasizing decentralizing activities in China's rural, agricultural sector (e.g., free market) and opening-up activities (e.g., the four special economic zones in Guandong and Fujian provinces) in China's open-door policy. While the open-door policy addressed China's external economic relationship, the agricultural reform and later the industrial and the macroeconomic structural reforms focused on China's internal economic conditions.

The two-way development approach is important for China's economic reforms because of the interaction between the internal and external markets. On the one hand, the foreign trade and investment generated from the open-door policy has been one of the major forces that promote the growth of agricultural and industrial sectors. On the other hand, the success of the agricultural and industrial reforms have resulted in the increase in agricultural and industrial products and the change of agricultural and industrial structure. The increase of the products and the change of the structure have promoted China's foreign trade, with more products exported to the foreign market and with foreign advanced industrial equipment and high-class consumer products imported to China's domestic market.

The adoption of the two-way development approach, especially the emphasis on the open-door policy, at the early stage of the reforms was certainly based on the reform leaders' consideration of economic development experience in China's neighboring countries and regions (e.g., Japan, South Korea, and Taiwan). Studies of economic development in East Asia (e.g., Kuznets, 1988) has identified one of the major factors that contribute to the success of economic development, that is, the use of export-oriented industries to promote and lead the domestic economic growth and development. Based on China's vast human resources and cheap labor cost, the Chinese government has followed a development pattern similar to that experienced in East Asian countries. The success of this development policy has also been related to the shift of production activities and the financial investment from China's neighboring countries and regions. For them, the opening up of China's market has provided a new frontier for both production and market because of the increase in government regulation and the rise of labor and land cost in their home societies.

The Strategy of Decentralization and Uneven-Development

Another important lesson in China's economic reforms has to do with the strategies of decentralization and uneven development. First, the decentralizing strategy has been emphasized in almost every aspects of China's economic reforms. Decentralization activities have been mentioned in China's agricultural, industrial, and macroeconomic structural reforms as well as in the changes in foreign trade policy, in regional development policy, and in China's administrative system. Unlike Mao's decentralization, the decentralization strategy in the post-Mao reforms means market decentralization, which has allowed local governments and producers to respond to their own market conditions and opportunities. During the reform years, local government units (both administrative and economic) have been very active in promoting economic growth-related activities. In fact, local officials' positive attitude toward and support of economic reform policies and programs has been considered one of the major factors contributing to China's successful development (Chen, Jefferson, & Singh, 1992; Liou, 1996; Yusuf, 1994; Waste, 1986).

Next, the post-Mao reformers have also accepted and emphasized an uneven development strategy. This uneven strategy represents a major change in China's regional development policy. The balanced development strategy emphasized in Mao's years attempted to balance regional development between coast and interior regions by providing a large portion of industrial development for the interior area. Recognizing the inefficiency problem of the earlier strategy, the reformers adopted the uneven-development strategy and allowed differential development among regions. The uneven-development strategy resulted in the dramatic increase of domestic and foreign investments in the coastal area.

Despite their positive contributions, both decentralization and uneven-development strategies have some negative effects. For example, the decentralization strategy has resulted in the increase of conflicts between China's central and local governments. The uneven-development strategy has caused the inequalities in China's regions and provinces and the rising income gap between the coastal and interior regions (Tsui, 1993; Yang, 1990). The combination of both decentralization and uneven development has caused an increase of localism among the rich regions, which may bring the possibility of China's disintegration.

The Kindred Development Model and Chinese Social Culture

One unique characteristic of China's post-Mao economic reforms and development is the important role of a kindred model developed during the reform process (Chen, Jefferson, & Singh, 1992). The kindred development model refers to the investment and contribution of overseas Chinese to the economic reforms. It has been noticed by many researchers (e.g., Ash & Kueh, 1993; Chang, 1995) that overseas Chinese, including Chinese in Hong Kong first and then Chinese in Taiwan, have been actively involved in China's economic development since the beginning of the open-door policy. The overseas Chinese contributed to China's development by promoting trade and direct foreign investment; transferring knowledge and skills on production, quality control, and logistics of exporting; and offering a model of the efficacy of the market (Chen, Jefferson & Singh, 1992; Yusuf, 1994; Whyte, 1995). It was estimated that investment by overseas Chinese (especially from Hong Kong and Taiwan) accounts for as much as 70 to 80 percent of China's total foreign direct investment (Tefft, 1994; Chang, 1995). The overseas Chinese enthusiastic attitude and participation in China's economic development is motivated not only by the profit incentive but also by deep patriotic emotions that are deeply rooted in Chinese culture.

Besides the kindred development model, the family patterns in Chinese traditional culture have also influenced economic development (Whyte, 1995). One of the major family patterns that affect economic development has been the rise of family firms in China's rural society during the reform years. The development of these family firms is closely related to the strong family localities that emphasized the traditional culture and survived in the pre-reform socialist experience. Whyte (1995: 1018-1019) suggested that a set of favorable conditions (e.g., the reform policies, a global economic situation) are important for the success of China's entrepreneurial familism and that the contributions of this family system are part of the explanation for China's recent economic success.

The Contribution of a Stable Political and Social Environment

As explained in the literature review of economic development, the importance of a stable political and social environment has been identified as one of the major factors contributing to the success of economic development. The experience of China's development provided evidence to support this argument from both negative and positive sides. On the negative side, the post-Mao reformers recognized that past political and class struggles emphasized in Mao's years disrupted the process of development and caused China's poor economic performance.

On the positive side, it has been noticed that the contribution of a peaceful and stable environment, both internal and external, led to China's post-Mao economic development. Internally, the reform leaders were very successful in building political consensus and support, among cadres and the public, about economic reforms at the beginning of the process. The leaders have been able to maintain that consensus and support during the entire period. Except for the 1989 Tiananmen Square incident, there have been no major political or social struggles and movements that resulted in social unrest. Major economic development policies and programs continued and even expanded after the Tiananmen Square incident.

Externally, the world economic environment has been stable since the beginning of China's development in the late 1970s. China has kept active political relationships with major developed countries and gained economic advantages from some of them (e.g., most favored nation status from the United States, continuous loans from the World Bank). The peaceful and stable social environment is especially important and attractive to overseas Chinese when they make decisions about their investment, trade, and touring activities. Except for a few incidents, the connection between China and Hong Kong as well as the informal relationship between China and Taiwan have progressed satisfactorily.

The Importance of Administrative Reforms

The examination of China's economic development has shown the importance of China's administrative reforms since the late 1970s. The reform measure of decentralization has been implemented not only in enterprise management but also in cadre management. The earlier reform measure of separation between economic enterprises and administrative agencies and the recent measure of reforming state-owned enterprises has changed the structure of China's administrative system.

The interest in economic development has also contributed to the emphasis on efficiency in China's public management. The reform measures about the improvement of the cadres' ability has resulted in the development of a civil service system in China. The new system emphasizes principles of scientific management and efficiency in issues related to personnel management (e.g., recruitment, performance appraisal, reward and discipline activities). The development of public administration association, education, and training has further added professionalism in China's administrative system. As indicated earlier, Chinese administrators, especially local administrators, have been one of the major factors that contribute to the success of economic reforms and development.

The importance of administrative reform is also evidenced in the existence of several negative issues that are related to economic reforms and development. The issues reviewed include, for example, administrative interference in enterprise management, price manipulation, and especially corrupt activities. To deal with these issues, the Chinese leaders have emphasized ethical standards for cadres' recruitment, evaluation, and promotion. In other words, the administrative reform emphasized not only the issue of efficiency but also the concern of ethics.

The Need for Monitoring and Control Mechanisms

The existence of negative issues in China's administrative and economic system suggests an important need for developing monitoring and control mechanisms. In addition to individual corrupt behavior, there have been some organization-wide problems (e.g., administrative interference and price manipulation) during the economic reform years. These problems stemmed from the economic and social transitions that are associated with the reforms. On the one hand, the reforms have removed or weakened some traditional monitoring and control mechanisms (e.g., the government's central planning mechanisms and the Party's control techniques). On the other hand, the reforms have not developed new control mechanisms or have not effectively implemented the established new mechanisms to monitor the problems.

As suggested by many researchers (e.g., Chen, Jefferson & Singh, 1992; Summers & Thomas, 1993), there is a need for institutional development to check and balance government interventions in an effective market economy. The institutional framework discussed include, for example, the emphasis on an autonomous banking system, the development of commercial and criminal law, especially rules governing property rights, the establishment of an independent legal system to enforce and interpret the law and rules, and an independent press to watch abusive officials and economic crimes.

Recognizing the importance of institutional support, Chinese leaders have emphasized many of these control mechanisms in their recent reforms of China's macroeconomic structures. These reforms, however, only focused on economic activities (e.g., banking reform) and did not cover social and political issues (e.g., political reform). Based on the experience of China's neighboring countries and regions, the leaders may need to address these issues in the near future after the economic conditions improve. One of the key issues is the role of the Chinese Communist Party in future development. That is, it is necessary and important to adjust the Party's role in the society and distinguish its activities from those of the government.

The Balance between Economic Growth and Social Development

Finally, the experience of China's post-Mao economic reforms has also indicated the importance of balancing economic growth and social development, one of the major issues in the economic development literature. As explained earlier, the reform strategies of decentralization and uneven development have contributed to the success of China's economic growth. These strategies, however, have also resulted in such negative effects as the confrontation between China's central and local governments, the increase of inequalities among China's regions, and the rise of an income gap within China's rural and urban societies. In addition, the success of economic growth has also been related to the deterioration of the quality of life in

Chinese society, including, for example, population increases, environmental pollution, labor disputes, bureaucratic corruption, and social crime and unrest.

It should be noted that the emergence of these problems during China's development is not a unique case. Similar issues and problems have also occurred during the process of economic development in other countries. For example, researchers (e.g., Pye, 1997) have noticed that the problem of corruption, emphasized and criticized by the public and officials, is also a major problem that relates to the process of economic development and democracy in China's neighboring countries and regions (e.g., Japan, South Korea, Taiwan). But, the problems and issues are especially challenging to Chinese policy makers because of China's past social and economic conditions. Under the traditional balanced-development model, for example, there were no major inequality issues between regions and provinces. Under control by the tight Party authority, there were relatively few cases of crime and social unrest (except during the time of political movement) and no official reports about these cases and problems (except for the purpose of political power struggles). Especially, people did not discuss these issues openly or challenge the authority for the problems.

Chinese leaders recognize the seriousness and consequences of these problems and have tried to deal with them. They have gradually abandoned several reform policies (e.g., the dual prices) that caused these problems and have developed new policies (e.g., the environment policy) that reduce the level of the old problems or prevent the occurrence of new ones. Again, the leaders emphasized the important role of the government (and the Party) in managing these issues and problems. They stressed the incorporation of the development of socialist culture and ideology into the overall plans of social and economic development. They argued against the position of seeking temporary economic development at the cost of the development of socialist culture and ideology (Li Peng, 1995).

THE FUTURE OF ECONOMIC REFORMS

Past development experience in China provides the basis for the discussion of the future development of China's economic reforms. As summarized in this chapter, the post-Mao economic reforms have been very successful in promoting economic growth, improving living standards, and transforming the economic structure and system. The economic reforms have also changed other aspects of individual and social values and activities, in both positive and negative ways. The success of China's economic reforms has been related to several important internal and external factors. Internal factors include reform strategies (e.g., the partial and gradual approach) and environmental factors (e.g., the support from the Chinese people and local officials, the stable political and social environment). External factors include the contribution of China's successful neighboring countries and regions (especially the overseas Chinese in Hong Kong and Taiwan) and the positive support from Western countries (e.g., the most favored nation status from the United States and continuous loans from the World Bank).

After reviewing the experience of China's economic reforms, two issues are important in the final analysis about the future development of the reforms. The first issue of interest focuses on China's political environment, which may significantly affect the future fate of the economic reforms. The second issue of interest has to do with future research on China's economic development and reform experience, which may contribute to not only our overall understanding of the Chinese experience but also the development of related theories and policies.

The Political Environment

The examination of China's post-Mao economic reforms in the previous chapters have briefly mentioned the contribution of political factors to the success of economic reforms and development. These include, for example, the political background of the reforms, the reformers' (especially Deng Xiaoping's) strategies to gain political power, the importance of a stable political environment without major power struggles in the Party, the incident at Tiananmen Square, the reaction of the Chinese leaders to the incident, and the changes in state-society relations.

While covering major political issues, the previous discussions of political issues, however, are inadequate in terms of understanding the overall development of Chinese politics during the reform years.[1] Many political issues that related to China's economic reforms and development were not analyzed in the present study, including, for example, the issue of China's political reforms and democratization (Goldman, 1994; Goodman, 1989; Lieberthal, 1984; Young, 1995), the relationship between national defense and economic development (Cheung, 1988), the political issues of greater China (Yahuda, 1993), the role and development of the Chinese People's Congresses (O'Brien, 1994), the political foundations of incremental reforms (Goldstein, 1995), the issue of China's threat (Roy, 1996), and the issue of succession politics (Bachman, 1996).

The issues of succession politics and the politics of greater China are especially important and worthy of further analyses because of several events that happened recently. First, the death of Deng Xiaoping in February 1997 indicated the beginning of China's development in the post-Deng era.[2] One of the immediate challenge issues for Chinese leaders is that of succession politics. The Chinese officials indicated that the transition of power from Deng to President Jiang Zemin, Deng's chosen successor, happened years ago and that Jiang has gathered up the reins of power in recent years. Most Chinese researchers believe that there will be no major changes of personnel, politics, or policy in the short term because of the leaders' concern for stability. In other words, Jiang and other members of the third-generation leadership (including for example, Premier Li Peng and Qiao Shi, the head of the People's National Congress) will continue to promote China's economic development on the one hand and preserve the country's one-party authoritarian rule on the other (Jiang, 1997).

Despite the official position, the issue of succession politics cannot be overlooked in the study of China's development. It is difficult to predict the future long-term development of China's leadership because of the past record of succession politics in China (and the Party) (Bachman, 1996). Most of the succession arrangements in the past have failed completely, including the arrangement of Liu

Shaoqi, Lin Biao, and Hua Guofeng during Mao's years. The rise of Deng Xiaoping to the ultimate power was based not on succession arrangements but on victory in the power struggles between Deng and Hua. Lacking the strong political background and power bases, Jiang may face challenges among the top Party leaders in the future if some difficult problems and events occur in Chinese society. Moreover, the succession issue in the future will certainly become more complicated than it used to be because of the changes in economic and social conditions that happened during the reform years.

Next, the political issue of greater China refers to the relationships between China, Hong Kong, and Taiwan. On the Taiwan issue, the political relationship between China and Taiwan reached a crisis situation in spring 1996, when China carried out military exercises close to Taiwan's territorial waters using live ammunition on maneuvers in the Taiwan Strait. Attempting to influence Taiwan's popular election of a president, the Chinese military activities have actually resulted in a consensus among the majority of Taiwan residents that it would be better for Taiwan to keep the current relationship of no independence or unification with China. The turbulent political relationship between China and Taiwan has negative effects on economic activities between the two sides. President Lee Teng-hui is especially concerned about the island's overdependence on the mainland for market outlets on the one hand and the increase of business investment on the mainland at the cost of undermining domestic investment on the other (Cheng, 1997).

Then, the political relationship between China and Hong Kong will also reach a new level as the June 1997 turnover of Hong Kong to China approaches. As explained before, Hong Kong has played a major role in China's economic development and has contributed to China's foreign trade, investment, and tourism development since the beginning of economic reforms, especially the implementation of the open-door policy. While interested in business opportunities on the mainland, the people of Hong Kong are very concerned about the political control of the Chinese government over them. The people's confidence in the Chinese government fell to the lowest level after the Tiananmen Square incident and has gradually increased since then. To assure the implementation of the Sino-British agreements and the "one country, two systems" policy, however, many issues, both internal (e.g., the interference of the Chinese government in the local issues of Hong Kong) and external (e.g., the role of Hong Kong in international or regional economic organizations), need to be resolved for China to reap the full benefits of the takeover of Hong Kong.

Despite their differences, both the Hong Kong and Taiwan issues will affect the future economic development of China and test the wisdom and leadership of China's new leaders. A smooth and successful transition for Hong Kong will reduce uncertainties among the Taiwanese and promote the development of a positive relationship between China and Taiwan in the near future. While providing further economic development, the democratic societies in both Hong Kong and Taiwan will also be very attractive to the Chinese people and may bring changes in China's political activities. After becoming rich, people begin to demand a say in their own governance. The experience of Hong Kong and Taiwan provides a good example for the Chinese people to seek more political rights. For example, many Chinese, especially young people, are aware of and envy the popular election of the president in Taiwan. It is very natural for them to ask, "If the people in Taiwan can elect their own president, why can't we?"

The Research Issue

Since the beginning of economic reforms in 1978, there have been many published studies (e.g., books, journal articles, and symposia) on the process and issues related to China's post-Mao economic development.[3] Despite the various disciplines involved, most of the earlier studies provided descriptions of the background, process, and strategies of China's reforms. Especially, the earlier studies tended to criticize China's partial and stop-and-go reform approach based on the analysis of the literature on economic development. Most of the later research on China's reforms focused on the evaluation of major achievements and problems of the reforms. Specifically, the later research tended to identify factors associated with the achievements and problems and to make suggestions about critical lessons learned from the Chinese reforms.

One of the major issues emphasized in the recent studies of China's economic reforms is the interpretation of the policy significance of the Chinese experience. For example, many researchers are interested in finding out whether the Chinese experience is relevant to other transitional economies, especially the reforms in Eastern Europe (e.g., Rawski, 1995; Walder, 1995). In general, they recognized the unique characteristics of the Chinese experience (e.g., the partial reform) and attributed China's success to many objective (e.g., the contribution of the overseas Chinese and China's rich neighbors) and subjective (e.g., the past decentralized experience and the background of China's social culture) factors. Emphasizing the importance of individual economic, political, and social conditions, they suggested that other ex-socialist nations might benefit from the Chinese experience by incorporating specific aspects of the Chinese reform patterns into their own reform strategies.

While studying different topics in various stages, all of the researchers of China's post-Mao economic reforms agreed that the studies of the Chinese reforms contribute to the existing literature in their disciplines. They indicated the importance of China as the world's leading social experiment for many reform ideas and theories because of many characteristics of the country's social backgrounds (e.g., the large population, the political system, and the complex society). With regard to the theory of economic development, for example, many researchers (e.g., Nolan, 1994; Nolan & Ash, 1995; Walder, 1995; Yusuf, 1994) have concluded that state involvement is necessary and important in managing the process of economic reforms or transformation. The challenge task in the reform process is not to criticize or abolish state involvement but to revise and improve the involvement according to the changing condition.

Finally, approaching their second decade, the Chinese economic reforms have moved to another critical stage. The new reform issues become more complex in their nature, involve many aspects of the society, and need to incorporate ideas and changes from different disciplines. For example, the task of reforming state-owned enterprises is very challenging because it covers changes not only in economic policies and issues but also in social institutions and behavioral issues because of the nature of China's state-owned enterprises. In addition, it is clear that we need to examine many economic-related issues in China's political, administrative, and social systems in order to address the new reform issues. The new challenging issues will again provide opportunities for the researchers of Chinese reforms to further test theories and policy options in their areas. The interdisciplinary nature of this book provides an example for the future researchers in their efforts to achieve an overall understanding of the Chinese reforms.

NOTES

1. The author did not fully present and discuss China's political development during the economic reform years because his intention in this book is to examine China's experience in managing economic development and reforms. Most of the issues examined are based on and related to theories and policies of economic development and public management.

2. Deng Xiaoping, the leader of the post-Mao economic reforms, passed away on February 19, 1997. Despite his controversial role in the Tiananmen Square incident, Deng's contribution to China's economic development and modernization has been perceived as beneficial by many Chinese researchers and observers. For a brief review of Deng's personal life and influence on the economic reforms, see, for example, *Beijing Review* (1997), Chua-Eoan and Walsh (1997), Forney (1997), and McGeary (1997).

3. For some publications about China's economic reforms and development, see the authors and topics listed in the bibliography section of this book.

Bibliography

Almond, G. A. & Powell, G. B. (1978). *Comparative Politics: System, Process, and Policy*. Second edition. Boston: Little, Brown.

Ash, R. F. (1992). "The Agricultural Sector in China: Performance and Policy Dilemmas during the 1990s." *The China Quarterly* 131 (September): 545-576.

Ash, R. F. & Kueh, Y. Y. (1993). "Economic Integration within Greater China: Trade and Investment Flows between China, Hong Kong and Taiwan." *The China Quarterly* 136 (December): 711-745.

Aufrecht, S. E. & Li, S. B. (1995). "Reform with Chinese Characteristics: The Context of Chinese Civil Service Reform." *Public Administration Review* 55, 2 (March/April): 175-182.

Bachman, D. (1986). "Differing Visions of China's Post-Mao Economy." *Asian Survey* 26, 3 (May): 292-321.

Bachman, D. (1996). "Succession Politics and China's Future." *Journal of International Affairs* 49, 2 (Winter): 370-389.

Beijing Review (1980). "Hua Guofeng's Speech at the Third Session of the Fifth National People's Congress." 23 (September 20): 20-24.

Beijing Review (1983). "Responsibility System Applied to Agriculture." 26, 48 (November 28): 19.

Beijing Review (1993a). "Big Cuts in Government Employees." 36, 13 (March 29-April 4): 8.

Beijing Review (1993b). "Big Embezzlers Sentenced to Death." 36, 41 (October 11-17): 6-7.

Beijing Review (1993c). "Measures Outlined to Fight Corruption." 36, 45 (November 8-14): 5-6.

Beijing Review (1993-1994). "Industrial Accident Prevention Stressed." 36, 52 (December 27, 1993-January 2, 1994): 6.

Beijing Review (1994). "China Set to Curb Organized Crime." 37, 49 (December 5-11): 5.

Beijing Review (1995a). "Renewed Campaign against Corruption." 38, 6-7 (February 13-19): 6.

Beijing Review (1995b). "China Keeps Crackdown on Corruption." 38, 13 (March 27-April 2): 6.

Beijing Review (1995c). "New Measures for Resource Protection." 38, 16 (April 17-23): 6.

Beijing Review (1996). "Cadres across China Target Training." 39, 37 (September 9-15): 5.

Beijing Review (1997). "Eternal Glory to Our Beloved Comrade Deng Xiaoping." 40, 10 (March 10-16): 4-13.

Bell, M. W., Khor, H. E., Kochhar, K., Ma, J., N'guiamba, S., & Lall, R. (1993). *China at the Threshold of a Market Economy*. Washington, DC: International Monetary Fund.

Bhalla, A. S. (1995). "Recent Economic Reforms in China and India." *Asian Survey* 35, 6 (June): 555-572.

Bickford, T. J. (1994). "The Chinese Military and Its Business Operations: The PLA as Entrepreneur." *Asian Survey* 34, 5 (May): 460-474.

Bing, S. (1992). "The Reform of Mainland China's Cadre System: Establishing a Civil Service." *Issues & Studies* 28 (October): 23-43.

Boxer, B. (1989). "China's Environmental Prospects." *Asian Survey* 29, 7 (July): 669-686.

Buchholz, R. A. (1992). *Business Environment and Public Policy: Implications for Management and Strategy*. Fourth Edition. Englewood Cliffs, NJ: Prentice Hall.

Burns, J. P. (1983). "Reforming China's Bureaucracy, 1979-82." *Asian Survey* 23, 6: 692-722.

Burns, J. P. (1987). "China's *Nomenklatura* System." *Problems of Communism*, 36: 36-51.

Burns, J. P. (1989). "Chinese Civil Service Reform: The 13th Party Congress Proposals." *The China Quarterly* 120 (December): 739-770.

Burns, J. P. (1993). "China's Administrative Reforms for a Market Economy." *Public Administration and Development* 13, 4 (October): 345-360.

Byrd, W. (1987). "The Impact of the Two-Tier Plan/Market System in Chinese Industry." *Journal of Comparative Economics* 11: 295-308.

Byrd, W. A. & Lin, Q. (Eds.). (1990). *China's Rural Industry: Structure, Development, and Reform*. Oxford: Oxford University Press.

Cabestan, J.-P. (1992). "Civil Service Reform in China: The Draft Provisional Order Concerning Civil Servants." *International Review of Administrative Sciences* 58, 4 (December): 421-436.

Caiden, G. E. (1982). "Postcript: Public Administration and Administrative Reform." In G. E. Caiden and H. Siedentopf (Eds.), *Strategies for Administrative Reform*. Lexington, MA: D.C. Heath and Company, pp. 221-231.

Caiden, G. E. (1988). "The Vitality of Administrative Reform." *International Review of Administrative Sciences* 54: 331-357.

Caiden, G. E. (1991). "What Really Is Public Maladministration?" *Public Administration Review* 51, 6 (November/December): 486-493.

Caiden, G. E. & Siedentopf, H. (Eds.). (1982). *Strategies for Administrative Reform*. Lexington, MA: D.C. Heath and Company.

Cannan, E. (Ed.). (1976). *Adam Smith: An Inquiry into the Nature and Causes of the Wealth of Nations*. Chicago: University of Chicago Press.

Caporaso, J. A. (1982). "The State's Role in Third World Economic Growth." *Annals of the American Academy of Political and Social Science* 459 (January): 103-111.

Chan, H. S. & Wong, K. K. (1994). "Environmental Attitudes and Concerns of the Environmental Protection Bureaucrats in Guangzhou, People's Republic of China: Implications for Environmental Policy Implementation." *International Journal of Public Administration* 17, 8: 1523-1554.

Chan, H. S., Wong, K.-K., Cheung, K. C. & Lo, J. M.-K. (1995). "The Implementation Gap in Environmental Management in China: The Case of Guangzhou, Zhengzhou, and Nanjing." *Public Administration Review* 55, 4 (July/August): 333-340.

Chan, K. W. (1996). "Post-Mao China: A Two-Class Urban Society in the Making." *International Journal of Urban and Regional Research* 20, 1: 134-150.

Chanda, N. (1995). "Withering State: The End Is Near." *Far Eastern Economic Review* 158, 8 (February 23): 48-50.

Chang, H. (1984). "The 1982-83 Overinvestment Crisis in China." *Asian Survey* 24, 12 (December): 1275-1301.

Chang, M. H. (1992). "China's Future: Regionalism, Federalism, or Disintegration." *Studies*

in Comparative Communism 25, 3 (September): 211.
Chang, M. H. (1995). "Greater China and the Chinese 'Global Tribe.'" *Asian Survey* 35, 10 (October): 955-967.
Chen, K. (1998). "Administrative Decentralisation and Changing State-Society Relations in China." *International Journal of Public Administration* (forthcoming).
Chen, K., Jefferson, G. H. & Singh, I. (1992). "Lessons from China's Economic Reform." *Journal of Comparative Economics* 16, 2 (June): 201-225.
Chen, K., Wang, H., Zheng, Y., Jefferson, G. & Rawski, T. (1988). "Productivity Change in Chinese Industry: 1953-1985." *Journal of Comparative Economics* 12, 4 (December): 570-591.
Cheng, C.-y. (1982). *China's Economic Development: Growth and Structural Change*. Boulder, CO: Westview Press.
Cheng, C.-y. (1990). *Behind the Tiananmen Massacre: Social, Political, and Economic Ferment in China*. Boulder, CO: Westview.
Cheng, C.-y. (1991). "Mainland China's Modernization and Economic Reform: Process, Consequences, and Prospects." *Issues & Studies* 27, 11 (November): 78-102.
Cheng, H.-S. (1993). "Foreign Trade." In W. Galenson (Ed.), *China's Economic Reform*. San Francisco, CA: The 1990 Institute, pp. 197-230.
Cheng, T.-j. (1997). "Taiwan in 1996." *Asian Survey* 37, 1 (January): 43-51.
Cheung, T. M. (1988). "Disarmament and Development in China: The Relationship between National Defense and Economic Development." *Asian Survey* 28, 7 (July): 757-774.
Chinese Academy of Social Sciences. (1989). *Information China*. Beijing: Pergamon Press.
Chinese Public Administration Society. (1993). *A Brief Introduction to Chinese Public Administration Society*. Beijing: Author.
Chow, G. C. (1994). *Understanding China's Economy*. Singapore: World Scientific Publishing Co.
Chow, K. W. (1991). "Perform of the Chinese Cadre System: Pitfalls, Issues, and Implications of the Proposed Civil Service System." *International Review of Administrative Sciences* 57 (March): 25-44.
Chow, K. W. (1993). "Conceptualizing Administrative Organization in China." In M. M. Mills and S. S. Nagel (Eds.), *Public Administration in China*. Westport, CT: Greenwood Press, pp. 31-47.
Chua-Eoan, H. & Walsh, J. (1997). "The Last Emperor." *Time* 149, 9 (March 3): 61-68.
Cohn, S. H. (1970). *Economic Development in the Soviet Union*. Lexington, MA: Lexington Books.
Croll, E. J. (1991). "The State and the Single Child Policy." In G. White (Ed.), *The Chinese State in the Era of Economic Reform*. Armonk, NY: M.E. Sharp, pp. 295-317.
Crook, F. (1986). "The Reform of the Commune System and the Rise of the Township Collective Household System." In Joint Economic Committee, U.S. Congress, *China's Economy Looks toward the Year 2000*, Vol. 1, *The Four Modernization*. Washington, DC: Government Printing Office.
Deng, X. (1984). *Selected Works of Deng Xiaoping*. Beijing: Foreign Languages Press.
Desai, P. (Ed.) (1983). *Marxism, Central Planning and the Soviet Economy*. Cambridge, MA: MIT Press.
Dicks, A. (1989). "The Chinese Legal System: Reforms in the Balance." *The China Quarterly* 119 (September): 540-576.
Doner, R. F. (1992). "Limits of State Strength: Toward an Institutionalist View of Economic Development." *World Politics* 44, 3 (April): 398-431.
Dong, F. (1980). "Some Problems Concerning the Chinese Economy." *The China Quarterly*

84 (December): 727-736.

Dong, F. (1988). "Development Theory and Problems of Socialist Developing Economies." In G. Ranis and T. P. Schultz (Eds.), *The State of Development Economics: Progress and Perspectives*. Oxford and New York: Basil Blackwell, pp. 235-241.

Easton, D. (1965). *A Framework for Political Analysis*. Englewood Cliffs, NJ: Prentice-Hall.

Edwards, R. R. (1984). "An Overview of Chinese Law and Legal Education." *Annals of the American Academy of Political and Social Science* 476 (November): 48-58.

Endean, E. (1991). "China's Foreign Commercial Relations." In Joint Economic Committee, U.S. Congress, *China's Economic Dilemmas in the 1990s: The Problems of Reforms, Modernization, and Interdependence*. Vol. 2, Washington, DC: Government Printing Office, pp. 741-769.

Falkenheim, V. C. (1980). "Administrative Reform and Modernization in Post-Mao China." *Public Affairs* 53, 1: 5-28.

Fan, Q. & Nolan, P. (Eds.). (1994). *China's Economic Reforms: The Costs and Benefits of Incrementalism*. London: Macmillan Press.

Fei, J. & Reynolds, B. (1987). "A Tentative Plan for the Rational Sequencing of Overall Reform in China's Economic System." *Journal of Comparative Economics* 11, 3: 490-502.

Ferdinand, P. (1996). "Social Change and the Chinese Communist Party: Domestic Problems of Rule." *Journal of International Affairs* 49, 2 (Winter): 478-492.

Field, R. M. (1992). "China's Industrial Performance since 1978." *The China Quarterly* 131 (September): 577-607.

Fisher, S. & Gelb, A. (1991). "The Process of Socialist Economic Transformation." *Journal of Economic Perspectives*, 5, 4 (Fall): 91-105.

Fisher, S., Sahay, R. & Vegh, C. A. (1996). "Stabilization and Growth in Transition Economies: The Early Experience." *Journal of Economic Perspectives* 10, 2 (Spring): 45-66.

Forney, M. (1996). "Don't Hold Your Breath: Will the Legal System Ever Be Free of Party Influence?" *Far Eastern Economic Review* 159, 10 (March 7): 24-28.

Forney, M. (1997). "Deng Xiaoping, 1904-1997." *Far Eastern Economic Review* 160, 10 (March 6): 22-29.

Fukasaku, K., Wall, D. & Wu, M. (1994). *China's Long March to an Open Economy*. Organization for Economic Cooperation and Development.

Galenson, W. (Ed.) (1993). *China's Economic Reform*. San Francisco, CA: The 1990 Institute.

Gao, S. (1996). *China's Economic Reform*. New York: St. Martin's Press.

Geng, Y. (1994). "Reforms of State Enterprises to Enter New State." *Beijing Review* 37, 47 (November 21-27): 4-5.

Gilley, B. (1996). "Irresistible Force: Migrant Workers Are Part of a Solution, Not a Problem." *Far Eastern Economic Review* 159, 14 (April 4): 18-20.

Glaeser, B. (Ed.). (1987). *Learning from China?* London: Allen & Unwin.

Gold, T. B. (1990). "Party-state versus Society in China." in J. K. Kallgren (Ed.), *Building a Nation-State: China After Forty Years*. Berkeley: Institute of East Asian Studies, University of California, Ch. 5.

Goldman, M. (1994). *Sowing the Seeds of Democracy in China: Political Reform in the Deng Xiaoping Era*. Cambridge, MA: Harvard University Press.

Goldstein, S. M. (1995). "China in Transition: The Political Foundations of Incremental Reform." *The China Quarterly* 144 (December): 1105-1131.

Goode, R. (1984). *Government Finance in Developing Countries*. Washington, DC: The Brookings Institution.

Goodman, D. S. G. (1989). "Review Article: Political Change in China: Power, Policy and Process." *British Journal of Political Science* 19, 3 (July): 425-443.

Goodman, D. S. G. (1994). "The Politics of Regionalism: Economic Development, Conflict and Negotiation." In D. S. G. Goodman and G. Segal (Eds.), *China Deconstructs: Politics, Trade and Regionalism*. New York: Routledge, pp. 1-20.

Goodman, D. S. G. & Hooper, B. (Eds.). (1994). *China's Quiet Revolution: New Interactions between State and Society*. New York: St. Martin's Press.

Goodman, D. S. G. & Segal, G. (Eds.). (1994). *China Deconstructs: Politics, Trade and Regionalism*. New York: Routledge.

Haggard, S. & Kaufman, R. (Eds.). (1992). *The Politics of Adjustment: International Constraints, Distributive Politics, and the State*. Princeton, NJ: Princeton University Press.

Haggard, S. & Webb, S. B. (1993). "What Do We Know about the Political Economy of Economic Policy Reform?" *The World Bank Research Observer* 8, 2 (July): 143-168.

Halpern, N. P. (1985). "China's Industrial Economic Reforms." *Asian Survey* 25, 10 (October): 998-1012.

Hamron, C. L. (1992). "The Party Leadership System." In K. Lieberthal and D. M. Lampton (Eds.), *Bureaucracy, Politics, and Decision Making in Post-Mao China*. Berkeley: University of California Press, pp. 95-124.

Han, B. (1993). "Development Strategy for Central and Western Regions." *Beijing Review* 36, 16 (April 19-25): 23-26.

Harding, H. (1981). *Organizing China: The Problem of Bureaucracy, 1949-1976*. Stanford, CA: Stanford University Press.

Harding, H. (1987). *China's Second Revolution: Reform after Mao*. Washington, DC: The Brookings Institution.

Harding, H. (1993). "The Concept of 'Greater China': Themes, Variations and Reservations." *The China Quarterly* 136 (December): 660-686.

Harding, H. (1994). "The Contemporary Study of Chinese Politics: An Introduction." *The China Quarterly* 139 (September): 699-703.

Heady, F. (1984). *Public Administration: A Comparative Perspective*. Third edition. New York: Marcel Dekker.

Holloway, N. (1995). "For Whom the Bell Tolls." *Far Eastern Economic Review* 158, 5 (February 2): 14-15.

Hong, Y. (1995). "China Makes Progress in Drug Control." *Beijing Review* 38, 1 (January 2-8): 15-19.

Hsiao, K. H. Y. (1984). *Money and Banking in the Chinese Mainland*. Taipei, Taiwan: Chung-Hua Institution for Economic Research.

Hua, S., Zhang, X. & Luo, X. (1993). *China: From Revolution to Reform*. London: Macmillan.

Huang, D. (1993). "Promoting the Quality of the Chinese Government." In M. K. Mills and S. S. Nagel (Eds.), *Public Administration in China*. Westport, CT: Greenwood Press, pp. 97-104.

Huang, F. (1987). "China's Introduction of Foreign Technology and External Trade." *Asian Survey* 27, 5 (May): 577-594.

Huang, W. (1996). "Continued Improvement in Chinese Legislation." *Beijing Review* 39, 2 (January 8-14): 22-24.

Huff, W. G. (1995). "What Is the Singapore Model of Economic Development?" *Cambridge Journal of Economics* 19, 6 (December): 735-759.

Hughes, H. (Ed.). (1988). *Achieving Industrialization in East Asia*. Cambridge: Cambridge University Press.

Huus, K. (1995). "The Reckoning Begins: Corruption Case Puts Red-chip Companies on Alert." *Far Eastern Economic Review* 158, 9 (March 2): 16.

Ishikawa, S. (1983). "China's Economic Growth Since 1949-An Assessment." *The China Quarterly* 94 (June): 242-281.

Jefferson, G. H. & Xu, W. (1991). "The Impact of Reform on Socialist Enterprises in Transition: Structure, Conduct, and Performance in Chinese Industry." *Journal of Comparative Economics* 15: 45-64.

Jiang, W. (1995). "A New Problem: Labor Relations in Foreign Enterprises." *Beijing Review* 38, 20 (May 15-21): 17-21.

Jiang, Z. (1997). "Memorial Speech at Deng Xiaoping's Memorial Meeting." *Beijing Review* 40, 10 (March 10-16): 14-22.

Kamath, S. J. (1990). "Foreign Direct Investment in a Centrally Planned Developing Economy: The Chinese Case." *Economic Development and Cultural Change* 39, 1 (October): 107-130.

Katz, S. M. (1971). "Exploring a System Approach to Development Administration." In F. W. Riggs (Ed.), *Frontiers of Development Administration*. Durham, NC: Duke University Press.

Kaye, L. (1994a). "Deafened by Decree: China's Currency and Tax Reforms Spread Confusion." *Far Eastern Economic Review* 157, 2 (January 13): 80-82.

Kaye, L. (1994b). "Pre-Emptive Cringe: China's Finance Minister Hints at Dangers Ahead." *Far Eastern Economic Review* 157, 12 (March 24): 48-50.

Kaye, L. (1994c). "Disorder under Heaven." *Far Eastern Economic Review* 157, 23 (June 9): 22-23.

Kaye, L. (1995a). "Withering State: Fire When Ready." *Far Eastern Economic Review* 158, 8 (February 23): 50-54.

Kaye, L. (1995b). "Vital Signs." *Far Eastern Economic Review* 158, 13 (March 30): 14-15.

Kaye, L. (1995c). "The Grip Slips." *Far Eastern Economic Review* 158, 19 (May 11): 18-20.

Keith, R. C. (1994). *China's Struggle for the Rule of Law*. London: Macmillan.

Kelliher, D. (1991). "Privatisation and Politics in Rural China." In G. White (Ed.), *The Chinese State in the Era of Economic Reform*. Armonk, NY: M.E. Sharpe, pp. 318-341.

Khan, A. R., Griffin, K., Riskin, C. & Zhao, R. (1992). "Household Income and Its Distribution in China." *The China Quarterly* 132 (December): 1029-1061.

Koo, A. Y. C. (1990). "The Contract Responsibility System: Transition from a Planned to a Market Economy." *Economic Development and Cultural Change* 38, 4 (July): 797-820.

Koo, A. Y. C., Li, E. H.-M. & Peng, Z. (1993). "State-Owned Enterprise in Transition." In W. Galenson (Ed.), *China's Economic Reform*. San Francisco, CA: The 1990 Institute.

Kornai, J. (1980). *Economics of Shortage*. Amsterdam: North-Holland.

Kornai, J. (1991). *The Socialist System: The Political Economy of Communism*. Princeton, NJ: Princeton University Press.

Kueh, Y. Y. (1992). "Foreign Investment and Economic Change in China." *The China Quarterly* 131 (September): 637-690.

Kueh, Y. Y. & Howe, C. (1984). "China's International Trade: Policy and Organizational Change and Their Place in the 'Economic Readjustment.'" *The China Quarterly* 100: 813-848.

Kuhn, A. (1994a). "Cops and Robbers." *Far Eastern Economic Review* 157, 23 (June 9): 26.

Kuhn, A. (1994b). "Private Guardians." *Far Eastern Economic Review* 157, 23 (June 9): 28-30.

Kuhn, A. & Kaye, L. (1994). "Bursting at the Seams: Rural Migrants Flout Urban Registration System." *Far Eastern Economic Review* 157, 10 (March 10): 27-28.

Kuznets, P. W. (1988). "An East Asian Model of Economic Development: Japan, Taiwan, and South Korea." *Economic Development and Cultural Change* 36 (April): S11-S44.

Lam, T. C. & Chan, H. S. (1995). "Designing China's Civil Service System: General Principles and Realities." *International Journal of Public Administration* 18, 8: 1297-1332.

Lam, T. C. & Chan, H. S. (1996). "Reforming China's Cadre Management System." *Asian Survey* 36, 8 (August): 772-786.

Lardy, N. R. (1992a). *Foreign Trade and Economic Reform in China, 1978-90*. Cambridge: Cambridge University Press.

Lardy, N. R. (1992b). "Chinese Foreign Trade." *The China Quarterly* 131: 691-720.

Lee, J. (1994). "Regional Differences in the Impact of the Open Door Policy on Income Growth in China." *Journal of Economic Development* 19, 1 (June): 215-234.

Lee, J. (1995). "Regional Income Inequality Variations in China." *Journal of Economic Development* 20, 2 (December): 99-118.

Lee, H. Y. (1978). *The Politics of the Chinese Cultural Revolution*, Berkeley, CA: University of California Press.

Lee, H. Y. (1984). "Evaluation of China's Bureaucratic Reforms." *Annals of the American Academy of Political and Social Science* 476 (November): 34-47.

Lee, H. Y. (1991). *From Revolutionary Cadres to Party Technocrats in Socialist China*. Berkeley, CA: University of California Press.

Lee, K. (1993). "Property Rights and the Agency Problem in China's Enterprise Reform." *Cambridge Journal of Economics* 17, 2 (June): 179-194.

Lehne, R. (1993). *Industry and Politics: United States in Comparative Perspective*. Englewood Cliffs, NJ: Prentice-Hall.

Li, D. (1994). "The Characteristics of and Reasons for the Floating Population in Contemporary China." *Social Sciences in China* (Winter): 65-72.

Li, F. (1993). "Recent Administrative Reform in China." In M. K. Mills and S. S. Nagel (Eds.), *Public Administration in China*. Westport, CT: Greenwood Press, pp. 49-60.

Li, N. (1995). "China's Bank Law Enforced." *Beijing Review* 38, 16 (April 17-23): 13-16.

Li, P. (1995). "Report on the Work of the Government." *Beijing Review* 38, 13 (March 27-April 2): I-XVI.

Li, T. (1994). "Inflation: Causes and Countermeasures." *Beijing Review* 37, 45 (November 7-13): 7-8.

Li, T. (1995). "15 years of Reform for State-Owned Enterprises." *Beijing Review* 38, 2 (January 9-15): 15-17.

Li, W. (1990). "Reform in the Chinese Public Personnel System." *Public Personnel Management* 19, 2 (Summer): 163-174.

Li, W. L. (1992). "Migration, Urbanization, and Regional Development: Toward a State Theory of Urban Growth in Mainland China." *Issues & Studies* 28, 2 (February): 84-102.

Li, Y. (1989). "China's Inflation: Causes, Effects, and Solutions." *Asian Survey* 29, 7 (July): 655-668.

Liao, Y. (1993). "Environmental Protection: Progress and Challenges." *Beijing Review* 36, 28 (July 12-18): 12-16.

Lieberthal, K. (1984). "China's Political Reforms: A Net Assessment." *Annals of the American Academy of Political and Social Science* 476 (November): 19-30.

Lieberthal, K. (1995). *Governing China: From Revolution through Reform*. New York: W. W. Norton & Company.

Lieberthal, K. G. & Lampton, D. M. (1992). *Bureaucracy, Politics and Decision Making in Post-Mao China*. Berkeley, CA: University of California Press.

Lieberthal, L. & Oksenberg, M. (1988). *Policy Making in China: Leaders, Structures, and Processes*. Princeton, NJ: Princeton University Press.

Lim, L. Y. C. (1983). "Singapore's Success: The Myth of the Free Market Economy." *Asian*

Survey 23, 6: 752-764.

Lin, J. Y. (1992). "Rural Reforms and Agricultural Growth in China." *American Economic Review* 82, 1 (March): 34-51.

Ling, L. H-M. (1988). "Intellectual Response to China's Economic Reforms." *Asian Survey* 28, 5 (May): 541-554.

Liou, K. T. (1994). *China's Economic Reforms: Achievements and Challenges*. Paper prepared for the 53rd American Society of Public Administration Annual Conference, July, Kansas City, MO.

Liou, K. T. (1996). *Strategies and Lessons of China's Post-Mao Economic Reforms*. Paper presented in the SECOPA, October, Miami, FL.

Liou, K. T. (1997). "Issues and Lessons of China's Civil Service Reform." *Public Personnel Management* (forthcomeing)

Liou, K. T. (1998). "The Role of Government in Economic Development: The Chinese Experience." *International Journal of Public Administration* (forthcoming).

Lippit, V. D. (1987). *The Economic Development of China*. New York: M.E. Sharpe.

Litan, R. E. & Nordhaus, W. D. (1983). *Reforming Federal Regulations*. New Haven, CT: Yale University Press.

Liu, A.P.L. (1983). "The Politics of Corruption in the People's Republic of China." *American Political Science Review* 77 (September): 602-623.

Liu, Y. (1993). "An Insider's Perspective: The Development of Chinese Administrative Science." In M. K. Mills and S. S. Nagel (Eds.), *Public Administration in China*. Westport, CT: Greenwood Press, pp. 133-143.

Lo, C.W.H. (1992). "Deng Xiaoping's Ideas on Law." *Asian Survey* 32, 7 (July): 649-665.

Lo, T. W. (1993). *Corruption and Politics in Hong Kong and China*. Philadelphia: Open University Press.

Lyons, T. P. (1987). *Economic Integration and Planning in Maoist China*. New York: Columbia University Press.

Lyons, T. P. (1991). "Interprovincial Disparities in China: Output and Consumption, 1952-1987." *Economic Development and Cultural Change* 39, 3 (April): 471-506.

Ma, G. (1994). "Income Distribution in the 1980s." In D. S. G. Goodman and B. Hooper (Eds.), *China's Quiet Revolution*. New York: St. Martin's Press, pp. 19-40.

Ma, S. K. (1989). "Reform Corruption: A Discussion on China's Current Development." *Pacific Affairs* 62, 1 (Spring): 40-52.

Ma, S. K. (1990). "Chinese Bureaucracy and Post-Mao Reforms: Negative Adjustment." *Asian Survey* 30, 11 (November): 1038-1052.

Manion, M. (1985). "The Cadre Management System, Post-Mao: The Appointment, Promotion, Transfer and Removal of Party and State Leaders." *The China Quarterly* 102: 203-233.

Manion, M. (1992). "The Behavior of Middlemen in the Cadre Retirement Policy Process." In K. G. Lieberthal and D. M. Lampton (Eds.), *Bureaucracy, Politics, and Decision Making in Post-Mao China*. Berkeley: University of California Press, pp. 216-244.

Mason, T. D. (1994). "Modernization and Its Discontents Revisited: The Political Economy of Urban Unrest in the People's Republic of China." *The Journal of Politics* 56, 2 (May): 400-424.

McGeary, J. (1997). "The Next China." *Time* 149, 9 (March 3): 50-56.

McKinnon, R. I. (1991). *The Order of Economic Liberalization*. Baltimore: Johns Hopkins University Press.

McMillian, J., Whalley, J., & Zhu, L. (1989). "The Impact of China's Economic Reforms on Agricultural Productivity Growth." *Journal of Political Economy* 97, 4: 781-807.

Meier, K. J. (1985). *Regulation: Politics, Bureaucracy, and Economics.* New York: St. Martin's Press.

Meyers, R. H. (1980). *The Chinese Economy: Past and Present.* Belmont, CA: Wadsworth.

Mills, M. K. & Nagel, S. S. (Eds.) (1993). *Public Administration in China.* Westport, CT: Greenwood Press.

Morgan, M. C. (1981). "Controlling the Bureaucracy in Post-Mao China." *Asian Survey* 21, 12 (December): 1223-1236.

Musgrave, R. A. & Musgrave, P. B. (1980). *Public Finance in Theory and Practice.* Third Edition. New York: McGraw Hill.

Myers, J. T. (1989). "China Modernization and 'Unhealthy Tendencies.'" *Comparative Politics* 21, 2 (January): 193-213.

Naughton, B. (1995a). *Growing Out of the Plan: Chinese Economic Reform, 1978-1993.* Cambridge: Cambridge University Press.

Naughton, B. (1995b). "China's Macroeconomy in Transition." *The China Quarterly* 144 (December): 1083-1104.

Nee, V. & Mozingo, D. (Eds.). (1983). *State and Society in Contemporary China.* Ithaca, NY: Cornell University Press.

Nolan, P. (1994). "Introduction: The Chinese Puzzle." In Q. Fan and P. Nolan (Eds.), *China's Economic Reforms: The Costs and Benefits of Incrementalism.* London: Macmillan Press Ltd., pp. 1-20.

Nolan, P. & Ash, R. F. (1995). "China's Economy on the Eve of the Reform." *The China Quarterly* 144 (December): 980-998.

O'Brien, K. J. (1994). "Chinese People's Congresses and Legislative Embeddedness: Understanding Early Organizational Development." *Comparative Political Studies* 27, 1 (April): 80-109.

Ogden, S. (1989). *China's Unresolved Issues: Politics, Development and Culture.* Englewood Cliffs, NJ: Prentice-Hall.

Pack, H. & Westphal, W. E. (1986). "Industrial Strategy and Technological Change: Theory versus Reality." *Journal of Economic Development* 11 (June): 87-128.

Park, Y. C. (1990). "Development Lessons from Asia: The Role of Government in South Korea and Taiwan." *American Economic Association Papers and Proceedings* 80, 2 (May): 118-121.

People's Daily, [*Renmin ribao*]. (1957). July 5.

People's Daily, [*Renmin ribao*]. (1978). December 7.

People's Daily, [*Renmin ribao*]. (1980a). June 28.

People's Daily, [*Renmin ribao*]. (1980b). July 22.

People's Daily, [*Renmin ribao*]. (1985). September 8.

Perkins, D. H. (1988). "Reforming China's Economic System." *Journal of Economic Literature* 26 (June): 601-645.

Perkins, D. H. (1994). "Completing China's Move to the Market." *Journal of Economic Perspectives* 8, 2 (Spring): 23-46.

Perry, E. J. (1993). "China in 1992: An Experiment in Neo-Authoritarianism." *Asian Survey* 33, 9 (January): 12-21.

Perry, E. J. (1994). "Trends in the Study of Chinese Politics: State-Society Relations." *The China Quarterly* 139 (September): 704-713.

Popkova-Pijasheva, L. (1990). "Why Is the Plan Incompatible with the Market?" *Annals of the American Academy of Political and Social Science* 507 (January): 80-90.

Potter, P. B. (1995). "Foreign Investment Law in the People's Republic of China: Dilemmas of State Control." *The China Quarterly* 141 (March): 155-185.

Prybyla, J. S. (1981). "Key Issues in the Chinese Economy." *Asian Survey* 21, 9 (September): 925-946.

Prybyla, J. S. (1982). "Economic Problems of Communism: A Case Study of China." *Asian Survey* 22, 12 (December): 1206-1237.

Prybyla, J. S. (1985). "The Chinese Economy: Adjustment of the System or Systemic Reform." *Asian Survey* 25, 5 (May): 553-586.

Prybyla, J. S. (1989). "Why China's Economic Reforms Fail." *Asian Survey* 29, 11 (November): 1017-1032.

Prybyla, J. S. (1990a). "Economic Reform of Socialism: The Dengist Course in China." *Annals of the American Academy of Political and Social Science* 507 (January): 9-17.

Prybyla, J. S. (Ed.). (1990b). "Privatizing and Marketizing Socialism." *Annals of the American Academy of Political and Social Science* 507 (January): 9-17.

Pye, L. W. (1986). "On Chinese Pragmatism in the 1980s." *The China Quarterly* 106 (January): 207-234.

Pye, L. W. (1991). "The State and the Individual: An Overview Interpretation." *The China Quarterly* 127 (September): 442-466.

Pye, L. W. (1997). "Money Politics and Transitions to Democracy in East Asia." *Asian Survey* 37, 3 (March): 213-228.

Qin, H. (1993). "China: 15 Years of Reform." *Beijing Review* 36, 43 (October 25-31): 20-24.

Rawski, T. G. (1979). *Economic Growth and Employment in China*. Oxford: Oxford University Press.

Rawski, T. G. (1994). "Chinese Industrial Reform: Accomplishments, Prospects, and Implications." *American Economic Association Papers and Proceedings* 84, 2 (May): 271-275.

Rawski, T. G. (1995). "Implications of China's Reform Experience." *The China Quarterly* 144 (December): 1150-1173.

Riskin, C. (1987). *China's Political Economy: The Quest for Development Since 1949*. Oxford: Oxford University Press.

Rivlin, A. M. (1971). *Systematic Thinking for Social Action*. Washington, DC: The Brookings Institution.

Rocca, J.-L. (1992). "Corruption and Its Shadow: An Anthropological View of Corruption in China." *The China Quarterly* 130 (June): 402-416.

Rondinelli, D. A. & Montgomery, J. D. (1990). "Managing Economic Reform: An Alternative Perspective on Structural Adjustment Policies." *Policy Sciences* 23: 73-93.

Root, H. (1996). "Corruption in China: Has It Become Systemic?" *Asian Survey* 36, 8 (August): 741-757.

Ross, L. (1984). "The Implementation of Environmental Policy in China: A Comparative Perspective." *Administration & Society* 15, 4 (February): 489-516.

Rossi, P. H., Freeman, H. E. & Wright, S. R. (1979). *Evaluation: A Systematic Approach*. Beverly Hills, CA: Sage.

Roy, D. (1996). "The 'China Threat' Issue: Major Arguments." *Asian Survey* 36, 8 (August): 758-771.

Sands, B. N. (1990). "Decentralizing an Economy: The Role of Bureaucratic Corruption in China's Economic Reforms." *Public Choice* 65: 85-91.

Selden, M. (1979). *The People's Republic of China: A Documentary History of Revolutionary Change*. New York: Monthly Review Press.

Selznick, P. (1952). *The Organizational Weapon*. New York: McGraw Hill.

Shambaugh, D. (1993). "Introduction: The Emergence of 'Greater China.'" *The China Quarterly* 136 (December): 653-659.

Shambaugh, David. (Ed.). (1995). *Greater China: The Next Superpower?* Oxford: Oxford University Press.

Shanor, D. & Shanor, C. (1995). *China Today*. New York: St. Martin's Press.

Shen, H.-S. (1993). "Foreign Trade." In W. Galenson (Ed.), *China's Economic Reform*. San Francisco, CA: The 1990 Institute, pp. 197-230.

Shih, C.-Y. (1995). *State and Society in China's Political Economy: The Cultural Dynamics of Socialist Reform*. Boulder, CO: Lynne Rienner Publishers.

Shirk, S. L. (1990). "Planning to the Provinces: Deng Xiaoping's Political Strategy of Economic Reform." *Studies in Comparative Communism* 23: 227-258.

Shirk, S. L. (1993). *The Political Logic of Economic Reform in China*. Berkeley: University of California Press.

Shue, V. (1988). *The Reach of the State: Sketches of the Chinese Body Politic*. Stanford, CA: Stanford University Press.

Sit, V. F. S. (1988). "China's Export-Oriented Open Areas: The Export Processing Zone Concept." *Asian Survey* 28, 6 (June): 661-675.

Solinger, D. J. (1981). "Economic Reform via Reformulation in China: Where Do Rightist Ideas Come From?" *Asian Survey* 21, 9 (September): 947-960.

Solinger, D. J. (1985). "'Temporary Residence Certificate' Regulations in Wuhan, May 1983." *The China Quarterly* 101: 98-103.

Solinger, D. J. (1993). *China's Transition from Socialism: Statist Legacies and Marketing Reforms*. Armonk, NY: M.E. Sharpe.

Solinger, D. J. (1995). "China's Urban Transients in the Transition from Socialism and the Collapse of the Communist Urban Public Goods Regime." *Comparative Politics* 27, 2 (Jan): 127-146.

State Statistical Bureau. (1986). *Statistical Yearbook of China 1986*. Beijing: China Statistical Information & Consultancy.

State Statistical Bureau. (1991). *China Statistical Abstract 1990*. Beijing: China Statistical Information & Consultancy.

State Statistical Bureau. (1993). *Statistical Yearbook of China 1993*. Beijing: China Statistical Publishing House.

State Statistical Bureau. (1994). *Statistical Yearbook of China 1994*. Beijing: China Statistical Publishing House.

State Statistical Bureau. (1996). *China Statistical Yearbook 1996*. Beijing: China Statistical Publishing House.

Stern, N. (1991). "Public Policy and the Economics of Development." *European Economic Review* 35, 2/3 (April): 241-271.

Stoltenberg, C. D. (1984). "China's Special Economic Zones." *Asian Survey* 24, 6 (June): 637-654.

Sullivan, L. R. (1988). "Assault on the Reforms: Conservative Criticism of Political and Economic Liberalization in China." *The China Quarterly* 114 (June): 198-222.

Summers, L. H. & Thomas, V. (1993). "Recent Lessons of Development." *The World Bank Research Observer* 8, 2 (July): 241-254.

Sun, Y. (1991). "The Chinese Protests of 1989: The Issue of Corruption." *Asian Survey* 31, 8 (August): 762-782.

Szelenyi, I. (1978). "Social Inequalities in State Socialist Redistributive Economies." *International Journal of Comparative Sociology* 16: 63-87.

Tanzi, V. (1990). "Fiscal Policy for Growth and Stability in Developing Countries: Selected Issues." In A. Premchand (Ed.), *Government Financial Management: Issues and Country Studies*. Washington, DC: International Monetary Fund, pp. 15-27.

Tefft, S. (1994). "The Rootless Chinese: Repatriates Transform Economy, Yet Endure Persistent Resentment." *Christian Science Monitor* (March 30): 11.

Tidrick, G. & Chen, J. (Eds.). (1987). *China's Industrial Reform*. Oxford: Oxford University Press.

Todaro, M. P. (1985). *Economic Development in the Third World*. New York: Longman.

Treadgold, D. W. (Ed.). (1967). *Soviet and Chinese Communism: Similarities and Differences*. Seattle: University of Washington Press.

Tsang, S.-k. & Cheng, Y.-h. (1994). "China's Tax Reforms of 1994." *Asian Survey* 34, 9 (September): 769-788.

Tsao, J. T. H. (1987). *China's Development Strategies and Foreign Trade*. Lexington, MA: D. C. Heath and Company.

Tsao, K. K. & Worthley, J. A. (1995). "Chinese Public Administration: Change with Continuity during Political and Economic Development." *Public Administration Review* 55, 2 (March/April): 169-174.

Tsui, K. Y. (1991). "China's Regional Inequality, 1952-1985." *Journal of Comparative Economics* 15, 1 (March): 1-21.

Tsui, K. Y. (1993). "Decomposition of China's Regional Inequalities." *Journal of Comparative Economics* 17, 3 (September): 600-627.

Tuan, F. C. & Webb, S.-E. H. (1993). "Agriculture: Past and Prospects." In W. Galenson (Ed.), *China's Economic Reform*. San Francisco, CA: The 1990 Institute, pp. 81-117.

Tzeng, F.-W. (1991). "The Political Economy of China's Coastal Development Strategy: A Preliminary Analysis." *Asian Survey* 31, 3 (March): 270-284.

Unger, J. (1994). "'Rich Man, Poor Man': The Making of New Classes in the Countryside." In D. S. G. Goodman and B. Hooper (Ed.), *China's Quiet Revolution*. New York: St. Martin's Press, pp. 43-63.

Walder, A. G. (1995). "China's Transitional Economy: Interpreting Its Significance." *The China Quarterly* 144 (December): 963-979.

Wang, H. (1994). *The Gradual Revolution: China's Economic Reform Movement*. New Brunswick: Transaction Publishers.

Wang, Z. (1993). "Some New Crime Trends in China: Their Impact on the United States." *Police Studies: The International Review of Police Development* 16, 1 (Spring): 11-19.

Waste, R. J. (1986). "Public Administration in China: Impressions of Some of the Changes since the Cultural Revolution." *Administration & Society* 17, 4 (February): 501-508.

White, G. (1987). "The Politics of Economic Reform in Chinese Industry: The Introduction of the Labor Contract System." *The China Quarterly* 111 (September): 365-389.

White, G. (1991). "Urban Government and Market Reforms in China." *Public Administration and Development* 11: 149-170.

White, G. (Ed.). (1991). *The Chinese State in the Era of Economic Reform: The Road to Crisis*. New York: M.E. Sharpe.

White, G. (1993). *Riding the Tiger: The Politics of Economic Reform in Post-Mao China*. Stanford, CA: Stanford University Press.

Whyte, M. K. (1995). "The Social Roots of China's Economic Development." *The China Quarterly* 144 (December): 999-1064.

Wiemer, C. & Lu, M. (1993). "Prices: The Two-Tier Transition Process." In W. Galenson (Ed.), *China's Economic Reform*. San Francisco, CA: The 1990 Institute, pp. 119-146.

Wiens, T. B. (1983). "Price Adjustment, the Responsibility System, and Agricultural Productivity." *American Economic Association Papers and Proceedings* 73, 2 (May): 319-324.

Wiens, T. B. (1987). "Issues in the Structural Reform of Chinese Agriculture." *Journal of*

Comparative Economics 11, 3 (September): 372-384.

Williams, O. (1993). "An Outsider's Perspective." In M. K. Mills & S. S. Nagel (Eds.), *Public Administration in China*. Westport, CT: Greenwood Press, pp. 145-153.

Wolken, L. C. (1990). "The Restructuring of China's Banking System under the Economic Reforms 1979-1989." *Columbia Journal of World Business* 25 (Spring/Summer): 53-63.

Womack, B. & Zhao, G. (1994). "The Many Worlds of China's Provinces: Foreign Trade and Diversification." In D. S. G. Goodman and G. Segal (Eds.), *China Deconstructs: Politics, Trade and Regionalism*. New York: Routledge, pp. 131-176.

Wong, C.P.W. (1986). "The Economics of Shortage and Problems of Reform in Chinese Industry." *Journal of Comparative Economics* 10 (December): 363-387.

World Bank. (1983). *World Development Report 1983*. Washington, DC: Author.

World Bank. (1988). *China: Finance and Investment*. Washington, DC: Author.

World Bank. (1990). *China: Macroeconomic Stability and Industrial Growth under Decentralized Socialism*. Washington, DC: Author.

World Bank. (1994). *China: Internal Market Development and Regulation*. Washington, DC: Author.

Wu, H. X. (1994). "Rural to Urban Migration in the People's Republic of China." *The China Quarterly* 139 (September): 669-698.

Wu, J. & Zhao, R. (1987). "The Dual Pricing System in China's Industry." *Journal of Comparative Economics* 11, 3 (September): 309-318.

Wu, N. (1993). "Realigning Government Bodies." *Beijing Review* 36, 33 (August 16-22): 14-17.

Wu, N. (1995). "95 Goals for Reform of State-Owned Enterprises." *Beijing Review* 38, 2 (January 9-15): 7-13.

Xue, M. (1979). *Economic Problems in Socialist China*. Beijing: People's Publishing House.

Xue, M. (1982). *Current Economic Problems in China*. K. K. Fung (Ed. & Trans.). Boulder, CO: Westview Press.

Yabuki, S. (1995). *China's New Political Economy: The Giant Awakes*. (Translated by S. M. Harner). Boulder, CO: Westview Press.

Yahuda, M. (1993). "The Foreign Relations of Greater China." *The China Quarterly* 136 (December): 687-710.

Yang, D. L. (1990). "Patterns of China's Regional Development Strategy." *The China Quarterly* 122 (June): 230-257.

Yang, D. L. (1991). "Reforms, Resources, and Regional Cleavages: The Political Economy of Coast-Interior Relations in Mainland China." *Issues & Studies* 27, 9 (September): 43-69.

Yang, D. L. & Wei, H. (1996). "Rising Sectionalism in China?" *Journal of International Affairs* 49, 2: 456-476.

Yeh, K. C. (1967). "Soviet and Communist Chinese Industrialization Strategies." In D. W. Treadgold (Ed.), *Soviet and Chinese Communism: Similarities and Differences*. Seattle: University of Washington Press, pp. 327-363.

Yeh, K. C. (1992). "Macroeconomic Issues in China in the 1990s." *The China Quarterly* 131 (September): 501-544.

Yeh, K. C. (1993). "Economic Reform: An Overview." in W. Galenson (Ed.), *China's Economic Reform*. San Francisco, CA: The 1990 Institute, pp. 11-32.

You, C. (1986). "Current Administrative Reform in China." *International Review of Administrative Sciences* 52, 1: 123-144.

Young, S. (1995). "Post-Tiananmen Chinese Politics and the Prospects for Democratization."

Asian Survey 35, 7 (July): 652-667.

Young, S. (1994). "Private Entrepreneurs and Evolutionary Change." In D. S. G. Goodman and B. Hooper (Eds.), *China's Quiet Revolution*. New York: St. Martin's Press.

Yusuf, S. (1994). "China's Macroeconomic Performance and Management during Transition." *Journal of Economic Perspectives* 8, 2 (Spring): 71-92.

Zafanoli, W. (1985). "A Brief Outline of China's Second Economy." *Asian Survey* 25, 7 (July): 715-736.

Zhang, C. F. (1993). "Public Administration in China." In M. K. Mills and S. S. Nagel (Eds.), *Public Administration in China*. Westport, CT: Greenwood Press, pp. 3-19.

Zhang, H. (1995). "Economic Reform Progresses Smoothly." *Beijing Review* 38, 38 (September 11-17): 13-16.

Zhang, Z. (1993). "Capital Gooods Turn to Free Market." *Beijing Review* 36, 27 (July 5-11): 13-16.

Zhao, Z. (1987). "Advance along the Road toward Socialism with Chinese Characteristics." *People's Daily*, [*Renin ribao*], November, 4, p. 2.

Zhou, X. (1995). "Partial Reform and the Chinese Bureaucracy in the Post-Mao Era." *Comparative Political Studies* 28, 3 (October): 440-468.

Zoo, G. & Wang, Z. (1993). "Marketization and Productivity Change." Unpublished paper, University of Southern California, Los Angeles.

Zweig, D. (1995). "'Developmental Communities' on China's Coast: The Impact of Trade, Investment, and Transnational Alliances." *Comparative Politics* 27, 3 (April): 253-274.

Index

About the Author

KUOTSAI TOM LIOU is Associate Professor of Public Administration at the University of Central Florida.

www.ingramcontent.com/pod-product-compliance
Ingram Content Group UK Ltd.
Pitfield, Milton Keynes, MK11 3LW, UK
UKHW041636031026
15587UKWH00001B/330

9 780275 957926